TRA

NEW ENGLAND

TRAVEL◆SMART™ TRIP PLANNER

Anne E. Wright

John Muir Publications
Santa Fe, New Mexico

For Randy, without whom this book would not have been possible.

Special thanks to Linda, Gail, my sister Martha, and my parents for their research assistance, and to Dianna Delling for her patience.

John Muir Publications, P.O. Box 613, Santa Fe, New Mexico 87504

Parts of this book were originally published as *2 to 22 Days in New England* © 1989, 1991, 1992, 1993, 1994, 1995 by Anne E. Wright

Printed in the United States of America.
First printing May 1996.

ISSN 1086-8127
ISBN 1-56261-256-5

Cover photo: Leo de Wys Inc./Sipa/Gamba
Back cover photos: Everett Johnson/Leo de Wys Inc.
Maps: American Custom Maps—Albuquerque, NM USA
Graphics Coordination: Sarah Horowitz
Editors: Dianna Delling, Peggy Schaefer
Design: Janine Lehmann, Linda Braun
Typesetting: Linda Braun
Production: Nikki Rooker, Janine Lehmann
Printing: R.R. Donnelley & Sons

Distributed to the book trade by
Publishers Group West
Emeryville, California

HOW TO USE THIS BOOK

This *New England Travel♦Smart™ Trip Planner* is organized in 18 destination chapters, each covering the best sights and activities, restaurants, and lodging available in that specific destination. Thanks to thorough research and experience, the author is able to bring you only the best options, saving you time and money in your travels. The chapters are presented in geographic sequence so you can follow an easy route from one to the next. If you were to visit each destination in chapter order, you'd enjoy a complete tour of the best of New England.

Each chapter contains:

• User-friendly maps of the area, showing all recommended sights, restaurants, and accommodations.

• "A Favorite Day" description—how the author would spend her time if she had just one day in that destination.

• Sightseeing highlights, each rated by degree of importance: ✯✯✯ Don't miss; ✯✯ Try hard to see; ✯ See if you have time; and No stars—Worth knowing about. (If the author considers a sight a waste of time, it isn't in this guide.)

• Selected restaurant, lodging, and camping recommendations to suit a variety of budgets.

• Helpful hints, fitness and recreation ideas, insights, and random tidbits of information to enhance your trip.

The Importance of Planning. Developing an itinerary is the best way to get the most satisfaction from your travels, and this guidebook makes it easy. First, read through the book and choose the places you'd most like to visit. Then, study the color map on the inside cover flap and the mileage chart (page 12) to determine which you can realistically see in the time you have available and at the travel pace you prefer. Using the Planning Map (pages 10–11), map out your route. Finally, use the lodging recommendations to determine your accommodations.

Some Suggested Itineraries. To get you started, six itineraries of varying lengths and based on specific interests follow. Mix and match according to your interests and time constraints, or follow a given itinerary from start to finish. The possibilities are endless. *Happy trails!*

SUGGESTED ITINERARIES

With the *New England Travel♦Smart™ Trip Planner* you can plan a trip of any length—a 1-day excursion, a getaway weekend, or a 3-week vacation—around any special interest. To get you started, the following pages contain six suggested itineraries geared toward a variety of interests. For more information, refer to the chapters listed—chapter names are bolded and chapter numbers appear inside black bullets. You can follow a suggested itinerary in its entirety, or shorten, lengthen, or combine parts of each, depending on your starting and ending points.

Discuss alternative routes and schedules with your travel companions—it's a great way to have fun, even before you leave home. And remember: don't hesitate to change your itinerary once you're on the road. Careful study and planning ahead of time will help you make informed decisions as you go, but spontaneity is the extra ingredient that will make your trip memorable.

Leo de Wys Inc./Danilo Boschung

New England in One to Three Weeks

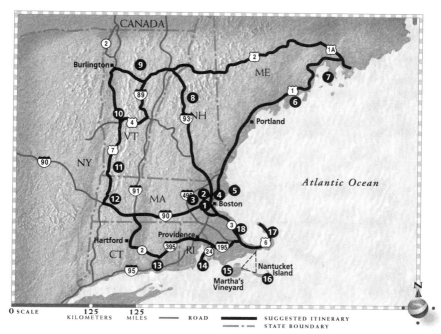

If you have one week to visit New England, see:

❶ Boston
❷ Cambridge
❸ Lexington and Concord
❹ Salem
❺ Cape Ann
❻ Coastal Maine

If you have two weeks to visit, add:

❼ Acadia National Park
❽ The White Mountains
❾ Northern Vermont
❿ Central Vermont
⓫ Southern Vermont
⓬ The Berkshires

If you have three weeks to visit, add:

⓭ The Heart of Connecticut
⓮ Newport
⓯ Martha's Vineyard
⓰ Nantucket
⓱ Cape Cod
⓲ Plymouth and the South Shore

New England: The Nature-Lover's Tour

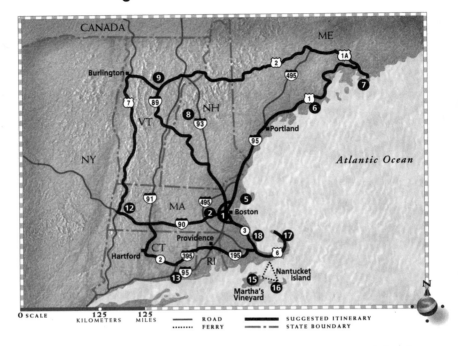

The nature lover's tour of New England offers variety, from the sandy beaches of the islands, to the forested peaks of the Green and White Mountains.

❶ **Boston** (The Arnold Arboretum, Boston's Harbor Islands)

❷ **Lexington & Concord** (Great Meadows Wildlife Refuge, Walden Pond)

❺ **Cape Ann** (The Parker River Wildlife Refuge, Plum Island)

❻ **Coastal Maine** (Monhegan Island)

❼ **Acadia National Park**

❽ **The White Mountains** (Franconia and Crawford Notch State Parks, Mt. Washington)

❾ **Northern Vermont** (Sky Line Drive, Mt. Mansfield, hiking)

⓬ **The Berkshires** (Mt. Greylock, Berkshire Botanical Garden, Bartholomew's Cobble)

⓭ **Heart of Connecticut** (Denison Pequotsepos Nature Center, Block Island)

⓯ **Martha's Vineyard** (beaches)

⓰ **Nantucket** (beaches)

⓱ **Cape Cod** (National Seashore)

⓲ **Plymouth and the South Shore** (wildlife refuges, World's End Reservation)

Time needed for this tour: 3 weeks. (For a 1 to 1½-week tour, visit only the first 5 recommended destinations, Boston–Acadia National Park.)

New England: The Art and Culture Lover's Tour

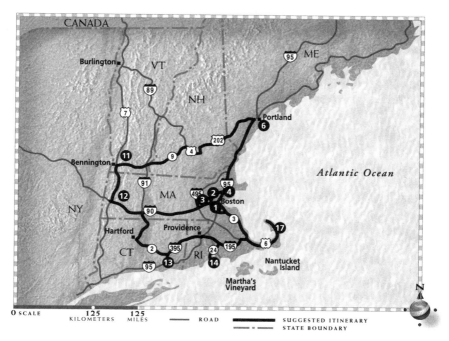

This tour exposes you to the lives and works of some of America's best-known literary figures and lets you take in fine performances of the Boston Symphony Orchestra, Boston Pops, and much more.

❶ **Boston** (museums, music)

❷ **Cambridge** (museums, Henry Wadsworth Longfellow's home)

❸ **Lexington and Concord** (The homes of Alcott and Emerson, the Thoreau Lyceum, the Wayside)

❹ **Salem** (Peabody Museum, the House of Seven Gables)

❻ **Coastal Maine** (museums)

⓫ **Southern Vermont** (museums)

⓬ **The Berkshires** (The Norman Rockwell Museum, Chesterwood, Tanglewood, Jacob's Pillow, Melville's Arrowhead, Wharton's The Mount)

⓭ **Heart of Connecticut** (The Wadsworth Athenaeum, the homes of Stowe and Twain, the Hill-Stead Museum, Yale Museums)

⓮ **Newport** (mansions)

⓱ **Cape Cod** (galleries and museums)

Time needed for this tour: 2 weeks

New England: Family Fun Tour

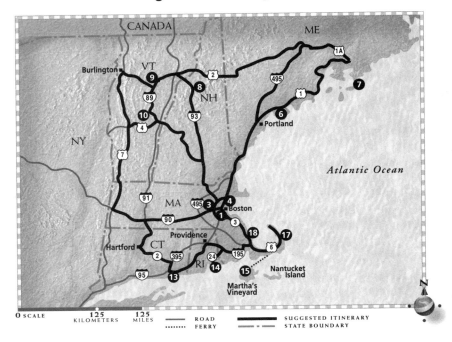

From hiking, biking, and beach-combing, to watching history brought to life in villages such as Sturbridge, Pioneer Village in Salem, Hancock Shaker Village, and Plimouth Plantation—a trip to New England can be active, educational, and fun for the entire family.

❶ Boston (museums, the Boston Tea Party Ship)

❸ Lexington and Concord (Walden Pond)

❹ Salem (wax museum, Pioneer Village)

❻ Coastal Maine (museums, Railway Village)

❼ Acadia National Park (outdoor activities)

❽ White Mountains (outdoor activities)

❾ Northern Vermont (Ben and Jerry's ice cream factory)

❿ Central Vermont (Sugarbush Farm, Quechee Gorge)

⓭ Heart of Connecticut (Mystic Sea port, train and riverboat rides)

⓮ Newport (Green Animals)

⓯ Martha's Vineyard (Flying Horses carousel)

⓱ Cape Cod (museums, seashore, Cape Cod chip factory)

⓲ Plymouth and the South Shore (history)

Time needed for this tour: 2 to 3 weeks. For a 1-week tour, end tour at Acadia National Park.

New England: The History-Lover's Tour

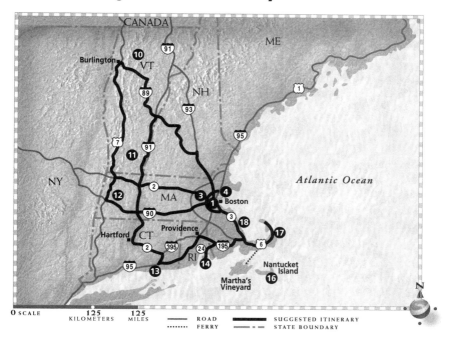

There is almost no better place in the United States to track our nation's history than New England.

● **Boston** (Freedom Trail, Kennedy Library, Tea Party Ship)

❸ **Lexington and Concord** (North Bridge, Sleepy Hollow Cemetery, the Concord Museum)

❹ **Salem** (Peabody Museum, Salem Witch Museum)

❿ **Northern Vermont** (Shelburne Museum)

⓫ **Southern Vermont** (Bennington Museum, Bennington Monument)

⓬ **The Berkshires** (historic Deerfield and Hancock Shaker Village)

⓭ **Heart of Connecticut** (Mystic Seaport)

⓮ **Newport** (mansions)

⓰ **Nantucket** (restored buildings)

⓱ **Cape Cod** (Heritage Plantation, museums)

⓲ **Plymouth and the South Shore** (Plimoth Plantation and the *Mayflower II*, Plymouth Rock)

Time needed for this tour: 2 to 3 weeks.

New England: The Literary Tour

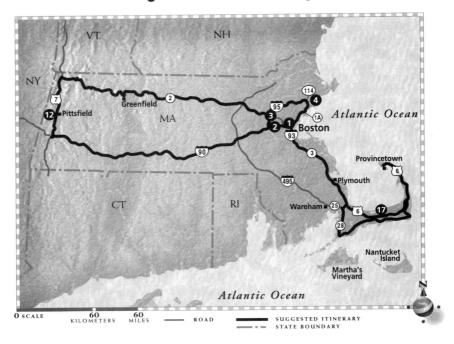

Concord, Massachusetts is the single most important stop on any literature lover's trip to New England as it was home to some of our country's most celebrated writers—Louisa May Alcott, Ralph Waldo Emerson, Henry David Thoreau, and Nathaniel Hawthorne.

❶ **Boston** (Old Corner Bookstore)

❷ **Cambridge** (The Longfellow National Historic Site)

❸ **Lexington and Concord** (The Concord Museum, the Thoreau Lyceum, the Wayside, the Old Manse, Emerson's House, Sleepy Hollow Cemetery, Walden Pond)

❹ **Salem** (The House of Seven Gables)

⓬ **The Berkshires** (Edith Wharton's The Mount, Herman Melville's Arrowhead)

⓱ **Cape Cod** (Thornton Burgess Museum, Green Briar Nature Center, the Seaman's Bethel)

Time needed for this tour: 1 to 1½ weeks

USING THE PLANNING MAP

A major aspect of itinerary planning is determining your mode of transportation and the route you will follow as you travel from destination to destination. The Planning Map on the following pages will allow you to do just that.

First, read through the destination chapters carefully and note the sights that intrigue you. Then, photocopy the Planning Map so you can try out several different routes that will take you to these destinations. (The mileage/time chart that follows will allow you to calculate your travel times and distances.) Decide where you will be starting your tour of New England. Will you fly into Boston, Hartford, or Providence, or will you start from somewhere in between? Will you be driving from place to place or flying into major transportation hubs and renting a car for daytrips? The answers to these questions will form the basis for your travel route design.

Once you have a firm idea of where your travels will take you, copy your route onto the Planning Map in the Appendix. You won't have to worry about where your map is, and the information you need on each destination will always be close at hand.

Planning Map: New England

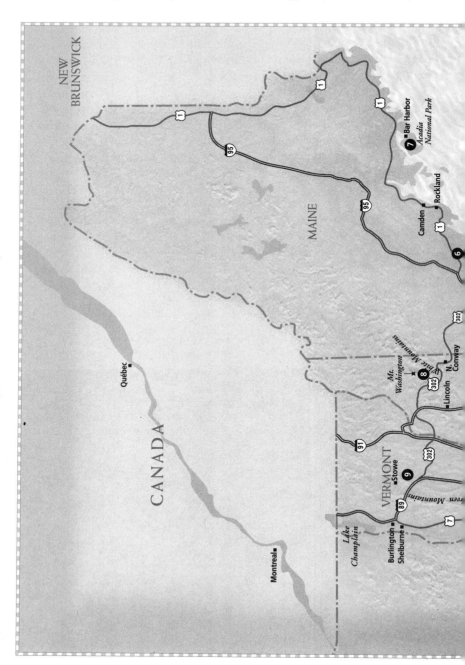

You have permission to photocopy this map.

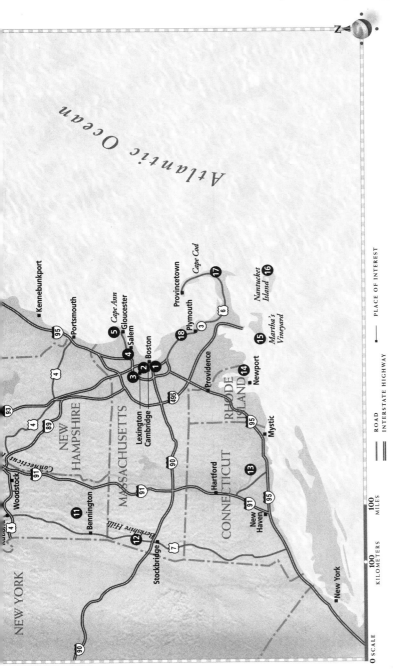

Atlantic Ocean

Kennebunkport
Portsmouth
Cape Ann
Gloucester
Salem
Boston
Cambridge
Lexington
Cape Cod
Provincetown
Plymouth
Providence
Nantucket Island
Newport
Martha's Vineyard
Mystic
Hartford
New Haven
Bennington
Berkshire Hills
Stockbridge
Woodstock
New York

NEW YORK
NEW HAMPSHIRE
MASSACHUSETTS
RHODE ISLAND
CONNECTICUT

Connecticut

SCALE
0   100
KILOMETERS
0   100
MILES

ROAD
INTERSTATE HIGHWAY
■ PLACE OF INTEREST

NEW ENGLAND MILEAGE CHART

	Boston	Concord	Salem	Cape Ann	Portland, ME	Acadia NP	North Conway	Burlington	Woodstock	Bennington	Stockbridge	Hartford	Newport	Martha's Vinyd	Nantucket	Cape Cod	Plymouth
Boston																	
Concord	20																
Salem	15	30															
Cape Ann	38	55	25														
Portland, ME	116	125	96	68													
Acadia NP	290	305	270	250	180												
North Conway	147	164	132	109	70	247											
Burlington	218	218	230	238	221	401	146										
Woodstock	175	175	190	139	155	335	141	100									
Bennington	152	132	168	169	198	378	235	123	96								
Stockbridge	141	131	156	179	249	429	288	169	142	46							
Hartford	100	98	115	142	201	381	251	220	140	111	65						
Newport	74	94	89	112	190	370	221	326	238	225	179	116					
Martha's Vinyd	108	128	123	146	224	404	255	326	284	260	250	217	116				
Nantucket	113	133	128	151	229	409	260	331	289	265	255	222	121	15			
Cape Cod	121	141	136	159	237	417	268	339	297	273	263	230	129	65	70		
Plymouth	40	60	55	78	156	336	187	258	216	192	182	149	90	68	73	81	

WHY VISIT NEW ENGLAND?

New England is the birthplace of our nation in many respects. The pilgrims landed here in 1620, the first battle of the Revolutionary War was fought on Massachusetts soil, Harvard University in Cambridge is the cornerstone of American education, and founding fathers such as John Adams spent their lives here. You'll feel history all around as you pause on centuries-old town greens, drive past crusty stone walls that define property lines, ramble over covered bridges, and visit time-weathered historic homes and monuments. Along the way, you'll see where Shakers worshipped, poets penned, colonists rebelled, whalers toiled, and presidents were born.

Nature has endowed New England with a beautiful landscape. Atlantic currents and Ice Age glaciers have sculpted this part of the country to near-perfection. During your holiday you'll have the opportunity to stretch out on sparkling white-sand beaches, picnic in rocky coves, watch playful seals in their natural habitat, hike pine-covered trails, stand atop the highest peak in the Northeast, swim in bubbling mountain streams, and dine on fish recently snatched from the ocean, all while you breathe in the salty sea air. If you visit in the fall, you'll also see the hills ablaze with vibrant colors as winter approaches.

This guide opens the door to your New England adventure.

HISTORY

New England unquestionably played a major role in our country's development, and is therefore one of the most historically rich regions of the United States. The arrival and settlement of the Pilgrims at Plymouth in 1620 established New England's place in our nation's history, while events a century and a half later solidified the region's reputation as a guiding force in the creation of our democracy.

In the 1760s, Britain imposed a series of taxes on the colonists. New Englanders—Bostonians in particular—were the most vocally opposed to the increasing tariffs. In 1770, a skirmish between British soldiers and angry colonists resulted in the deaths of five colonists—since referred to as the Boston Massacre. Three years later another act of defiance, the Boston Tea Party, further escalated the hostility between the British and the colonists which eventually culminated in the Revolutionary War.

In April of 1775, Paul Revere made his fabled ride from Boston to Lexington and Concord to warn the revolutionary minutemen of the

advancing British troops. The next day the first shots of the
Revolutionary War were fired. During the course of the war, a number
of key battles took place on New England soil, such as the battle of
Bunker Hill and a confrontation at Bennington in 1777 where the
colonists soundly defeated the British.

New England contributed to the country's growth in other areas
as well. In the early days, the region's whaling operations and foreign
trade helped produce a thriving economy for the infant nation. With
the advent of the industrial revolution, area factories began to churn
out yards upon yards of fabric from southern-grown cotton, further
contributing to the country's economic stature. In more recent years,
New England-based high-tech firms have helped to bring about a revolution of a completely different nature.

Finally, New England has been the site of at least one regrettable
but highly memorable incident in our nation's history—the Salem
Witch Trials. In 1692, some 200 residents of the town of Salem,
Massachusetts were accused of being witches. Nineteen of the accused
met their fate at the gallows before the governor stepped in to stop the
paranoia. The infamous event no doubt helped to shape our constitution when it came to a U.S. citizen's right to a fair trial.

CULTURES

As New England was often the first U.S. gateway that immigrant
groups entered, the region is naturally culturally diverse. Long
before the Pilgrims arrived in 1620, New England was inhabited by
Native American groups such as the Penobscots in what is now Maine,
the Pequots in what is now Connecticut, and the Wampanaogs in what
is now Massachusetts.

Until the mid-1800s, the cultural heritage of most New
Englanders was primarily British. Then many Irish came to New
England in search of a better life after the potato famine of 1846, and
African-Americans began moving to the north to escape the oppressive
slavery of the south. Several decades later the Boston area became a
popular destination for large numbers of Italian immigrants, and Portuguese, often drawn by a thriving fishing industry, settled in places such
as New Bedford and Rhode Island. Closer to home, clusters of French-
Canadians relocated from Canada to Vermont and New Hampshire.

Representatives from all of these cultures still reside in New
England today, and each group, in its own way, has affected the societal
tenor of the region as a whole.

THE ARTS

While the arts are celebrated throughout New England—there are outdoor concerts on the town green during the summer in Bar Harbor, and regular theatrical performances in season in places such as the Dorset Playhouse in Southern Vermont and the Goodspeed Opera House in East Haddam, Connecticut—Massachusetts has the highest concentration of prestigious artistic organizations in the region. Those organizations are based primarily in two regions: the Berkshires and metropolitan Boston.

Boston is a regular stop for traveling productions of Broadway musicals, and top-notch dance companies such as Alvin Ailey. The Boston Ballet has made *The Nutcracker* a requisite part of many area residents' annual holiday celebrations, while the Boston Pops Orchestra, led in the past by legendary conductors Arthur Fiedler and John Williams, has been a long-time favorite. The Boston Symphony Orchestra, considered one of the best in the country, spends its winter season in the city then moves to Tanglewood in the Berkshires for the summer months.

The BSO at Tanglewood is one of the best-known attractions in the Berkshires, but lovers of the arts will have no trouble filling up their calendars with performances during a summer visit to the area. For dance, there's Jacob's Pillow; for theatrical performances, the Williamstown Theatre Festival, the Berkshire Theatre Festival, and the Mount.

CUISINE

Boston baked beans, Parker House rolls (named for Boston's famed Parker House Hotel), Boston cream pie, and New England clam chowder—each of these celebrated foods is deeply rooted in New England. The traditional fare of the region developed for the most part from food sources and ingredients that were readily available, and therefore as a rule tends to have fewer spices than cuisine native to other regions of the United States.

Clams are plentiful in New England. Fried or steamed, the clams on Cape Ann are often considered to be the best in the world. Of course, no trip to New England would be complete without succulent Maine lobster either broiled or steamed, then dipped in melted butter. Clams and lobster are the two main ingredients in a typical New England clambake—along with juicy corn-on-the-cob. Yet another seafood dish, broiled scrod, is a New England staple because of its availability.

Native fruits have left their mark on the regional cuisine as well. Bountiful fields of Maine blueberries are transformed into baked blueberry muffins, pancakes, and pies. As the prime cranberry-growing region is located in southern Massachusetts, cranberries were an important part of the Pilgrim's first Thanksgiving—as was native turkey—and both still appear on Thanksgiving tables everywhere to this day.

New England cuisine also reflects the area's English and Irish cultural heritage. You're probably more likely to find properly British roast beef and Yorkshire pudding on a New England menu than elsewhere in the country, and the so-called New England boiled dinner, consisting of corned beef, cabbage, and potatoes, was really brought over by Irish immigrants and is traditionally eaten on St. Patrick's Day.

FLORA AND FAUNA

With temperatures that can dip well below freezing during the winter months, particularly in the northernmost part of the region, you're not going to find palm or citrus trees in New England. Nor will you see cacti and other plants that favor an arid climate, or blooming beauties such as orchids that require a tropical environment. New England flora depends on ample rainfall, yet the plantlife must be hardy enough to withstand occasionally harsh winters. Variations in climate and elevation within the region also dictate what you'll ultimately see on your trip.

In coastal areas such as Cape Cod, and islands like Nantucket and Martha's Vineyard, beach roses and spiky beach grass cover sandy dunes. Inland, forest floors are blanketed with lush, leafy ferns; and maple trees, interspersed with white birches, offer a colorful show during the autumn months. In Maine, where the climate is more severe, the evergreen is the dominant tree. Blueberries are also abundant in Maine, while the marshy terrain of southern Massachusetts provides the perfect environment for cranberry bogs. Corn grows successfully in every New England state, and wildflowers thrive in all rural areas during the summer months.

Deer are common throughout the region, as are small animals such as woodchucks, raccoons, rabbits, squirrels, and skunks. If you travel deep into the Maine wilderness, you may spot moose and bear. Atlantic whales are the largest mammals to inhabit New England, while clams, lobster, and bluefish, are among the abundant sea-life that shares the coastal waters with the gentle giants.

Seagulls make their home all along the coast, while robins and bluejays are the common types of birds you'll see further inland. The New Hampshire lakes, such as Squam and Winnipesaukee, are especially hospitable to loons, and hawks can sometimes be seen soaring over New England's more mountainous areas.

THE LAY OF THE LAND

A tour of New England will reveal a landscape that is as interesting and as beautiful as it is varied. The southern and central part of the region bordering the Atlantic, including eastern Connecticut, eastern Massachusetts, and Rhode Island, is typical of many coastal areas on the eastern seaboard. The land is relatively flat leading out to a shore lined with white-sand beaches. Traveling northward along the Maine coast, the shoreline becomes increasingly more rugged and rocky, reaching a crescendo at Acadia National Park, which contains both Cadillac Mountain, the highest point on the Atlantic coast, and Somme Sound—the only natural fjord on the eastern coast.

Farther inland Maine becomes more mountainous, and the almost completely landlocked states of Vermont and New Hampshire (a tiny section of southeastern New Hampshire does touch the sea) are all but dominated by the majestic Green and White Mountain ranges, respectively. New Hampshire lays claim to Mt. Washington— the tallest mountain in the northeast, at over 6,000 feet, and while the Berkshires of western Massachusetts do not reach such lofty heights, they are a respectable mountain range nonetheless. Traveling south from the Berkshires, the mountains give way to the more subtle rolling hills of western Connecticut. In central Connecticut, the Connecticut River cuts a swath across the middle of the state leading to the Atlantic once again.

OUTDOOR ACTIVITIES

Naturally, in terrain as varied as New England's, outdoor activities are plentiful and diverse enough to suit all tastes. Hundreds of miles of shoreline insure that surfers, swimmers, windsurfers, and sailors have ample opportunities to pursue their hobbies. Inland lakes, rivers, and streams provide outlets for fishing, kayaking, rafting, and canoeing enthusiasts; while thousands of acres of mountainous forests offer the perfect setting in which to hike the Appalachian Trail, rock climb, backcountry camp, hunt, or mountain bike.

In certain parts of New England, hot-air balloon trips are now possible, and the coastal waters are popular for whale-watching. Bird-watchers will find numerous wildlife sanctuaries throughout the region. In the winter, the Berkshires and the White and Green Mountains come to life with snowmobilers as well as downhill and cross-country skiers.

PRACTICAL TIPS

HOW MUCH WILL IT COST?

The cost of your trip to New England will be determined by a number of factors, such as how long you will be visiting the region, how many people are in your party, whether you fly to New England or drive from a neighboring state, whether you rent a vehicle or travel in your own car, whether you eat primarily in restaurants or prepare your own meals, and whether you camp or stay in expensive hotels. What you spend depends on the style in which you travel. I have listed average costs for car rentals, lodging, and meals in the Transportation, Camping and Lodging, and Food sections of this chapter. More-specific price information is provided throughout the book for lodgings, restaurants, and sights to help you plan your trip budget in greater detail.

WHEN TO GO

The best time to visit New England is between mid-May and mid-October. Many historical sites, restaurants, and hotels listed here are open only during those months when the climate is at its best. Of course, New England is known worldwide for its spectacular fall foliage, which generally reaches its peak in Vermont and New Hampshire in early October. Winter skiing is also a popular attraction there. Do keep in mind that if you visit New England for the foliage or for skiing, many of the suggested sightseeing highlights will already be closed for the season.

July and August are the busiest months in terms of tourists, and the most expensive—particularly in the coastal regions. Vermont and New Hampshire are naturally very crowded during peak leaf-peeping season, when places like North Conway in the Mt. Washington valley of New Hampshire turn into veritable parking lots on Columbus Day weekend. If you plan to travel during peak periods, advance lodging reservations are a necessity. I've been told that churches have had to open their doors to stranded tourists, or worse, weary travelers have spent frosty New England nights upright in their cars. For your trip to run as smoothly as possible, I recommend calling ahead for reservations.

In my experience, the best time to see New England is in September. The weather is usually sunny and pleasant without the heat and humidity of July and August, ocean temperatures are at their warmest, and many sites are still operating on their extended summer schedules. You may miss the foliage at its peak (although I'll bet you'll see a few leaves turning in the northern regions), but you'll also miss many of the summer tourists, and off-season rates begin just after Labor Day in some coastal towns.

June is another good time to travel and avoid the crowds, but the weather is less predictable than in September, and high-season rates generally go into effect on Memorial Day weekend.

TRANSPORTATION

Just about all of the major airlines have several daily nonstop flights to Boston from most major U.S. airports. Prices vary depending upon your departure city, but fares from airline to airline are generally comparable. Your travel agent can help get you the lowest-price flight available for your desired departure date. It is usually best to purchase your ticket at least 30 days in advance to secure the lowest fare.

NEW ENGLAND'S CLIMATE

Average daily high and low temperatures in degrees Fahrenheit, plus monthly precipitation in inches.

	Boston	Portland	Hartford	Burlington
Jan.	37/23	32/12	36/18	27/10
	3.6	3.5	3.4	1.8
March	46/31	41/25	45/27	38/20
	3.7	3.7	3.6	2.2
May	67/50	64/42	71/47	66/44
	3.3	3.6	4.1	3.1
July	82/65	79/57	85/62	81/59
	2.8	3.1	3.2	3.7
Sept.	73/57	69/47	75/52	69/49
	3.1	3.1	3.8	3.3
Nov.	52/36	48/30	52/32	44/30
	4.2	5.2	4.0	3.1

While the metropolitan Boston area is readily accessible by public transportation and a network of commuter trains and buses, the rest of New England is not. Greyhound, Bonanza, Peter Pan, and Vermont Transit bus companies serve the more rural areas of New England to some extent, but you will find it hard to travel to all the sights once you reach each destination by bus.

This book is designed for those traveling by car, RV, or motorcycle. With the exception of Sargent Drive along Somme Sound in Maine, all suggested routes are open those types of vehicles. However, the auto roads to Cadillac Summit in Acadia National Park and to Mt. Washington in New Hampshire may be too precarious for larger motor homes and too demanding for older cars.

You'll find that states such as Maine, New Hampshire, and Vermont are very good about providing directional and mileage signs for historical sites, lodging, and eating establishments that are off secondary roads.

If this is your first trip to New England, it may also be your first experience with rotary traffic circles. A word of caution: these circular intersections—found most often in Massachusetts when three or more roads come together—can be dangerous, so approach them carefully. A Massachusetts driver's approach to rotaries is, "Close your eyes and go." While this is not recommended, neither is timidity. Many unaccustomed drivers get hit because they hesitate too long. Try to blend into rotary traffic as easily as possible, moving at a slow but steady speed. Do not stop in the middle of a rotary! If you miss your exit, just continue on around and exit on your next circuit.

Renting a Vehicle: All major car rental agencies have offices in Boston. Compact cars generally run about $225 per week with unlimited mileage, and midsize cars can rent for up to $250 per week or more. Subcompacts are somewhat cheaper and get better gas mileage but can feel cramped when you spend a lot of time inside them.

CAMPING AND LODGING

Country inns are one of the best ways to truly immerse yourself in New England tradition. Inns, some of which have been operating for 100 years or more, serve regional specialties, are often furnished with priceless antiques, and generally offer comfortable to exceptional lodging, sometimes at little more than the cost of a motel room. A night in a country inn will generally be at least $100 for two during the summer, and can be as little as $60 in the off-season (of course, rates vary greatly depending upon location and type of accommodation offered). In many cases, the room rate includes a full breakfast, making the cost more appealing. Motels in the area average about $55 for two but often provide only half as much in the way of amenities and atmosphere. However, if you're traveling with a family, motels may be the only affordable lodging other than camping. For those who want to travel lavishly, I have also listed luxury accommodations.

Camping is a much cheaper alternative to staying in either bed and breakfasts or motels, although many campgrounds on the itinerary are not as convenient to the sights. Campgrounds operated by state, national, and municipal park services usually charge less than private campgrounds—about $12 per night. Park-run campgrounds tend to be more wooded and less crowded than private ones but often don't have facilities such as hot showers, grocery stores, playgrounds, or swimming pools on the premises, as many private camping areas do. Of course, there is a price to pay for convenience: nightly rates at private camp-grounds run at least $15—or more. To get the most satisfaction from your trip, choose the type of lodging that best suits your lifestyle and budget.

FOOD

Preparing your own meals is the most economical way to eat on your trip, and you shouldn't have any trouble finding adequate provisions at any point along the way. If you're not equipped for food preparation or prefer to leave that task to others while on vacation, be prepared to spend an average of $5 for breakfast, $7 for lunch, and at least $10 for dinner, per person, when eating out. The restaurants I suggest are ones that I've personally enjoyed, or that have local reputations for their food quality, uniqueness, convenience, or price. Fresh seafood is what comes to mind first when one thinks of New England cuisine, but places like Boston and Cambridge offer the visitor a wide variety in ethnic dining as well.

An ice chest or a inexpensive Styrofoam cooler, stocked with soda, juice, yogurt, cheese, and other snacks, can save both money and time. If your bed and breakfast sends you off with a hearty morning meal, you can often get by until dinner with just a yogurt in the early after-noon. If your lodging establishment doesn't provide breakfast, a chilled fruit cup from the cooler may be just the thing to start the day. By cut-ting out one restaurant meal a day, you can reduce your total trip cost significantly. Having the cooler will also save time since you won't have to pull off the highway every time you feel a pang of hunger or thirst. Besides, the less time you spend looking for a place to eat, the more time you'll have to explore the New England you came to see.

LICENSES

Since campfire and fishing regulations vary from state to state, it is wise to check with each state prior to engaging in either activity. Most states require fishing licenses (Maine sells theirs at the Tourist Information Center in Kittery), and in some areas, permits are required for campfires.

WHAT TO BRING

Mark Twain once said, "One of the brightest gems in the New England weather is the dazzling uncertainty of it." There couldn't be a truer statement, so the best way to deal with New England weather is to come prepared. Even in the hottest summer months, it is possible to run into cool evenings in parts of Maine, Vermont, and New Hampshire. Bring at least one heavy sweater no matter what season you plan to visit the area. The sweater will also come in handy any time you are out on the Atlantic, whether it's on a whale-watching vessel, the ferry to Nantucket, or a small pleasure craft; the ocean breezes can be quite chilling.

Although I hope you won't have occasion to use it, rain gear is a must when traveling through New England. It is unlikely that you'll be able to spend a week or two in the area without encountering some form of precipitation, even if it's only a soft island mist on Martha's Vineyard. I recommend packing a lightweight hooded poncho to use while cycling or hiking and a fold-up umbrella for city sight-seeing.

Binoculars will help bring the scenic vistas and wildlife of Acadia and the White Mountains National Forest into closer view, so make room in your suitcase for a pair. You wouldn't want to miss seeing the seals basking on the rocks just off the Maine coast.

Also pack a small empty knapsack or day-pack. It should be large enough to hold your sweater, poncho, guidebook, map, camera, and binoculars, but lightweight enough to carry easily on your back. You'll find it invaluable when hiking, traveling to the islands, or simply transporting a picnic lunch.

RECOMMENDED READING

Reading (or rereading) *The House of Seven Gables* by Nathaniel Hawthorne, *Little Women* by Louisa May Alcott, *Ethan Frome* by Edith Wharton, and *Walden* by Henry David Thoreau will complement your New England sojourn as you visit the haunts and homes that inspired these great American literary classics. The many layers of Newport, Rhode Island, society were the basis for Thornton Wilder's enjoyable *Theophilus North*, while Henry Beston spent a Thoreau-like year in a tiny house on Nauset Beach in Cape Cod recording the passage of nature in his book, *The Outermost House*; either book will add an extra dimension to your trip. Robert McCloskey's *Make Way for Ducklings*, a delightful tale of a duck family living in the Boston Public Gardens, will help the city come alive for young children.

RESOURCES

Connecticut Tourism Office: (800) CT-BOUND
Maine Publicity Bureau: (207) 623-0363
Massachusetts Office of Travel and Tourism: (617) 727-3201
New Hampshire Office of Travel and Tourism: (603) 271-2666
Rhode Island Tourism Division: (800) 556-2484
Vermont Chamber of Commerce: (802) 223-3443

1
BOSTON

Boston was established in 1630, and you get a sense of its long history the moment you arrive. It's hard to walk more than a block in downtown Boston without seeing some kind of historic marker. If it weren't for the parked cars, a walk at dusk along Beacon Hill's gaslit brick sidewalks and cobblestone streets might convince you that you'd traveled back in time to the nineteenth century. With the exception of Back Bay, a former tidal marsh area that was filled in and laid out in the mid-nineteenth century, Boston's complex network of narrow streets, distinct neighborhoods, and old brick buildings give it more the feel of a European city than a modern American metropolis.

However, you need only look at the number of glass skyscrapers in the financial district to realize that progress has by no means passed Boston by. In addition to the thriving financial community, countless high-tech firms have their headquarters in the Boston area. Boston Harbor, once the city's mainstay, is still a busy port. Long a center of learning, Boston boasts one of the greatest concentrations of higher-education institutions in the nation and is on the cutting edge of medical research. Consequently, it is an interesting, culturally diverse, and attractive city, steeped in its past yet vibrantly alive in its present. ◨

BOSTON

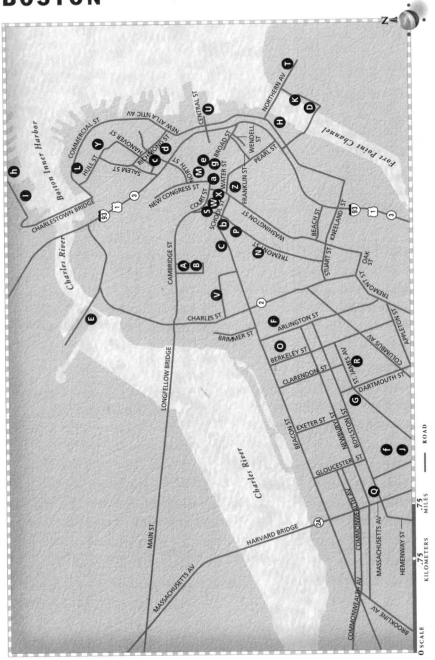

Boston Inner Harbor

Fort Point Channel

Charles River

Charles River

COMMERCIAL ST
HULL ST
SALEM ST
HANOVER ST
RICHMOND ST
NORTH ST
NEW ATLANTIC AV
CENTRAL ST
NEW CONGRESS ST
COURT ST
SCHOOL ST
WATER ST
BROAD ST
FRANKLIN ST
WENDELL ST
PEARL ST
WASHINGTON ST
TREMONT ST
CAMBRIDGE ST
CHARLES ST
BRIMMER ST
ARLINGTON ST
BERKELEY ST
CLARENDON ST
ST JAMES AV
DARTMOUTH ST
COLUMBUS AV
APPLETON ST
BEACON ST
EXETER ST
NEWBURY ST
BOYLSTON ST
GLOUCESTER ST
COMMONWEALTH AV
MASSACHUSETTS AV
HEMENWAY ST
BROOKLINE AV
MAIN ST
STUART ST
BEACH ST
KNEELAND ST
OAK ST
TREMONT ST
NORTHERN AV
CHARLESTOWN BRIDGE
LONGFELLOW BRIDGE
HARVARD BRIDGE

0 SCALE
.75 KILOMETERS
.75 MILES

ROAD

Sights

A African Meeting House

B The Black Heritage Trail

C The Boston Athenaeum

D Boston Children's Museum

E Boston Museum of Science

F The Boston Public Gardens

G The Boston Public Library

H Boston Tea Party Ship & Museum

I The Bunker Hill Pavilion and Monument

J Christian Science Center

K The Computer Museum

L Cop's Hill Burial Ground

M Faneuil Hall

N The Freedom Trail

O Gibson House Museum

P Granary Burying Ground

Q Institute of Contemporary Art

R The John Hancock Observatory

S King's Chapel

T The Massachusetts Bay Brewing Company

U New England Aquarium

V Nichols House Museum

W Old City Hall

X Old Corner Bookstore

Y Old North Church

Z Old South Meeting House

a Old State House

b Park Street Church

c Paul Revere House

d Pierce/Hicborn House

e Quincy Market

f The Skywalk at the Prudential Building

g State House

h USS Constitution Museum

A PERFECT DAY IN BOSTON

Boston has so much to offer, and I've had so many wonderful days there over the years, that it is truly hard for me to focus on one single favorite day. The city can accommodate visitors with so many different interests that your perfect day might be vastly different from mine. For instance, if you're interested in science, then your ideal day would probably include visits to the science and computer museums. If you're drawn to the sea, then a tour of the aquarium, the USS *Constitution*, and a harbor cruise might be your ultimate day in Boston. Since I'm a lover of the arts, I would spend mine in the city's superb art museums.

My favorite day would begin with a breakfast picnic in the Boston Public Gardens—enjoying the beauty of the flowers and birds in the quiet calm of the early morning. Then I'd hop on the T and travel to the Museum of Fine Arts to be one of the first ones through the door when the museum opens at 10 a.m. After a few hours wandering through its galleries and visiting the MFA's gift shop (making a few purchases, no doubt), I'd break for lunch in the museum's fine restaurant. After lunch I'd walk over to the Gardner museum and leisurely linger in its divine courtyard. Following the Gardner, I'd head to Newbury Street and browse through its shops and galleries—perhaps finding a treasured used book at the Victor Hugo Bookshop (at number 339) or the latest bestseller at Waterstones' (on the corner of Newbury and Exeter). Just before dusk I'd go up to the observation deck of either the Prudential or John Hancock Buildings (depending on which building was closer at the time), and watch the lights come on all over the city. From there, I'd travel across town to the North End for a marvelous Italian meal. If I had any energy left after dinner, I'd stroll through Quincy Market to see whatever street acts might still be performing, or unwind to music in a piano bar.

ARRIVING IN BOSTON

Although Logan Airport is only 2½ miles from downtown Boston, getting to the downtown area can often be an exhausting experience. (If you're renting a car for your trip through New England, I recommend waiting to pick it up until after you've visited Boston and Cambridge. Driving in the city can be confusing at best, and parking is both limited and expensive.) From the airport, cab fare into the city will run at least $10, and can be very expensive if you get stuck in traffic, which you're bound to do—but a taxi may be your only option if you have a lot of luggage. Share a cab if possible. Some downtown hotels will pick up guests from the airport, so you may want to call and check with your lodging to see if they offer such a service before jumping into a taxi.

If you are traveling light, the MBTA (Massachusetts Bay Transportation Authority) is the fastest and least expensive means to reach the downtown area. A free shuttle bus that stops regularly at all airline terminals will take you to the Blue Line subway stop. A subway token is 85 cents, and in 10 minutes you'll be in the heart of Boston. Board the train on the "Inbound" side of the tracks. A map of the entire subway system is clearly posted in every subway station to help guide you to your destination.

Another option when traveling to downtown is to take the Water Taxi from Logan Airport. This is a quick and scenic method, but unless your hotel is located on the waterfront, you'll still have to transfer to some other mode of transportation once across the harbor.

Amtrak trains arrive at South Station several times a day from New York and points south. South Station is on the main subway line, and no doubt your hotel will only be a short subway or cab ride away.

Greyhound operates a terminal in the city, providing access to Boston from many smaller towns. The depot is near the Arlington Street subway stop of the Green Line in Back Bay.

By car, Boston can be reached from the west by the Massachusetts Turnpike, from the north by Interstate 95 to Route 1, and from the northwest and south by Interstate 93, known locally as the Southeast Expressway.

GETTING AROUND BOSTON

Walking is the preferred form of transportation in this compact city. Be sure to wear comfortable shoes, since many of the old brick and cobblestone streets were in place long before high heels came into vogue.

The subway system is the oldest in the country and sometimes operates like an antique. Subway stations are marked by a "T" symbol. The network of lines (Red, Green, Blue, and Orange) is quite extensive in the heart of the city, but check your street map before hopping on the system. Often three stops on the subway are only three physical blocks apart, and it would take more time to wait for the train than to walk the distance yourself. The farther you're going from the city center, the more sense it makes to travel by subway, but it is best to avoid subway travel at rush hour. Although tokens cost 85 cents, in some areas additional fare is required. If you plan to use the subway often, short-term visitor passes can be purchased at the Greater Boston Convention & Visitor's Bureau at the Prudential Tower, or ask at any MBTA office for additional sales locations.

If you drove to Boston, it's probably best to leave your car parked at your hotel. Since Boston has been settled for more than 350 years, a great number of existing thoroughfares were laid down over old cow-paths that follow no logical design. The haphazard pattern of streets can be a nightmare for out-of-town drivers, and parking spaces are hard to come by. Don't try to demystify Boston driving, or to tame Boston drivers, in a few short days. You'll have fewer headaches and enjoy the city much more if you travel on foot.

SIGHTSEEING HIGHLIGHTS

★★★ **The Freedom Trail** • The trail, which is a 3-mile walking tour of many of Boston's most important historical sites, may be the best way for a first-time visitor to become acquainted with the city's roots. The trail begins at the information booth in Boston Common on Tremont Street between the Park Street and Tremont Street subway stations. Walking the trail and visiting all of the sites in one day requires too much standing for some. Sightseeing tours also travel the 3-mile route. You can get tour information from the visitor informa-tion kiosk as well. Should you decide to tackle the trail on your own, it is well-marked by a red line on the pavement, but it's a good idea to get a trail map at the information booth in case you decide to stray from the main route at all. In addition, the map contains background information on each site.

The first stop on the Freedom Trail is the "new" **State House**, designed by respected architect Charles Bullfinch and built in 1795. The Capitol was built on land belonging to John Hancock's family, and Samuel Adams laid the cornerstone. With its gleaming golden dome, it has long been a cherished Boston landmark. Hours: Open Monday through Friday from 10 a.m. to 4 p.m.

The next stop is the **Park Street Church** and **Granary Burying Ground**, where John Hancock and Samuel Adams lie buried near vic-tims of the Boston Massacre. A little farther down Tremont Street is **King's Chapel**, built in 1754. Behind the chapel on School Street is the **Old City Hall**, now home to a marvelous French restaurant,

Maison Robert, and a commemorative statue of Benjamin Franklin. Several doors down, on the corner of School and Washington Streets, is the **Old Corner Bookstore** in a lovely brick building that dates back to 1712. Now known for its fine selection of regional and travel titles, the store is steeped in literary history: such notable figures as Henry David Thoreau, Henry Wadsworth Longfellow, Ralph Waldo Emerson, and Judge Oliver Wendell Holmes met there in the 1800s to discuss topics of the day.

Diagonally across from the Old Corner Bookstore at the **Old South Meeting House** you can view a multimedia presentation on the building's role in history: Boston Tea Party rallies were held here. The meeting house was built in 1729. Admission is $2.50 for adults, $2 for seniors and students, $1 for children 6 to 18. Hours: Open 9:30 a.m. to 5 p.m. daily April through October; 10 a.m. to 4 p.m. weekdays, and 10 a.m. to 5 p.m. weekends during the rest of the year.

The **Old State House**, the next stop on the trail, was built in 1712 and currently houses exhibits on Boston history. Just outside the State House is the site of the Boston Massacre, where five colonists were slain by British soldiers in 1770, foreshadowing the Revolutionary War. Hours: Open daily from 9:30 a.m. to 5 p.m. Admission to the museum is $3 for adults, $2 for seniors and students, $1.50 for children 6 to 18. Address: Washington and State Streets.

From the State House you'll pass through **Faneuil Hall** and **Quincy Market**, old buildings that have been refurbished to serve as a major focal point for entertainment, dining, and shopping in the city. Because of the number of dining options this could be a good place to stop, have lunch, and recharge your batteries for completing the rest of the trail. If you find the shops tempting, you can always return in the evening for a more leisurely visit; many of the stores stay open late.

From Quincy Market, cross under Interstate 93 to Boston's thriving North End district where a large Italian population keeps their customs alive through restaurants, groceries, and bakeries. If you didn't dine at Quincy Market, you may want to treat yourself to a memorable lunch in one of the North End's fabulous bistros while you're here. Paul Revere was perhaps the North End's most famous former resident, and his home at 19 North Square is the next stop along the Freedom Trail. The **Paul Revere House**, built in 1676, is the oldest building still standing in the city of Boston. On exhibit in the home are Revere documents, memorabilia, and, of course, silver. Admission to the house is $2.50 for adults, $2 for seniors and students, $1 for children 5 to 17. Hours: Open daily from 9:30 a.m. to 5:15 p.m. mid-April through October, from 9:30 a.m. to 4:15 p.m. during winter. The Revere House is closed on Mondays January through March. **The Pierce/Hicborn House** next door, circa 1711, can be toured with the Revere House for a combined admission charge of $3.25 for adults, $2.25 for students and seniors, $1 for children.

From the Revere house, follow the trail to the **Old North Church** where the famed lanterns ("one if by land, two if by sea") warned of the British arrival the night of Paul Revere's ride. Farther up Hull Street you'll pass the old **Cop's Hill Burial Ground**, where Edward Hartt, the builder of the USS *Constitution*, was buried. Cross the Charlestown Bridge to the Charlestown Navy Yard to view his creation, also known as "Old Ironsides." The ship was built in 1797, saw active duty in the War of 1812, and is the oldest commissioned warship afloat today. Guided tours of the ship are given from 9:30 a.m. to 3:50 p.m., but if you get there after 3:50 p.m. you can still tour the top deck of the ship on your own until sunset. There is also a **USS Constitution Museum**, open year-round. Admission is $4 for adults, $3 for seniors and students, and free for children under 6, but the ship itself is free. Hours: Open 9 a.m. to 6 p.m. in summer, 9 a.m. to 4 p.m. in winter, 9 a.m. to 5 p.m. in spring and fall; closed Thanksgiving, Christmas, and New Year's Day.

Just outside the entrance to the Navy Yard you can see a multimedia re-creation of the battle of Bunker Hill at **The Bunker Hill Pavilion**. Reenactments are shown every half hour, and the pavilion is open daily from 9:30 a.m. to 4 p.m., and until 5 p.m. during the summer months. Admission is $3 for adults, $2 for seniors, $1.50 for children 5 and up, $8 for families. Then walk up the hill to the 220-foot-tall **Bunker Hill Monument** that commemorates the major Revolutionary War battle. Hours: Open 9:30 a.m. to 6 p.m. June through August, from 9:30 a.m. to 4 p.m. September through May. Admission to the monument is free.

Once you've reached the end of the trail there is no need to retrace your steps back into town. MBTA buses run frequently from Charlestown to downtown Boston. (All day)

★★★ **Boston Museum of Fine Arts** • This is one of the most highly respected art museums in the country. The collection consists of ancient Greek, Roman, Egyptian, and Oriental art, with classic European and American artists represented as well. There are also American period rooms, early American furniture, silver, and fine musical instruments. The West Wing addition, designed by I. M. Pei, houses changing exhibits, an attractive restaurant, and a superlative museum gift shop. Courtyard dining adjoins the lower-level cafeteria. Hours: Open Tuesday through Sunday 10 a.m. to 5 p.m., Wednesday until 10 p.m. The West Wing is open until 10 p.m. on Thursday and Friday evenings. Admission is $8 for adults, $6 for seniors and students, $3.50 for children 6 to 17. Everyone is admitted free of charge on Wednesday from 4 p.m. to 9:45 p.m. Address: 465 Huntington Avenue, across from Northeastern University. The Huntington Avenue branch of the Green Line stops right in front of the museum. (2½ hours)

✶✶ **Boston Museum of Science** • Test your strength, then discover the power of electricity. Learn about the earth's gravitational force, then explore faraway planets in the planetarium. You can spend hours in this fascinating museum unearthing the secrets of nature's unseen energy sources as well as those that are visible to the naked eye, and seeing how man tries to tame and control them. Many of the exhibits are participatory. Hours: Open daily from 9 a.m. to 5 p.m. (until 7 p.m. during the summer) and Friday evening until 9 p.m. Admission to the museum and the Omni Theater is $7 for adults, $5 for children 4 to 14 and for seniors. Admission to the planetarium is separate, but combination tickets are available. Address: The museum has its own subway stop on the Lechmere branch of the Green Line. (2 hours)

✶✶ **The Boston Public Gardens** • Founded in 1897 and designed by Frederick Law Olmstead, who also created New York's Central Park, these are the oldest public gardens in the United States. The gardens are in full bloom from April through October, but the stately trees and beautiful landscaping make them a pleasure to visit in any season. Children will love the *Make Way for Ducklings* sculpture, depicting a scene from the book of the same name, and a ride on Boston's own Swan Boats. A swan boat ride is a relaxing way for adults to get perspective on the city as well. A small fee is charged. Swan boats operate from 10 a.m. to 4 p.m. mid-April through mid-June and 10 a.m. to 5 p.m. mid-June through Labor Day. Phone: (617) 635-4505. (It only takes a few minutes to walk through the gardens. Allow more time if you plan to picnic or take a boat ride.)

✶✶ **The Computer Museum** • With the influence of the high-tech industry in Boston, and nearby Massachusetts Institute of Technology turning out computer geniuses of the future, it is no wonder that Boston had the first museum devoted to the history of the computer.

Get a close-up look at the first computers, then test your skills in the PC gallery. Hours: Open daily from 10 a.m. to 6 p.m. during summer months, Friday evening until 9 p.m.; Tuesday through Sunday from 10 a.m. to 5 p.m. September through May. Address: On Museum Wharf next to the Children's Museum. Admission is $7 for adults, $5 for students and seniors, free for children under 4. Admission is half-price on Sundays from 3 p.m. to 5 p.m. (2 hours)

✪✪ **Isabella Stewart Gardner Museum** • My favorite museum in Boston, this Venetian-style palazzo on the Fenway just 2 blocks from the Museum of Fine Arts houses Ms. Gardner's extraordinary private collection. Imagine having a chapel in your home with a thirteenth-century stained-glass window and living with not one but three Rembrandts. Ms. Gardner, an avid patron of the arts, made it her life's work to amass this collection, ranging from early Italian religious paintings to American and French impressionists of the last century to beautifully intricate European laces. The courtyard, complete with Roman statues and mosaics, is abloom with flowers in every season and makes a splendid haven from the outside world. Concerts are given frequently in the halls, usually on Sunday afternoons at 3 p.m. There is also a café on the premises. Despite the much-publicized theft of some of the museum's most famous works in 1990, it remains a treasure well worth unearthing. Hours: Open Tuesday through Sunday from 11 a.m. to 5 p.m. Admission is $7 for adults, $5 for students and senior citizens, $3 for kids 12 to 17, and free for children under 12. (2 hours)

✪✪ **The John Hancock Observatory** or **The Skywalk at the Prudential Building** • From the top of either the John Hancock Tower in Copley Square or the Prudential Building nearby, you'll see magnificent views of the city and beyond on clear days and the city sparkling as night falls. Observatory hours: Monday through Saturday from 9 a.m. to 10 p.m., Sunday from noon to 10 p.m. Admission is $3.75 for adults, $2.75 for seniors and children 5 to 15. The Skywalk at the Prudential Building just down the street is not as tall but has views in all directions (the Hancock is closed off on one side). Skywalk hours: Open Monday through Saturday from 10 a.m. to 10 p.m., Sunday from noon to 10 p.m. Admission is $2.75 for adults and $1.75 for seniors, students, and children 5 to 15. (1 hour)

✪✪ **John F. Kennedy Library and Museum** • Your visit begins with a film on Kennedy in an imposing building designed by noted architect

I. M. Pei. Then it's on to the exhibits, which include Kennedy's presidential desk, video presentations of the former president on the campaign trail, and important speeches from his term in office. More than just a tribute to one man, the library gives you a fascinating look into our recent past. Hours: Open daily from 9 a.m. to 5 p.m., except Thanksgiving, Christmas, and New Year's Day. The last film of the day starts at 3:50 p.m. Admission is $6 for adults, $4 for seniors and students, and $2 for children. Address: In the Columbia Point section of Boston. Phone: Call (617) 929-4523 for directions. (2 hours)

✹✹ **New England Aquarium** • What trip to the coast would be complete without a look at the inhabitants of the sea? The aquarium has a magnificent cylindrical glass tank several stories high. You can view hundreds of species of sea life, including sharks, barracudas, and giant sea turtles, as you wind your way down the spiral ramp. Dolphin shows are included in your admission. If you don't have time to go in the museum, at least take a few minutes as you stroll along the waterfront to watch the seals play at the outside entrance to the aquarium. Hours: Open daily from 9 a.m. to 5 p.m., later in the summer. Times vary depending upon the season. Address: On Central Wharf, 3 blocks from Faneuil Hall Marketplace next to the Aquarium T stop on the Blue Line. Phone: (617) 973-5200 for current hours during your visit. Admission is $8.50 for adults, $7.50 for seniors, $4.50 for children 3 to 11. (1½ hours)

✹ **Boston Children's Museum** (✹✹✹ **if you are travelling with children**) • The museum is known for its "hands-on" exhibits, Native American collection, and Japanese home painstakingly moved here piece by piece from Kyoto. Children magically become hushed when they enter the Japanese house, but in the rest of the museum laughter prevails as they try on clothes in Grandmother's Attic, scramble up and down over several levels in the climbing structure, and blow bubbles as big as they are. Teens will enjoy "faultless jamming" in the clubhouse designed especially for them, with electronic musical instruments that sound good together no matter how they are played. Hours: Open daily from 10 a.m. to 5 p.m., Friday evening until 9 p.m. Closed on Monday from Labor Day through June, and on New Year's, Thanksgiving, and Christmas. Admission is $7 for adults, $6 for seniors and children 2 to 15, $2 for 1-year-olds. Admission Friday evenings from 5 p.m. to 9 p.m. is only $1 for everyone. Address: On Congress Street at Museum Wharf. (3 hours)

✸ **Boston Tea Party Ship & Museum** • You get to throw a tea chest overboard in protest of the British tax on this replica of the eighteenth-century ship where the famous revolt took place. (The chests aren't actually filled with tea and are connected by rope, but at least you get to feel like a rebel.) Admission is $6.50 for adults and $3.50 for children over age 5. Hours: Open daily from 9 a.m. to 6 p.m. during the summer, until 5 p.m. the rest of the year. Closed December through March. Address: 300 Congress Street on Museum Wharf. (1 hour)

Arnold Arboretum • For an outdoor excursion, a visit to the Arboretum at the Arborway in Jamaica Plain is well worthwhile—especially during lilac season. The 265-acre landscaped Arboretum has more than 7,000 varieties of trees and boasts the second-largest collection of lilacs in all of North America, with over 400 varieties. Hours: The visitor's center is open from 10 a.m. to 4 p.m., the grounds from sunrise to sunset. Phone: (617) 524-1718. Admission is free.

The Black Heritage Trail • Similar to the Freedom Trail, this walking tour highlights significant places in Boston's black history. The **African Meeting House**, the oldest standing black church in the United States, is one of the stops on the trail. Hours: Daily from 10 a.m. to 4 p.m. Address: The African Meeting House is at 8 Smith Court. Other sites on the trail can be visited only with an organized tour. Phone: (617) 742-5415 for information.

The Boston Athenaeum • At 10½ Beacon Street near the State House, the Athenaeum is a long-standing Boston institution. The library's collection includes early American publications and an exhibit gallery of American art.

The Boston Beer Company • The brewery is known for local favorite Samuel Adams Lager. Hours: Tours are held Thursday and Friday at 2 p.m.; tours run continuously from noon to 2:30 p.m. on Saturday. A $1 donation is requested Phone: (617) 522-9080.

The Boston Public Library • Located in Copley Square, the library was designed by the highly regarded architectural firm of McKim, Mead & White.

Christian Science Center • This headquarters of the First Church of Christ is architecturally impressive. The *Christian Science Monitor* is published here, and the 30-foot stained glass globe called the Mapparium, inside one of the center's buildings, is frequented by tourists. Address: On Huntington Avenue behind the Prudential Building. Admission is free.

Gibson House Museum • An 1859 Victorian home. Tours at 2 p.m., 3 p.m., and 4 p.m. Wednesday through Sunday, May through October, and November through April on Saturday and Sunday at the same hours. No tours are given on major holidays. Address: 137 Beacon Street in Back Bay. Admission is $3.

Institute of Contemporary Art • This museum features changing exhibits of contemporary art. Admission is $5 for adults, $3 for students, $2 for seniors and children under 16. Free Thursday evenings. Hours: Open Wednesday through Sunday from noon to 5 p.m., staying open until 9 p.m. on Thursday evenings. Address: 955 Boylston Street.

The Massachusetts Bay Brewing Company • This company also runs brewery tours on Tuesday, Friday, and Saturday. Phone: (617) 574-9551.

Museum of the National Center of Afro-American Artists • This museum focuses on visual arts by Afro-Americans. Hours: Tuesday through Saturday from 1 p.m. to 5 p.m., and until 6 p.m. in the summer months. Address: 300 Walnut Avenue in the Roxbury section of Boston. Admission is $4 for adults. Phone: (617) 442-8614.

Nichols House Museum • This 1809 period home that once belonged to Rose Standish Nichols is at 55 Mt. Vernon Street atop Beacon Hill. Hours: During the summer, Tuesday through Saturday from noon to 5 p.m.; hours are more limited during the rest of the year. Phone: Call (617) 227-6993 if you are interested in visiting during the off-season. Admission is $4.

FITNESS AND RECREATION

S ince Boston is a compact and walkable city, and most sights are best reached on foot, you'll probably get plenty of exercise just walking around sightseeing. However, facilities do exist if you desire an even more active vacation. A bike trail begins at the Museum of Science and ends at Watertown Square. If you're adventurous or a frequent bicyclist, the 17-mile distance should not be challenging, but most visitors stick to the section that runs along the banks of the Charles River from the Esplanade to the far end of Back Bay. This portion of the path is also favored by runners and roller bladers. Bicycles can be rented from **Earth Bikes** at 35 Huntington Avenue near Copley Square, (617) 267-4733.

For those who wish to try their hand at sailing or windsurfing on the Charles, **Community Boating** (617-523-1038) offers programs for short-term visitors (a 2-day membership runs about $50, a 7-day membership is around $70). The boat dock is located on the river near the Charles Street MBTA station, and is open April through October.

The MDC operates a number of ice skating rinks in the metropolitan area, and public skating hours are built into the schedule. The most convenient rink to downtown Boston is located on the far side of the North End.

FOOD

While Boston has no shortage of good restaurants, four eateries have remained popular for more than 100 years. The **Locke Ober Cafe** (617-542-1340), down an alley off Winter Street, was established in 1875. It is an old-money institution with dark wood paneling, hard-backed leather chairs, and a men's-club atmosphere. Menu items include lobster Savannah, Wiener schnitzel, and expensive prices. **Jacob Wirth's** (617-338-8586), across from the New England Medical Center on Stuart Street near Chinatown, has changed little over the last century. The wooden floors are well worn, the home-brewed beer (both light and dark) is full-bodied, the hearty meals have a German flavor, and prices are moderate. **Durgin Park** (617-227-2038) in Faneuil Hall Marketplace is yet another Boston landmark noted for New England-style meals, large portions, and surly waitresses. The restaurant originally served the men who worked the docks (big meals at low prices), and has tried to retain the same atmosphere—although prices are no longer dirt cheap. Just around the corner, the **Union Oyster House** (617-227-2750), established in 1826, has a raw oyster bar and specializes in seafood. Entrees range from $15 to $25. The quality of the food has slipped somewhat in recent years at Locke Ober, Durgin Park, and the Union Oyster House, and the restaurants seem to be riding on their reputation a bit. However, they are still worth visiting for tradition's sake.

Although **Maison Robert** and **Cafe Budapest** aren't a century old, they've still been around long enough to become venerated Boston eateries. Maison Robert, at 45 School Street, is located in lovely Old City Hall, and fine French fare is the restaurant's specialty (617-227-3370). Continental cuisine, with an emphasis on Hungarian dishes, is the focus of Cafe Budapest's menu. A violinist in the evening adds a touch of romance to the atmosphere (90 Exeter Street, 617-266-1979). Expect to pay a price for dining at either restaurant, but Maison Robert does operate a more moderately priced café downstairs from its main restaurant. On the trendy side, Boston has a **Hard Rock Cafe** (131 Clarendon, 617-424-7625). While not as much a novelty as these cafes once were when there were only a few, a meal at the Hard Rock can still be a fun experience if you're a rock 'n' roll fan—and of course the memorabilia is different in each restaurant.

Anthony's Pier 4 at 140 Northern Avenue overlooking the harbor and Boston serves seafood on a grand scale. In size, Anthony's is more like a factory than a restaurant, and while its standards are not what they used to be, it manages to maintain a pleasant atmosphere. Tasty dishes from the sea come with freshly baked popovers, and if you have room for dessert, the baked Alaska is sure to please. Try to get a seat outdoors in the summer. Call (617) 423-6363 for reservations, and expect to pay at least $20 per person at dinner.

The **Boston Sail Loft** at 80 Atlantic Avenue also specializes in seafood and overlooks the water, but in a crowded yet relaxed milieu. The menu includes sandwiches, chowder, salads, and pub fare at moderate prices. About a 5-minute walk from Faneuil Hall, it is a popular night spot with local young professionals. Even more casual and crowded is **No Name** in the wharf area of the waterfront. What it lacks in ambiance, No Name makes up for in low prices and the freshness of its seafood. Call (617) 338-7539 for directions since the restaurant is hard to find, and be prepared to wait in line—they do not take reservations. **Skipjack's**, a relative newcomer, is quickly gaining acceptance for its innovative seafood dishes. The fresh-baked rolls that accompany meals are a nice touch, and on Sundays the restaurant has a jazz brunch (199 Clarendon Street, telephone 617-536-3500).

You'll be able to get fresh fish most anywhere in New England. What you won't find in many other parts of New England is the variety of excellent ethnic restaurants that Boston has to offer. Try several of them while you're here. The **King & I** restaurant at 145 Charles Street on Beacon Hill (617-227-3320) has delicious Thai cuisine with reasonable prices. The spicy aroma of **Kebab 'n' Kurry**, at Massachusetts Avenue and Beacon Street, can easily entice you into

GREATER BOSTON

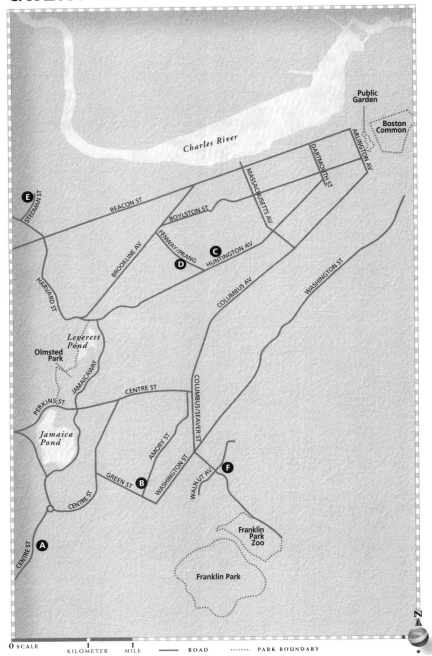

Public Garden

Boston Common

Charles River

ARLINGTON AV

DARTMOUTH ST

MASSACHUSETTS AV

BEACON ST

BOYLSTON ST

STEDMAN ST

E

BROOKLINE AV

FENWAY / PRANG

HUNTINGTON AV

C

D

COLUMBUS AV

WASHINGTON ST

HARVARD ST

Leverett Pond

Olmsted Park

JAMAICAWAY

CENTRE ST

COLUMBUS / SEAVER ST

PERKINS ST

Jamaica Pond

AMORY ST

WASHINGTON ST

CENTRE ST

GREEN ST

B

WALNUT AV

F

CENTRE ST

A

Franklin Park Zoo

Franklin Park

N

0 SCALE   1 KILOMETER   1 MILE   ——— ROAD   ········ PARK BOUNDARY

Greater Boston Sights

Ⓐ Arnold Arboretum

Ⓑ The Boston Beer Company

Ⓒ Boston Museum of Fine Arts

Ⓓ Isabella Stewart Gardner
Museum

Ⓔ John F. Kennedy Library and
Museum

Ⓕ Museum of the National
Center of Afro-American
Artists

ordering more than you can possibly eat, and everything you sample will be delectable. The basement Indian restaurant is casual and affordably priced. Try the samosas and chicken saga. Call (617) 536-9835 for hours of operation. A bit pricier, **Casa Romero** specializes in gourmet Mexican and southwestern dishes. The restaurant, located in the alley just off Gloucester and Newbury Streets, is open Monday through Saturday. Reservations are recommended, since the chef's talents are renowned in the area (617-536-4341). **Jae's Cafe** (617-421-9405) on revitalized Columbus Avenue in the South End serves delicious Korean noodle and rice dishes, and prices are reasonable. At **Nara**, on Wendell Street deep in the heart of the financial district (call 617-338-5935 for directions), a wide variety of sushi selections are rolled to order. The teriyaki dishes are also terrific. Busy during weekday lunch hours, this cozy restaurant is refreshingly quiet in the evenings.

The North End is the place to go for Italian cuisine. **Felicia's** (617-523-9885) and **Villa Francesca** (617-367-2948) on Richmond Street are somewhat expensive, but the food, particularly at Francesca's, is worth its price. **La Piccola Venezia** (617-523-3888) at 263 Hanover Street serves traditional Italian specialties such as cannelloni, manicotti, veal parmigiana, and lasagna in an informal setting. The menu is written on chalkboards throughout the tiny restaurant. Prices are moderate, and bring a hearty appetite because the portions are huge! Prices are also moderate at **L'Osteria** (617-723-7847), just down the street at 109 Salem. The restaurant serves melt-in-your-mouth eggplant parmigiana or, if you like shrimp, try the savory shrimp Francese. It is not unusual to see lines of people waiting outside North End restaurants on weekend nights since most do not take reservations. If you visit Boston during the summer, you may be lucky enough to come upon one of the neighborhood's Italian festivals. You can literally eat your way through the streets! Call (617) 536-4100 for festival information.

Chinatown (which has the third-largest Chinese population in the country) has a wide selection of Oriental restaurants, enough so that you can walk down the street and eat at whichever one appeals to you the most.

As cold as the region gets in winter, oddly enough New England has the highest per-capita consumption of ice cream in the country. New Englanders are passionate about their ice cream! Almost every town has at least one ice-cream parlor. You will be able to locate them easily by the trail of eagerly slurping patrons. Bostonians are connoisseurs; hence a number of locally famous rival parlors vie for business.

Wherever you decide to sample the sweet frozen dessert, you're bound
to be pleased.

Steve's, possibly the best known of the lot, has locations throughout the area, including Quincy Market and on Massachusetts Avenue in
Back Bay. Try their mix-ins: crushed Oreos, Heath bars, chocolate
chips, and the like are hand-blended into fresh ice cream made the
old-fashioned way. Their hot fudge sundaes are amazing. Steve
Herrell, who originally founded Steve's and later sold the company, is
back with his own parlor, **Herrell's**, on Dunster Street in Cambridge.
Emack & Bolio's on upper Newbury Street also turns out a good
product. For basic family-style ice cream, **Brigham's** operates several
restaurants in the city.

LODGING

Cosmopolitan city that it is, Boston has plenty of high-class hotels
to bathe you in luxury. Lodging in downtown Boston can be quite
pricey but many of the hotels listed here have special weekend packages, making them a little more affordable than during the week. **Le
Meridien** (617-451-1900 or 800-543-4300) in the financial district has
one of the better restaurants in the city—**Julien's**. Doubles start at
$245. The hotel also has an indoor swimming pool. The **Bostonian**
(617-523-3600 or 800-343-0922), adjacent to Quincy Market and
Haymarket, and a short walk from the North End, has one of the best
locations in the city for sightseeing. Doubles range from $215 to $255.
The hotel also has a "Boston Kids" package that includes milk, cookies,
popcorn, videos, and board games for children, and a complimentary
continental breakfast for up to four people. The **Ritz-Carlton**,
(617-536-5700 or 800-241-3333) overlooking the Public Gardens, has
been accommodating guests since 1927. Its high tea is a classy affair,
and this is where visiting heads of state stay when they come to town.
Double rooms average $260 to $380. The **Four Seasons** (617-338-4400
or 800-332-3442) is also adjacent to the Public Gardens. Doubles start
at $195 on weekends, and run upwards of $400 for a deluxe suite during the week. Special amenities for children with the hotel's "weekend
with the kids" package include child-size robes and Nintendo games.
The hotel also has a lap pool and sauna. The **Copley Plaza**
(617-267-5300 or 800-996-3426) has one of the most sumptuous lob-
bies in Boston and is conveniently located in Copley Square. Doubles
range from $210 to $260 per night. For families, the hotel has a suite
with two bedrooms and a connecting bath, and kids can borrow books

BOSTON

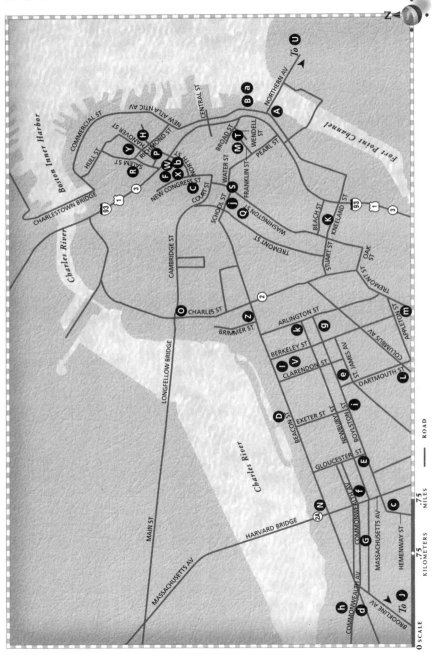

Food

(A) Anthony's Pier 4

(B) Boston Sail Loft

(C) Brigham's

(D) Cafe Budapest

(E) Casa Romero

(F) Durgin Park

(G) Emack & Bolio's

(H) Felicia's

(I) Hard Rock Cafe

(J) Herrell's

(K) Jacob Wirth's

(L) Jae's Cafe

(M) Julien's

(N) Kebab n' Kurry

(O) King & I

(P) La Piccola Venezia

(Q) Locke Ober Cafe

(R) L'Osteria

(S) Maison Robert

(T) Nara

(U) No Name

(V) Skipjack's

(W) Steve's

(X) Union Oyster House

(Y) Villa Francesca

(Z) Beacon Hill Bed & Breakfast

Lodging

(a) The Boston Harbor Hotel

(b) Bostonian

(c) The Boston International Hostel

(d) The Buckminster

(e) Copley Plaza

(f) The Eliot Hotel

(g) Four Seasons

(h) Howard Johnson's

(m) Le Meridien

(i) The Lenox Hotel

(j) The Omni Parker House

(k) Ritz-Carlton

(m) YWCA

Note: Items with the same letter are located in the same place.

and games from the hotel's lending library. **The Boston Harbor Hotel** (617-439-7000 or 800-752-7077) on the waterfront is an elegant new addition to the Boston lodging scene. Water taxis from the airport stop right at its doorstep. Double rooms with a city view start at $285, and those with a harbor view start at $335. If you're traveling with a family, ask about the hotel's family-vacation packages where kids under 18 stay free in the room with parents—and the hotel is super convenient to the kid-friendly Children's Museum, Tea Party Ship, Computer Museum, and Aquarium.

The Lenox Hotel at 710 Boylston Street at Copley Square (617-536-5300 or 800-225-7676) and **The Omni Parker House** (617-227-8600 or 800-843-6664), which is on the Freedom Trail just a few blocks from Quincy Market, are more reasonably priced than the hotels listed above and are still convenient to sights—as is **The Eliot Hotel** (617-267-1607 or 800-443-5468) on Commonwealth Avenue next door to the Harvard Club in Back Bay. Suites at the Eliot are comfortable and elegant with chintz fabrics, antiques, botanical prints, and Italian marble baths. Guest rooms at the Eliot start at $145, one-bedroom suites at $175, and two-bedroom suites at $300—all for double occupancy. Doubles at the Parker House, which tend to be on the small side, start at $205, while double-occupancy rooms at the Lenox start at $190. The Lenox also has a family rate which includes breakfast for two adults and two children, and four one-day passes to the subway.

Even more of a bargain are two hotels in Kenmore Square—**The Buckminster** and **Howard Johnson's**. Rates at the Buckminster, including breakfast, start at $55. The hotel is accessible to wheelchairs, and several rooms have been especially designed to accommodate travelers with disabilities. Rates at the Howard Johnson's (617-267-3100 or 800-654-2000) range from $95 to $165, and kids under 16 stay free in the same room with their parents. For a homier atmosphere, try **Beacon Hill Bed & Breakfast** at 27 Brimmer Street on the residential "flats" of Beacon Hill near the Charles River. Rooms including breakfast start at $140 per night (617-523-7376). The B&B has only three guest rooms, so reservations should be made well in advance.

The Boston International Hostel at 12 Hemenway Street offers basic dormitory accommodations for only $15 per night for AYH members, and $18 per night for non-members. The hostel is close to the Boylston subway stop on the Green Line, to Newbury Street, and to the Prudential Center, and only a 5-minute walk from the Museum of Fine Arts. It has a fully equipped kitchen and showers, and is handicapped accessible (617-536-9455). The **YWCA** in the South End at

40 Berkeley Street has budget accommodations for women only. Rooms with shared baths run about $40 per night, and long term rates are available (617-482-8850).

For a more complete listing of hotels in the area, write the **Massachusetts Lodging Association** at 148 State Street, Suite 400, Boston, MA 02109. They produce a free lodging directory. **Bed & Breakfast Agency of Boston** (617-720-3540 or 800-248-9262) can help you find a bed and breakfast in the area that's right for your needs. In general, if you are willing to stay outside the city, you'll probably find a wider range of inexpensive hotels. You will not, of course, have the convenience of the city at your doorstep.

NIGHTLIFE

If you're in a bar-hopping mood, the Quincy Market area is a good place to start because of its high concentration of drinking establishments. **Houlihan's** is primarily a restaurant but has a dance floor that packs them in after dinner. **Cricket's** attracts the business-suit set; and **Lily's** has a piano bar and outdoor seating, and is a great place to people-watch on hot summer nights. Near Faneuil Hall, **The Black Rose** is a lively Irish pub, and the place to go on St. Patrick's Day, if you can get in.

Back Bay has a number of popular night spots including **Friday's**, on Newbury Street, which has a fun menu, tasty appetizers, and a crowded bar area in which to mix and mingle. **Daisy Buchanan's**, also on Newbury Street, used to be a Red Sox hangout but is now dominated by swinging singles. **The Eliot Lounge**, on Massachusetts and Commonwealth Avenues, sports a relaxed and casual atmosphere. This is where the runners flock after completing the Boston Marathon. **The Top of the Hub**, atop the Prudential Building, has a terrific view of the city. The drinks aren't cheap, but the view is worth it. If your tastes run to Broadway show tunes, try **Diamond Jim's** piano bar at the Lenox Hotel. Patrons are welcome to stand up and try their hand at a song or two.

On Beacon Hill, one of my favorites is **The Seven's Pub** at 77 Charles Street. They serve great sandwiches with homemade potato salad at rock-bottom prices, and have a good selection of imported beer. The milieu is smoky and very casual. The clientele is mixed but always friendly. Hidden away on lower Chestnut Street (#75) is the **Charles Restaurant**, a classy establishment with an intimate bar. Several blocks away on Beacon Street, **The Bul 'n' Finch Pub** inspired the TV sitcom *Cheers*. Although it has lost some of its neighborhood appeal to fame, it is still a fun place to go, especially if you were a fan of the show. For more elegant sipping, try upstairs in the lounge at **The Hampshire House**.

Landsdowne Street, across from Fenway Park, is lined with nightclubs catering to a young crowd, one of the most popular being **Venus de Milo** at number 11 (617-421-9595). If Venus de Milo is packed, you may want to try **Avalon** at 15 Landsdowne (617-262-2424). **Zanzibar** at 1 Boylston Place is a Caribbean-themed nightspot complete with palm trees and exotic drinks.

If you prefer comedy to dancing, the **Comedy Connection** in Quincy Market's upper rotunda features comics nightly. Call (617) 248-9700 for schedule and cover charge information. **Shear Madness**, a "whodunit" that's more comedic than mysterious, has been running in Boston since the 1970s. For show times, call the box office at (617) 426-5225.

Music lovers should not miss the world-famous **Boston Pops** or the **Boston Symphony Orchestra's** more traditional classical performances. Both make their home in Symphony Hall, except during the summer when the BSO travels to Tanglewood and the Pops give their annual Fourth of July concert at the Esplanade on the Charles River. Call (617) 266-1492 for ticket information. Boston also has its own ballet company, the **Boston Ballet**. Call (617) 695-6950 for their schedule. Annual performances of *The Nutcracker* are a holiday favorite.

The **BOSTIX** booth in Faneuil Hall Marketplace sells tickets for all major theatrical productions. Check with them to see what's in town during your visit. It is sometimes possible to get reduced ticket prices there the day of performance. Call (617) 482-2849 for up-to-date schedule and ticket information.

SPORTS

If you enjoy a good game of baseball, you'll especially appreciate watching one in **Fenway Park**, home of the **Boston Red Sox**. The ballpark's relatively small size makes attending a game more a participatory than a spectator sport. Call (617) 267-1700 for schedule and ticket information.

Wintertime visitors can catch either the **Boston Celtics** or the **Boston Bruins** at the **Fleet Center**, which replaced the aging Boston Garden in 1995. You can call the Fleet Center's phone number for event information (617-624-1000), but tickets can be purchased only in person at the center's box office or by calling Ticketmaster at (617) 931-2000.

Racing buffs will be drawn to **Suffolk Downs** (617-568-3225) for horse racing and **Wonderland** for dog racing. Both tracks have their own stops on the Blue Line subway. Hard-core sports enthusiasts can now visit the **Sports Museum of New England**, located in the Cambridge Side Galleria near the Lechmere stop on the MBTA's Green Line. Call (617) 577-7678 for hours and information.

SHOPPING

B oston shopping affords enough variety so that any visitor should be able to find what he or she is looking for. The best shopping is clustered in five different sections of the city.

Newbury Street—This handsome street in the heart of Back Bay runs from the edge of the Public Gardens to Massachusetts Avenue and is home to the city's chic boutiques and art galleries. Sumptuous shops range from the trendy to antiques, and traditional favorites such as Burberry's and Laura Ashley. You can find several interesting second-hand clothing stores toward the Massachusetts Avenue end of the street. Along the way are plenty of sidewalk cafés catering to weary shoppers. Pucker Gallery, and the Copley Society are among my favorite stops on Newbury Street.

Copley Place—This high-class shopping mall is anchored by the Westin and Marriott Hotels at opposite ends of the mall. Tiffany, Neiman Marcus, and Gucci are all located here, as well as an excellent newsstand carrying a wide variety of American and continental magazines, a six-cinema movie complex that features the fine *Where's Boston* documentary film on one screen, and a Rizzoli's bookstore. Saks Fifth Avenue and Lord & Taylor are nearby at the Prudential Center.

Downtown Crossing—This is the area of Washington Street 1 block east of Park Street station. Though not a visually appealing place to shop, the "World Famous Filene's Basement" is worth a stop, especially for bargain hunters. (It's important to note that there is no tax on clothing in Massachusetts, making the bargains at Filene's even more affordable to many out-of-state visitors.) Barnes and Noble operates a large bookstore here, and fast-food addicts can have their fill at either The Corner or the fast-food hall upstairs at Lafayette Place.

Quincy Market—The market is a good place to browse after sightseeing, since many of the stores are open until 9 p.m. The specialty carts adjacent to the food hall sell everything from Celtics souvenir shirts to batik sarongs.

Haymarket—This open-air fruit and vegetable market is held every Friday and Saturday alongside Interstate 93 between Quincy Market and the North End. Many of the vendors are true characters, and the market is a ritual that has remained unchanged through the years. Haymarket can be a good place to stock up on fresh fruit and nuts for your trip, but beware: some vendors display gorgeous merchandise at rock-bottom prices but fill your bag with overripe fruit from the back of the pile. Make sure you pick what you want before you hand over the money. The best selection is in the morning, while the best prices are at the end of the day when the vendors try to unload their wares rather than carry them home.

HELPFUL HINTS

If a foreigner walks up to you on the streets of Boston and asks you, "Where is this place that you have war?" they are probably not referring to the Bunker Hill area but to an area known locally as the Combat Zone. The Zone lies between the theater district and Chinatown, and is comparable to New York City's Times Square district. Although the Zone is shrinking due to new development, what remains is a strip of X-rated movie houses, and is best avoided.

SIDE TRIPS FROM BOSTON

A quick and refreshing way to get out of the city is to take a cruise in Boston Harbor. There are dinner cruises, brunch cruises, jazz cruises, cruises to the harbor islands, and sightseeing cruises. The cost depends upon the length and type of cruise you select, but the view of the city from the harbor is almost always impressive. If you plan to venture out to the harbor islands you may want to bring along a picnic lunch and make a day of it. A number of companies operate harbor cruises, and each has its own schedule and list of specialty cruises. **Bay State Cruises**, (617) 723-7800, and **Boston Harbor Cruises**, (617) 227-4321, are located on Long Wharf. **Massachusetts Bay Lines**, (617) 542-8000, and **Odyssey Cruises**, (617-654-9700), are located at Rowes Wharf.

If you wish to travel further afield, one of New England's foremost attractions is **Old Sturbridge Village** about an hour west of Boston. A living museum that re-creates everyday life in an 1830s New England village, Sturbridge has more than 40 restored buildings on 200 acres. A Friends Meetinghouse, a print shop, gristmill, and nineteenth-century school are among the structures in the village; and crafts demonstrated by costumed guides include candle making, blacksmithing, and woodworking. Although children especially enjoy the village, adults will certainly be impressed as well. The village is open year-round (10 a.m. to 4 p.m. during the winter; 9 a.m. to 5 p.m. the rest of the year), except for major holidays and Mondays during winter months. Admission is high—$15 for adults, $7.50 for children 6 to 17—but the visit is an all-day event. From Boston, take the Massachusetts Turnpike (Interstate 90) west to Exit 9 and follow signs to the village.

The Sturbridge area is also one of the largest apple-growing regions in the state and many of the orchards have "pick your own" programs, making a Sturbridge outing fun for the whole family, especially on a crisp, clear autumn day. The trip from Boston is about 60 miles each way. If you want to spend the night in Sturbridge, the **Publick House & Country Motor Lodge** is a popular spot. Call (508) 347-3313 or 800-787-5425 for reservations.

2
CAMBRIDGE

Cambridge, like Boston just across the Charles River, has been around for more than 350 years. Remarkably, Harvard University has been in existence almost as long, and its influence is felt in just about every aspect of Cambridge life—particularly in bustling Harvard Square, which is the focal point for most travelers when they visit the city.

In addition to Harvard's superb museums, visitors will find a good selection of shops and restaurants in the "Square." From there it is only a short walk to the river to watch crew teams ply the river in racing sculls, or to Brattle Street, where handsome residences belie the urban locale. History buffs might want to include a visit to Mount Auburn Cemetery, while budding scientists should take in the exhibits at Cambridge's other renowned university—MIT. ◣

CAMBRIDGE

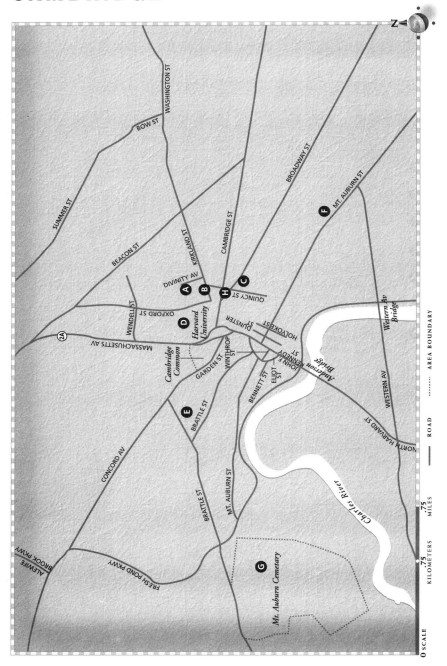

N

O SCALE

KILOMETERS .75

MILES .75

—— ROAD   ········ AREA BOUNDARY

Sights

Ⓐ Botanical Museum

Ⓑ Busch Reisinger Museum

Ⓒ Fogg Art Museum

Ⓓ Harvard University

Ⓔ Longfellow National Historic Site

Ⓐ Mineralogical and Geological Museum

Ⓕ MIT Museum

Ⓖ Mount Auburn Cemetery

Ⓐ Museum of Comparative Zoology

Ⓐ Peabody Museum of Archaeology and Ethnology

Ⓗ Sackler Museum

Ⓐ Semitic Museum

Note: Items with the same letter are located in the same place.

A PERFECT DAY IN CAMBRIDGE

My day would begin with a pastry from Au Bon Pain in Harvard Square while I sat and watched commuters on their way to work, and students on their way to class, enjoying the fact that with my day of leisure ahead of me I was doing neither. Then I would divide my morning between the Fogg Art Museum and the Busch Reisinger at Harvard. After lunch at the Wursthaus, I'd stroll down Brattle Street past some of Cambridge's loveliest homes to Longfellow's house. After touring the home I would head back to the square and spend what was left of the afternoon browsing in the many shops there—especially the bookstores. Dinner would be casual, either a salad from Grendel's salad bar, or a Chinese meal at Yenching. I'd end the day with an art film at the Brattle Theater, and an ice cream from Herrell's.

SIGHTSEEING HIGHLIGHTS

★★★ **Harvard University** • This is the oldest university in the United States. Its ivy-covered buildings and quiet courtyards (in some areas of the school) make it one of the prettiest as well. Stop in at Widener Library as you walk through "The Yard"; it has one of the most extensive collections of any library in the country. The library has a small exhibit depicting Cambridge history that may help put the city in perspective.

Harvard's huge endowment has given the school outstanding museums and innumerable buildings of interest. The **Fogg Art Museum** (32 Quincy Street) with its fine collection of impressionist works, including a Degas ballerina and Romanesque and medieval works, is my favorite Harvard museum. At the **Busch Reisinger** (29 Kirkland Street), the specialty is German expressionism. The **Sackler** (Quincy Street and Broadway), the newest of the Harvard museums, concentrates on Far Eastern and Islamic works of art. Hours: Daily 10 a.m. to 5 p.m.; free to children under 18 and all visitors on Saturdays from 10 a.m. noon. Admission is $5 for adults, $4 for seniors, $3 for students, and covers all three museums. (3 hours)

Also operated by Harvard are the **Botanical Museum**, with its unusual glass flowers exhibit, the **Peabody Museum of Archaeology and Ethnology**, the **Museum of Comparative Zoology**, the **Mineralogical and Geological Museum**, and the **Semitic Museum**. These museums are located on Oxford Street and Divinity Avenue. Semitic Museum Hours: Monday through Friday 11 a.m. to 5 p.m.,

Sunday 1 p.m. to 5 p.m. Other museum hours: Open Monday through Saturday 9 a.m. to 4:30 p.m., Sunday from 1 p.m. to 4:30 p.m. All museums are closed on major holidays. Phone: (617) 495-3045 for additional information. Admission is $4 for adults, $3 for seniors and students, $1 for children 3 to 13, and free to everyone on Saturday mornings from 9 a.m. to 11 a.m.

✸✸ **Longfellow National Historic Site** • This was the home of poet Henry Wadsworth Longfellow for 45 years, until his death in 1882. His major works were written here, among them *Hiawatha* and *Evangeline*. The house was built in 1759 and has additional historic significance as George Washington's headquarters during the siege of Boston in 1776. Hours: Daily from 10 a.m. to 4:30 p.m. except for Thanksgiving, Christmas, and New Year's Day; it's just one of many beautiful homes along Brattle Street. Address: 105 Brattle Street. Admission is $2. There is no charge for seniors and children under 16. (1½ hours)

✸ **MIT Museum** • In addition to exhibits on holography, engineering, science, and architecture—exhibits you'd expect from a university that has produced some of the world's greatest scientific minds—this museum also has an art collection and a model ship gallery. Museum Hours: Tuesday through Friday from 9 a.m. to 5 p.m. and on weekends from 1 p.m. to 5 p.m. Address: 265 Massachusetts Avenue, near Central Square. Admission is $2 for adults. The Compton Gallery is in Building 10 of the school's main campus. Gallery Hours: Monday through Friday 9 a.m. to 5 p.m. The Hart Nautical Galleries are in Building 5. Hours: Daily 8 a.m. to 8 p.m. (1 hour)

✸ **Mount Auburn Cemetery** • This is one of the most beautifully landscaped urban cemeteries anywhere. There's even a small lookout tower where you can view the surrounding cities of Cambridge and Boston. Charles Bullfinch (the architect who designed the Massachusetts State House), American artist Winslow Homer, Henry Wadsworth Longfellow, and Oliver Wendell Holmes are all buried here. Address: 580 Mt. Auburn Street. It is a bit of a walk from Harvard Square, but may be worthwhile if you appreciate historic tombstones. (½ hour)

CAMBRIDGE

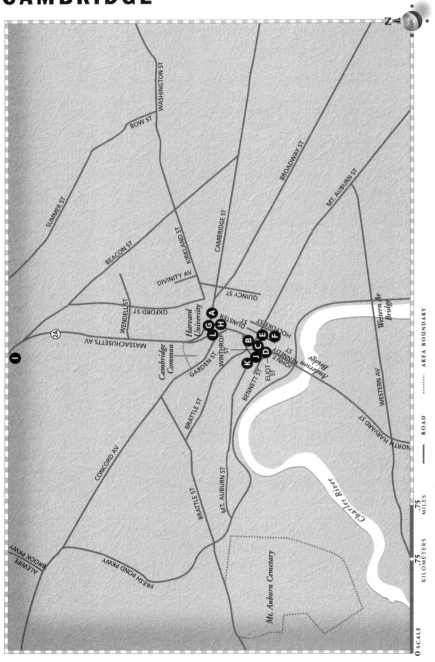

Food

(A) Au Bon Pain

(B) Border Cafe

(C) Cafe Aventura

(C) Formaggio's

(C) The Garage

(D) Grendel's Restaurant

(C) John Harvard's Brew House

(E) Leo's Place

(F) Upstairs at the Pudding

(G) The Wursthaus

(H) Yenching

Lodging

(I) A Cambridge Bed & Breakfast Inn

(J) Charles Hotel

(K) Harvard Manor House

(L) Inn at Harvard

Note: Items with the same letter are located in the same place.

FOOD

Harvard Square's restaurants run the gamut from fast-food establishments to upscale bistros. **The Wursthaus** (617-491-7110) on JFK Street, which has been around for generations, serves excellent lox, bagels, and cream cheese; cold-cut platters; and a marvelous selection of beers from around the world. Try **Yenching** (617-547-1130) on Massachusetts Avenue near the T station for good Chinese food at moderate prices. **Au Bon Pain**, next to Yenching, is the place to people-watch at outdoor tables. Study chess players intent on their game as you sample croissants in every flavor imaginable, gourmet sandwiches such as tarragon chicken or chicken with bernaise, and creamy soups from Au Bon Pain's kitchen for under $5 per meal. **Grendel's Restaurant** (617-491-1050), at JFK and Winthrop Streets, has a terrific salad bar, good Greek combination plates, and a pleasant atmosphere. Prices are reasonable. Popular with the young set, the **Border Cafe** packs them in for tasty fajitas and other Mexican dishes. Expect long lines, scruffy wooden tables, and a spirited crowd if you choose to dine there.

The Garage on the corner of Mt. Auburn, JFK, and Dunster Streets is filled with out-of-the-ordinary fast-food restaurants. **Formaggio's** creates unique sandwiches with fillings such as ratatouille and boursin cheese on fresh homemade bread. Upstairs, **Cafe Aventura** serves great pizza for a song. In the basement, on the Dunster side of the complex is **John Harvard's Brew House** (617-868-3585). The restaurant serves home-brewed beer and pub grub, and smoked meats are the house specialty. Prices range from $5.95–$15.95. **Leo's Place** (617-345-9192), across the street from The Garage, is very casual and offers the best basic Swiss burger and fries around at a reasonable price.

At the other end of the spectrum is **Upstairs at the Pudding** (617-864-1933) for fine dining. The "Pudding"—as in Harvard's notorious Hasty Pudding Club—is at 10 Holyoke Street. The restaurant has an herb-garden terrace, and reservations are recommended. Meals are expensive.

LODGING

If you want to be in the heart of things, then Harvard Square is really the best place to stay in Cambridge—there is always something happening in the square. The **Charles Hotel** (617-864-1200 or 800-882-1818) is the upscale lodging choice, with doubles ranging from $199 to $259, while the **Harvard Manor House** (617-864-5200 or 800-458-5886) across the street offers no-frills motel-style accommodations for $110 to $135 per night. One of the newest lodgings to grace Harvard Square is the **Inn at Harvard** (617-491-2222 or 800-222-8733). With its elegant atrium lounge and attractive guest rooms, the inn is both comfortable and convenient (doubles $129–$239). On Massachusetts Avenue beyond Harvard Square in North Cambridge, **A Cambridge House Bed & Breakfast Inn** offers romantic lodging in a nineteenth-century home. Rooms have large, inviting canopy beds, and a gourmet breakfast is included in the room rate ($119–$225 for two people). Call (800) 232-9989 or (617) 491-6300 for reservations.

NIGHTLIFE

Ryles Jazz Club in Inman Square has long been recognized as one of the Boston area's best jazz bars (617-876-9330). The **Regattabar** at the Charles Hotel in Harvard Square also has live jazz most evenings. Blues musicians perform nightly at actor Dan Ackroyd's **House of Blues** at 96 Winthrop Street (617-491-2583). The cover charge varies, and there's a gospel brunch on Sundays. The **Brattle Theatre** (617-876-6837) on Brattle Street in Harvard Square shows current art films, revives old film classics, and occasionally runs film festivals.

SHOPPING

Because of its proximity to Harvard University, Harvard Square has more than its share of bookstores. **The Coop** (Harvard Cooperative Society), Harvard University's main bookstore, also has a considerable music and art-print department. **Wordsworth** and the **Harvard Square Bookstore** are two bookstores where you can browse to your heart's content, since both are open late. When you run out of bookstores, there are plenty of clothing stores and specialty shops, particularly in the **Galleria** and **Charles Hotel** shopping complexes, to keep even the most determined shopper busy for hours. Don't miss the newsstand in the center of Harvard Square: its selection of magazines and newspapers seems endless.

HELPFUL HINTS

The Cambridge Discovery Booth next to the T station in Harvard Square sells historic walking tour maps of the area for $1. The booth is open 9 a.m. to 5 p.m. Monday through Saturday, 1 p.m. to 5 p.m. on Sunday mid-June through Labor Day, on weekends only through October. Call (617) 497-1630 for information.

3
LEXINGTON AND CONCORD

The famous "shot heard 'round the world" was fired in Concord on April 19, 1775. During the hundred years that followed, Concord was also home to some of America's foremost literary figures—Ralph Waldo Emerson, Nathaniel Hawthorne, Louisa May Alcott, and Henry David Thoreau. As a result of Thoreau's strong naturalist influence, parts of Concord have been set aside as nature preserves. It is still easy to see what inspired writers to live in such a charming village.

Neighboring Lexington also has its share of charm and history. The first battle of the Revolutionary War took place in Lexington on that same April day in 1775. Some of the buildings that played an important role in that initial skirmish (such as the Munroe Tavern, which served as a field hospital for the retreating British) are still standing today. ◪

LEXINGTON AND CONCORD

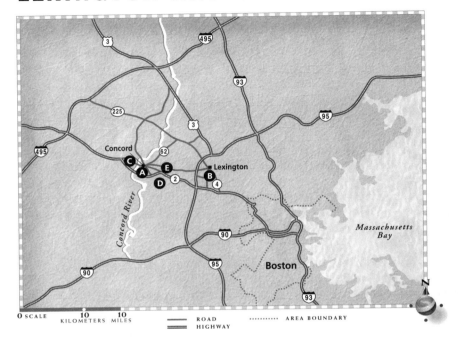

Sights

- Ⓐ Concord Museum
- Ⓐ Emerson's House
- Ⓐ Great Meadows Wildlife Refuge
- Ⓑ Museum of Our National Heritage
- Ⓒ The North Bridge
- Ⓐ The Old Manse
- Ⓐ Orchard House
- Ⓐ Sleepy Hollow Cemetery
- Ⓐ Thoreau Lyceum
- Ⓓ Walden Pond
- Ⓔ The Wayside

Note: Items with the same letter are located in the same town or area.

A PERFECT DAY IN CONCORD

To set the stage for the day to come, I would begin at North Bridge in Concord. Then I would tour the Concord Museum. I would spend the better part of midday picnicking, swimming, and hiking at Walden Pond. After enjoying the out-of-doors for a few hours, I'd head back inside, catching the last tour of the Alcott family home—Orchard House. For a relaxing end to the day, I'd dine in the historic Colonial Inn in the center of Concord.

SIGHTSEEING HIGHLIGHTS

★★ **Concord Museum** • The museum brings together Concord's military and literary histories. Items of interest on the museum tour include Paul Revere's lantern, which hung in the Old North Church in Boston the night of his famous ride, and personal articles of Henry David Thoreau and Ralph Waldo Emerson, who were friends as well as fellow writers. Hours: 10 a.m. to 5 p.m. Tuesday through Saturday, 1 p.m. to 5 p.m. Sunday. Hours are shortened to 11 a.m. to 4 p.m. Monday through Saturday, and 1 to 4 p.m. on Sunday, January through March. Closed on major holidays. Address: 200 Lexington Road, just east of the intersection of Routes 2 and 2A. Admission is $6 for adults, $4 for seniors and students, $2 for children. (1½ hours)

★★ **The North Bridge** • On this site, British and Revolutionary troops first clashed. Visit the bridge more for its historical significance than for what you'll see here today. *The Minute Man* statue now stands at the site in memory of that fateful battle. The statue was created by noted sculptor Daniel Chester French, whose grave is in nearby Sleepy Hollow Cemetery. The visitor center on the hill above the bridge houses a gift shop and replicas of military attire that the minutemen used. Address: Monument Street, just under a mile from the center of Concord. There is no admission fee to the site. (½ hour)

★ **Emerson's House** • Ralph Waldo Emerson lived here for almost 50 years, until his death in 1882. Many of the writer's personal artifacts are on display, including a desk he used and part of his personal library. Hours: Mid-April through October: Thursday through Saturday from 10 a.m. to 4:30 p.m., Sunday from 2 p.m. to 4:30 p.m. Address: On Cambridge Turnpike just across from the Concord Museum. Admission is $3.50 for adults and $2 for children 6 to 17. (1 hour)

✩ **Great Meadows Wildlife Refuge** • This marshy area was frequented by Thoreau in his study of nature. Today you can follow the 1¾-mile Dike Trail loop and perhaps see a fox, muskrat, or weasel in addition to the various species of waterfowl that nest in the wetlands. To get to there from Sleepy Hollow Cemetery, continue on Bedford Road for about three-fourths of a mile, then turn left onto Monsen Road. Stay on Monsen Road to the refuge entrance.

✩ **Museum of Our National Heritage** • The museum is devoted to preserving and showing virtually all facets of America's heritage through changing exhibits that range from antique quilts to decorative arts to early military paraphernalia. Hours: Monday through Saturday 10 a.m. to 5 p.m., Sunday noon to 5 p.m., closing only for Thanksgiving, Christmas, and New Year's Day. Address: 33 Marrett Road on Route 2A in Lexington. Admission is free. (1 hour)

✩ **The Old Manse** • On Monument Street just below the North Bridge, the Old Manse was built in 1770 and was, at different times, home to both Emerson and Nathaniel Hawthorne. Hours: June through October, Mondays and Wednesday through Saturday 10 a.m. to 4:30 p.m., Sundays 1 p.m. to 4:30 p.m. Admission is $4.50 for adults, $2.50 for senior citizens, $1.50 for children 6 to 16. (1 hour)

✩ **Orchard House** • This was the home of Louisa May Alcott from 1858 to 1877 and the setting for her famous novel, *Little Women*. Many actual Alcott furnishings are on display, including sketches done by an Alcott sister which still remain on one of the bedroom walls. The chapel in back of the house was built in 1884 to house meetings of the Concord School of Philosophy. The school was founded by A. Bronson Alcott, Louisa's father. Hours: April through October 10 a.m. to 4:30 p.m. Monday through Saturday, Sundays and holidays from 1 p.m. to 4:30 p.m. Address: On Route 2A (Lexington Road) traveling toward Lexington. Phone: Call (508) 369-4118 for winter hours. Admission is $4.50 for adults, $4 for senior citizens and students 13 to 18, $3 for children 6 to 12. (1 hour)

✩ **Sleepy Hollow Cemetery** • As you travel back toward Concord center from the North Bridge, turn left onto Bedford Street. The entrance to the cemetery will be on your left. Follow signs to Author's Ridge. Ralph Waldo Emerson, Henry David Thoreau, Nathaniel

Hawthorne, Louisa May Alcott, and sculptor Daniel Chester French are all buried here. (½ hour)

⭐ **Thoreau Lyceum** • The Lyceum is filled with Thoreau memorabilia and includes a bookshop and library specializing in Thoreau's works and a replica of his house at Walden Pond. Hours: 10 a.m. to 5 p.m. Monday through Saturday, 2 p.m. to 5 p.m. on Sunday. Closed on holidays. Address: 156 Belknap Street. Admission is $2 for adults, $1.50 for students, and free for children under 8. (1 hour)

⭐ **Walden Pond** • Henry David Thoreau's famous retreat from "civilization" is now a popular escape for Boston city-dwellers and their suburban counterparts. Being relatively mud-free compared to most ponds, and much warmer than the Atlantic, Walden Pond is a preferred place to swim in the area. The pond can get crowded on a hot summer day, but the farther you walk from the main beach, the better chance you have of finding a secluded pond-side picnic spot. In recent years there has been a major crusade to save the woods surrounding Walden Pond from developers. Spearheaded by celebrity musician Don Henley, the effort to save the woods is an action of which Thoreau himself would no doubt have approved. There is a model of Thoreau's house next to the parking lot, and the actual house site is about a 10-minute walk in from Route 126. There is a charge for the parking lot, and it is the only legal spot to park within walking distance. Address: Follow Walden Street from Concord center south for about a mile. You will cross Route 2, and the pond will be on your right, the parking lot on your left. (The length of your visit will depend on whether you want just a glimpse of the famous pond, you plan to picnic there, or you want to spend a leisurely day swimming and hiking.)

⭐ **The Wayside** • Louisa May Alcott and Nathaniel Hawthorne both lived in this nineteenth-century home. Hours: Open seasonally, and admission is charged. Phone: Call (508) 369-6975 for hours it is open during your visit. (1 hour)

FOOD

If the weather is nice, it would be hard to resist picnicking either at Walden Pond or Great Meadows Wildlife Refuge. Luckily there are a number of roadside farm stands in the area if you are looking to

LEXINGTON AND CONCORD

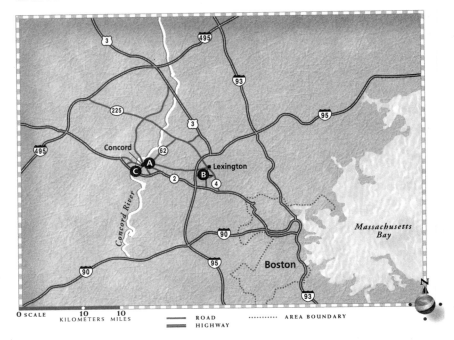

Food

Ⓐ Merchant's Row

Ⓑ Lemon Grass

Ⓑ Mario's

Ⓑ Yangtze's

Lodging

Ⓑ Holiday Inn Express

Ⓑ Sheraton Tara Lexington Inn

Ⓒ Colonel Roger Brown House

Ⓐ Colonial Inn

Note: Items with the same letter are located in the same town or area.

augment your picnic basket. Otherwise, for fine indoor dining in Concord, **Merchants Row** restaurant at the Colonial Inn is the place to go. In addition to breakfast, lunch, and dinner, the restaurant also serves an afternoon tea, and a buffet brunch on Sunday. Reservations are recommended (508-369-9200).

Lexington has a handful of restaurants that offer ethnic variety at reasonable prices. For Thai food, try the **Lemon Grass** at 1710 Massachusetts Avenue (617-862-3530). **Mario's**, on Massachusetts Avenue in the center of Lexington, is popular with families because it offers large portions of Italian dishes at low prices. The restaurant is casual, and often crowded and lively. Entrées are generally under $7 (617-861-1182). For Chinese, try **Yangtze's** evening buffet. The restaurant is also in the center of town and the buffet costs $10.95 per person.

LODGING

The **Colonial Inn** (508-369-9200 or 800-370-9200) on Monument Square in the center of Concord is one of the best-known inns in the area. The oldest part of the inn dates back to 1716, and at various times has been everything from a general store to a storehouse during the Revolutionary War. It's been run as a hotel for the last century, and guest rooms are attractively appointed with colonial style and country furnishings. Room prices range from $85 to $200 with the price depending upon the season, type, and location of the room within the inn (rooms in the oldest section are the most expensive). For families, connecting rooms are available in the Prescott wing, and the Cottage has two two-bedroom suites each with a full kitchen. About 3 miles from Concord center, the **Colonel Roger Brown House** (1694 Main Street, 508-369-9119 or 800-292-1369) offers bed and breakfast accommodations in a relaxed atmosphere. The home was built in 1775 by minuteman Colonel Roger Brown, but today each guest room has a private bath and color television. A continental buffet breakfast is included in the room rate ($75–$90), but best of all for active travelers, guests get a complimentary membership to the health club next door during their stay.

If you prefer to stay in chain hotels, try the **Sheraton Tara Lexington Inn** (617-862-8700 or 800-325-3535) or **Holiday Inn Express** (617-861-0850 or 800-465-4329) in Lexington. The Sheraton is located at 727 Marrett Road; the Holiday Inn is at 440 Bedford Street. Doubles at the Sheraton run about $150 per night, and rooms at the Holiday Inn are in the $70–$100 range.

SIDE TRIPS FROM LEXINGTON AND CONCORD

Adjacent to both Concord and Lexington, Lincoln is another attractive town in the area. In Lincoln, the **DeCordova Museum and Sculpture Park** is worth a visit if you have time. Exhibits change regularly but focus on twentieth-century American art, and the grounds are always lovely. The museum is open Tuesday through Friday from 10 a.m. to 5 p.m., and on weekends from noon to 5 p.m. Admission is $4 for adults and $3 for children and seniors. Call (617) 259-8371 for current exhibit information.

Lowell, northwest of Lexington and Concord, was once a major center for textile manufacturing, and today almost 40 restored buildings related to the industry survive as part of the **Lowell National Historical Park** (call 508-970-5000 for information). Also in Lowell is **The New England Quilt Museum** (508-452-4207) and artist James McNeill Whistler's birthplace (508-452-7641).

4
SALEM

S alem is both beguiling and bewitching. It is a small city struggling to preserve its past glory while striving to keep pace with the twentieth century. The infamous witch trials of 1692 took place in Salem, and the House of Seven Gables immortalized by Hawthorne is here. Fewer people know about Salem's prominence in early America's foreign trade network. All facets of Salem's past are worth exploring.

In 1692, mass hysteria gripped the city of Salem when several girls were said to have been bewitched by a West Indian servant named Tituba. This started a rash of accusations, and just about anyone exhibiting strange behavior was said to be a witch. More than 200 townsfolk in all were arrested for allegedly practicing witchcraft. Nineteen of the accused were hanged before Massachusetts Governor William Phipps put a stop to the executions in 1693. However, the events of 1692 were so traumatic that Salem is known, even today, as the "witch city." ◥

SALEM

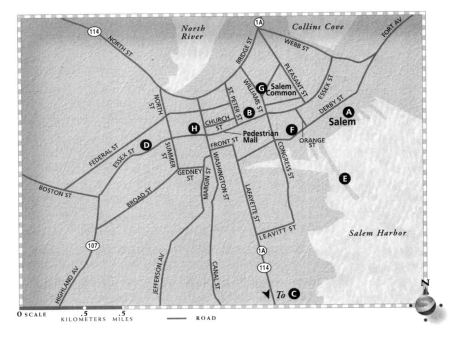

Sights

A The House of Seven Gables

B The Peabody Essex Museum

C Pioneer Village

D Ropes Mansion

E Salem Maritime National Historic Site

F Salem Wax Museum of Witches and Seafarers

G The Salem Witch Museum

H The Witches Dungeon

A PERFECT DAY IN SALEM

My day would start at the wonderful Peabody Essex Museum. Lunchtime would find me at Victoria Station for waterside dining. In the afternoon I'd visit the House of Seven Gables, which was so vividly portrayed in Hawthorne's book, and then tour the Witch House or watch the Witch Museum's media show. If I had time to spare, I'd window-shop at Pickering Wharf before heading to nearby Marblehead for an Italian dinner at Rosalie's.

SIGHTSEEING HIGHLIGHTS

✵✵✵ **The Peabody Essex Museum** • The Peabody is a gem, with extraordinary depth for a small city museum. There are exhibits of nautical paintings and instruments and ships' figureheads, as one might expect in a city whose livelihood came from the sea. However, the most fascinating exhibits are those devoted to goods brought back to this country through foreign trade. The collection includes fine china from the Orient, tribal artifacts from the Pacific islands, exotic furniture, silver, and even a miniature Taj Mahal carved in ivory. For children, there are several rooms devoted to natural history. Plummer Hall houses a collection of art, silver, dolls, toys, and military artifacts from Essex County, as well as special exhibits. Hours: Monday through Saturday 10 a.m. to 5 p.m., Sunday noon to 5 p.m., and Thursday evenings until 8 p.m. Address: 132 Essex Street. Admission is $7 for adults, $6 for senior citizens and students, $4 for children 6 to 16, and $18 for a family of four. The museum also offers tours of historic homes dating from 1690 to 1819. Combination tickets to the galleries and homes can be purchased. (3 hours)

✵✵ **The House of Seven Gables** • This house on the water inspired Nathaniel Hawthorne's well-known novel by the same name. Built in 1668, the home harbors a secret staircase. The house in which Hawthorne was born has been moved to the grounds in recent years and the complex includes two other buildings dating back to the 1600s. Hours: The complex is open 9:30 a.m. to 5:30 p.m. July 1 through Labor Day and from 10 a.m. to 4:30 p.m. during the rest of the year. The house is closed Christmas, New Year's, Thanksgiving, and the first two weeks in January. Address: 54 Turner Street. Admission is $7 for adults, $4 for students, $3 for children 6 to 12. The tour includes a short introductory film. (2 hours)

✯✯ **Pioneer Village** • Grazing sheep, thatched cottages, black-smithing, hand-churned butter, as well as hand-spun wool, are a few of the things you'll see in this re-created 1630s village. Costumed guides reenact the Puritan way of life here, and 12 structures are spread throughout the village's four acres. Hours: Daily from late May through October, 10 a.m. to 5 p.m. Monday through Saturday, and from noon to 5 p.m. on Sunday. Address: The village is located at Forest River Park. Admission to the village is $4.50 for adults, $3.50 for seniors and youths 13 to 17, and $2.50 for children 6 to 12. Family rates are available, as are combination tickets to the village and the House of Seven Gables. (2 hours)

✯✯ **The Salem Witch Museum** • In a Romanesque style building that's hard to miss on Salem Common, the museum features an audio-visual presentation of the events of 1692. It is an engaging introduction to the history of the witch trials. Hours: Daily from 10 a.m. to 5 p.m., to 7 p.m. during July and August. Admission is $4 for adults, $3.50 for seniors, and $2.50 for students and children 6 to 14. The presentation is shown on the hour and half-hour. (½ hour)

✯ **Salem Maritime National Historic Site** • Run by the National Park Service, the site includes the Custom and Derby houses, along with several wharves and warehouses illustrating Salem's former dominance as a port. Hours: Daily September through June 8:30 a.m. to 5 p.m. and July 1 through Labor Day 8:30 a.m. to 6 p.m. Admission is free. Address: 174 Derby Street.

✯ **Salem Wax Museum of Witches and Seafarers** • Wax figures represent Salem's past in a variety of historical scenes that depict the founding of Salem, the witch trials, and the city's prosperous seafaring days in this museum. A 23-minute multimedia show on the witch trials is included in the admission price of $4 for adults, $3.50 for seniors, and $2.50 for children under 14. Hours: Daily 10 a.m. to 6 p.m. July through October, and 10 a.m. to 4:30 p.m. during the rest of the year (weekends only, January through March). Address: 288 Derby Street. (1 hour)

✯ **The Witches Dungeon** • The trial of Sarah Goode, one of the accused witches, is reenacted in a re-creation of the dungeon where alleged witches awaited hanging. Hours: Daily from 10 a.m. to 5 p.m. May through November. Address: 16 Lynde Street. Admission is $4 for adults, $3.50 for seniors, $2.50 for children 6 to 14.

FITNESS AND RECREATION

For beach-goers, **Devereux Beach** runs along the narrow strip of land that connects the town of Marblehead to Marblehead Neck about 6 miles from Salem. There are facilities at Devereux, but since the beach tends to be a little rocky, some residents prefer a tiny slip of a beach set back in a cove within walking distance from downtown Marblehead. If Devereux does not appeal to you, perhaps you can persuade one of the locals to give you directions to his "secret" beach.

FOOD

In Salem, **Pickering Wharf** has the highest concentration of restaurants, generally fast-food and take-out operations ranging from Chinese to pizza. **Victoria Station** (508-745-3400), at Pickering Wharf on the water, has outdoor seating in summer and good steak and seafood dinner entrées that run from $8 to $22. Lunch prices are moderate. Seafood gets top billing at the **Chase Restaurant** (508-744-0000), also at Pickering Wharf. In an attractive building on Church Street (#43), the **Lyceum Bar and Grill** offers fine fare. Baked scrod, grilled pork tenderloin, and fish chowder are all specialties at this popular restaurant (508-745-7665).

The **Barnacle** (617-631-4236) and **The Landing** (81 Front Street, call 617-631-1878 for reservations) both overlook Marblehead harbor and serve fresh seafood. Prices are moderate to expensive. **The King's Rook** at 12 State Street is a cozy coffeehouse that serves copious salads and tasty desserts (617-631-9838). Chocolate lovers must find their way to **Stowaway Sweets** candy shop at 154 Atlantic Avenue. The "chocolate meltaways" are positively out of this world (617-631-0303).

LODGING

In Salem, the following inn establishments are all close to the main tourist attractions. **The Salem Inn** at 7 Summer Street is in an attractive brick Federal-style building constructed in 1834 by a local sea captain. Rooms are furnished with antiques, and suites with fully equipped kitchens are available. The inn is diagonally across from the Witch House. Double rooms start at $109, and suites run $119–$179 (508-741-0680 or 800-446-2995). The **Hawthorne Hotel**, an elegant small hotel on the town common, keeps company with Salem's

SALEM

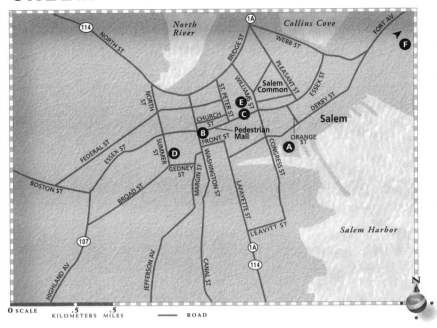

O SCALE
.5   .5
KILOMETERS MILES — ROAD

Food

- **A** Chase Restaurant
- **B** Lyceum Bar and Grill
- **A** Pickering Wharf
- **A** Victoria Station

Lodging

- **C** Hawthorne Hotel
- **D** The Salem Inn
- **E** Stepping Stone Inn

Camping

- **F** Winter Island Maritime Park

Note: Items with the same letter are located in the same town or area.

MARBLEHEAD

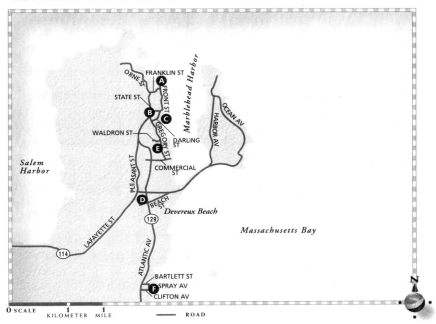

Food

Ⓐ The Barnacle

Ⓑ The King's Rook

Ⓒ The Landing

Ⓓ Stowaway Sweets

Lodging

Ⓔ Harborside House

Ⓕ Spray Cliff

stateliest homes. Doubles start at $92 per night (508-744-4080 or 800-729-7829). The **Stepping Stone Inn** (508-741-8900 or 800-338-3022), adjacent to the Witch Museum at 19 Washington Square, is a cozy bed and breakfast with a cheery breakfast room, and central location ($75–$95 including continental breakfast). The Salem Inn and Hawthorne Hotel both have decent restaurants as well.

While staying right in Salem is certainly convenient for sight-seeing, you may wish to travel 6 miles to the charming seaside town of Marblehead for lodging. A stroll down its winding streets, a seafood dinner overlooking the water, and a drive out onto affluent Marblehead Neck are all excellent ways to relax after a busy day of sightseeing. Two bed and breakfasts that overlook the ocean are **Spray Cliff** (617-631-6789 or 800-626-1530) at 25 Spray Avenue and **Harborside House** (617-631-1032) at 23 Gregory Street. The Spray Cliff has a Tudor exterior, and a crisp, airy feel inside. Innkeepers Sally and Roger Plauche welcome their guests with wine and cheese, and guests are always free to help themselves to soft drinks or refreshments from the bar. In the morning a continental breakfast with home-baked goods is served, and all are included in the room rate of $169 to $189. A continental breakfast is also included in Harborside's rates, which range from $65 to $85. For a $15 booking fee, **Bed & Breakfast Marblehead & North Shore** (617-964-1606 or 800-832-2632) can help you locate a bed and breakfast suited to your tastes in Marblehead, Salem, or anywhere you may be visiting on the North Shore.

CAMPING

There are campsites at **Winter Island Maritime Park** at 50 Winter Island Road in Salem. Sites are $15 to $18, and the campground is open May through October. The Salem Trolley stops at the campground, and can take you to Salem's historic sights. Call (508) 745-9430 for information.

SIDE TRIPS FROM SALEM

Marblehead, founded in 1629, is such a delightful town that you may wish to spend a few hours exploring its narrow streets lined with handsomely restored homes and quaint shops. One historic home of particular note, **The Lee Mansion**, is open to the public from mid-May through mid-October. Built in 1768 by Colonel Jeremiah Lee, the Georgian residence is now home to the Marblehead Historical Society.

The house hosted famous guests such as George Washington and John Adams, and the decor includes exquisite hand-painted wallpaper, antique pewter tableware, and an engaging primitive oil painting of Marblehead harbor. Hours: 10 a.m. to 4 p.m. during the week, and from 1 p.m. to 4 p.m. on weekends. Admission is charged.

If you'd like to get out on the water, **East India Cruise Company** of Salem operates whale-watch, harbor, and "attitude adjustment" cruises May through October. Address: The ticket booth and dock are located at Pickering Wharf across from Victoria Station restaurant. Phone: Call (508) 741-0434 or 800-745-9594 for current departure times and ticket price information.

5

CAPE ANN

Cape Ann is not as famous as Cape Cod, yet it's closer to Boston and its rugged coastline typifies traditional New England scenery. The area boasts enchanting villages (many originally settled in the 1600s) and first-rate beaches, yet tourism is much subtler here than in other New England communities.

On Cape Ann's south end, the most scenic drive to the ocean is Route 127 through lovely towns such as Manchester-by-the-Sea, where New England aristocrats hide stately homes behind stone walls and vast lawns. Pride's Crossing railroad station has two waiting benches, one marked "Democrats" and one "Republicans." Often the most interesting sights are just off Route 127, so try a few side streets.

In Manchester, you can take an invigorating dip at Singing Beach, named for the sound of the wind on moving sand. (Warning to visitors: the ocean north of Boston may be a trifle colder than you expect— enter the water cautiously.) To the north is Gloucester, long a fishing port and now home to Hammond Castle. Rockport, at Cape Ann's outer tip, was an art colony for many years. Although now somewhat commercial, the town retains much of its original charm. Nearby, sleepy Annisquam has beautiful oceanside homes. Antique-lovers should not miss the shops on Route 133 between Gloucester and Rowley. Ipswich, where colonists first exclaimed, "No taxation without representation!", claims more seventeenth-century homes still standing than any other town in America. Newburyport, at Cape Ann's north end, boasts fine Federalist homes and the beautiful Parker Wildlife Refuge. ∎

CAPE ANN

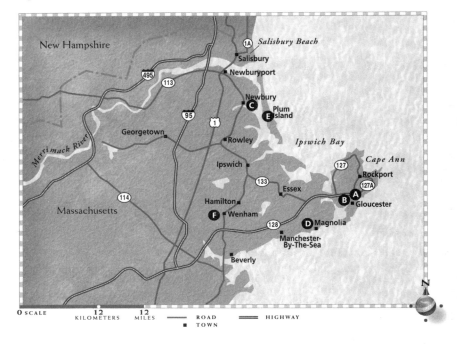

Sights

- **A** Beauport House
- **B** Cape Ann Historical Museum
- **C** The Coffin House
- **C** Dole-Little House
- **D** The Hammond Castle Museum
- **E** Plum Island and Parker River National Wildlife Refuge
- **C** Spencer-Pierce-Little Farm
- **C** Swett-Ilsley House
- **F** Wenham Museum

Note: Items with the same letter are located in the same town or area.

A PERFECT DAY ON CAPE ANN

I would start my day walking the nature trails at Plum Island, and then perhaps rest on the beach there for a spell. Then I would travel south to Essex for a heaping fried-clam plate at Woodman's for lunch before visiting Hammond Castle in Gloucester. I would end the day strolling the shop-laden lanes of Rockport.

SIGHTSEEING HIGHLIGHTS

☆☆☆ **The Hammond Castle Museum** • Constructed during the late 1920s, much of the building and its contents actually date to medieval and Renaissance Europe. The castle was built for John Hays Hammond, Jr. Though not a household name, he holds more than 400 patents and is credited with many inventions that have shaped modern life, ranging from radio control systems to shaving cream. The castle interior includes an organ with more than 8,000 pipes and, in the center of a medieval courtyard, a reflecting pool that Hammond used to dive into from his second-floor bedroom window. Another unique fixture in the castle is a rain-making system, which Hammond installed in the roof over the courtyard to water his plants. On Route 127, the turnoff to Hesperus Avenue is about 4½ miles from Manchester center on your right. The street sign is not well-marked from this direction, so keep your eyes peeled. Hours: Open daily from 9 a.m. to 5 p.m. (last tour at 4 p.m.), but you may want to call ahead to verify hours during your visit; the castle sometimes closes early for special events. The castle is closed Thanksgiving, Christmas, and New Year's Day. Address: 80 Hesperus Avenue. Phone: (508) 283-7673. Guided tours are $5.50 for adults, $4.50 for students and seniors, $3.50 for children 6 to 12. (1½ hours)

☆☆ **Plum Island and Parker River National Wildlife Refuge** • This superb wildlife refuge offers miles of golden sand beaches to walk on, and bird-watchers have the opportunity to see various species in their natural habitat. The entrance fee is $5 per car, but the number of cars entering the refuge is sometimes restricted for environmental reasons. One word of caution: in early July, the beaches in this area are visited by "greenheads," a type of horsefly with a nasty bite. The greenhead season only lasts about two weeks and I've been told bug spray will repel them. Come prepared and you can still appreciate this beautiful park. Address: Turn right onto Rolfe's Lane from Route 1A in Newbury and follow the signs. (1 hour–½ day)

Cape Ann Historical Museum • Devoted to Cape Ann's history, decorative arts, home furnishings, and maritime heritage, the museum is run by the Cape Ann Historical Association; exhibits include an 1804 period home and a collection of paintings by nineteenth-century artist Fitz Hugh Lane. Hours: Tuesday through Saturday from 10 a.m. to 5 p.m. Address: 27 Pleasant Street in downtown Gloucester. Admission is $3.50 for adults, $3 for seniors, $2 for students, and children under 6 are admitted free. (1 hour)

Wenham Museum • A small museum with period rooms and a doll collection. Hours: Open year-round Monday through Friday 11 a.m. to 4 p.m., Saturday 1 to 4 p.m., Sunday 2 to 5 p.m. Closed on holidays. Address: 132 Main Street, in the center of Wenham. Admission is $3 for adults, $2.50 for seniors, and $1 for children 3 to 14. (½ hour)

The Society for the Preservation of New England Antiquities (SPNEA) • This society operates more than 40 historic sites in New England and a number of them are on Cape Ann. **Beauport** is a gabled, turreted home designed by Henry Davis Sleeper, who is probably best known for his design of Winterthur in Delaware. The 40-room mansion is filled with Sleeper's unique architectural features as well as fine Chinese porcelain and Chippendale furnishings that belonged to Charles and Helena McCann, who bought the home after Sleeper's death in 1934. Hours: 10 a.m. to 4 p.m. Monday through Friday and 1 p.m. to 4 p.m. weekends mid-May through mid-October; weekdays only the rest of the year. Tours leave on the hour (with additional tours on the half-hour during July and August) and the last tour of the day is at 4 p.m. Address: 75 Eastern Point Boulevard in Gloucester. Admission is $5 for adults, $4.50 for seniors, and $2.50 for children 6 to 12.

   The Coffin House and the **Spencer-Pierce-Little Farm** are also run by SPNEA. The Coffin House dates back to 1654 and has seventeenth-, eighteenth-, and nineteenth-century period rooms. Crops from Spencer-Pierce-Little Farm are still harvested as they have been for more than 350 years and visitors can see exhibits on early farm life in the late seventeenth-century home that still stands on the property. Hours, Coffin House: Open for tours on the hour from noon to 4 p.m. Thursday through Sunday June through mid-October. Tours are $4 for adults, $3.50 for seniors, and $2 for children 6 to 12. Address: Route 1A, Newbury. Hours, Spencer-Pierce-Little Farm: Open the same dates and times as the Coffin House, and admission prices are also comparable. Address: 5 Little's Lane in Newbury.

Two other SPNEA homes in Newbury, the **Dole-Little House** and the **Swett-Ilsley House**, are open by appointment. Contact SPNEA at (617) 227-3956 for additional information.

FITNESS AND RECREATION

Essex River Basin Adventures** runs guided kayak tours on the Essex River and sea-kayaking trips to offshore islands. Less strenuous tours are offered for inexperienced kayakers and instruction is provided. Call 508-768-3722 or 800-529-2504 for information.

FOOD

Cape Ann is fried-clam country. As Lawrence "Chubby" Woodman invented the fried clam back in 1914, **Woodman's** (508-768-6451), on the causeway in Essex, is quite naturally the most well-known place to get this regional specialty. Serving phenomenal fried clams, Woodman's is a Cape Ann institution. Although their prices are no longer dirt-cheap, portions are so large that two people should have no problem splitting a dinner. Parents need not worry about bringing their children to Woodman's as the atmosphere is extremely casual—patrons dine on picnic tables and are frequently seen diving into fried-clam platters hands first. The restaurant's slogan is "eat in the rough," and they mean it. Another popular place for clams is **The Clam Box** on High Street in Ipswich. Fittingly, the restaurant is shaped like a clam box, and the owners take pride in their preparation—only the best fresh clams are used, and the frying oil is changed frequently (508-356-9707).

If fried clams are not for you, **Chipper's River Cafe** (508-356-7956) on Market Street in Ipswich has delicious, out-of-the-ordinary sandwiches at reasonable prices. **The Wenham Tea House** (508-468-1398) serves simple home-cooked meals and corn muffins that will carry you back to your childhood. Rockport has plenty of eateries to choose from on Bearskin Neck and along Beach Street in the center of town. In Newburyport, **The Grog** (15 Middle Street, 508-465-8008), is the fun place to go for pub grub and **Jacob Marley's** offers a varied menu in a pleasant environment (23 Pleasant Street, 508-465-5598).

CAPE ANN

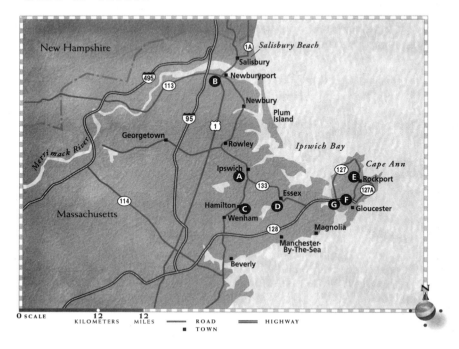

Food

- **B** Chipper's River Cafe
- **A** The Clam Box
- **B** The Grog
- **B** Jacob Marley's
- **C** The Wenham Tea House
- **D** Woodman's

Note: Items with the same letter are located in the same town or area.

Lodging

- **E** Addison Choate Inn
- **D** George Fuller House Bed & Breakfast Inn
- **E** The Linden Tree Inn
- **E** Rocky Shores
- **E** Seacrest Manor
- **E** Tuck Inn

Camping

- **F** Annisquam Campground
- **G** Camp Ann Camp Site

LODGING

B ed and breakfasts are the most popular form of lodging on Cape Ann, and Rockport has the highest concentration of them. The lovely shingled **Seacrest Manor** at 131 Marmion Way is about a mile from Bearskin Neck and the center of Rockport. At the manor, friendly hosts pride themselves on the inn's lawns and gardens, and rooms are comfortably furnished. Room rates of $82–$124 (ocean-view rooms in season are the most expensive) include a full breakfast, nightly turndown, and a morning newspaper (508-546-2211). Across from the inn is a 9-acre nature preserve. **Rocky Shores** on Eden Road is another inn overlooking the sea. There are bed and breakfast-style accommodations in the turn-of-the century inn, and 11 housekeeping cottages on the grounds have kitchens, making them a good option for traveling families. Double rooms at the inn range from $76 to $110; weekly rates for the cottages start at $640 for a two-bedroom and $785 for a three-bedroom cottage (508-546-2823 or 800-348-4003).

The **Tuck Inn**, in a 1790 Colonial on High Street, is within walking distance of Bearskin Neck. A plentiful, home-baked breakfast buffet is included in your stay, as is use of the inn's own swimming pool. Rates run from $47 to $87 in the off-season, and from $67 to $107 in high season (508-546-7260). The **Addison Choate Inn**, at 49 Broadway, also has a swimming pool and breakfast buffet. Many people appreciate the inn for its colorful gardens alone, and all guest rooms in the Greek Revival home have private baths. Doubles start at $91 in the summer and $75 in the winter, with discounts for long-term stays (508-546-7543 or 800-245-7543). **The Linden Tree Inn** at 26 King Street gets its name from the majestic linden tree that shades the inn's lawn. Home-baked goodies such as sour-cream chocolate cake, pineapple walnut bread, and pumpkin chocolate-chip bread often appear as part of the inn's continental breakfast. Doubles are in the $90 range (508-546-2492 or 800-865-2122).

In nearby Essex, the **George Fuller House Bed & Breakfast Inn** overlooks a salt marsh. Rooms in the 1830 Federal-style home are furnished with a mix of antiques and period reproductions. Several guest rooms have their own working fireplaces. Doubles range from $70 to $100, and full country breakfasts—with dishes such as French toast topped with brandied lemon butter, or piña colada pancakes—are included in the room rate. The inn also has a sailboat for guests to enjoy (508-768-7766).

CAMPING

Camp Ann Camp Site in West Gloucester has almost 300 camp-sites, and hook-ups are available. The campground is about a mile from Wingersheek Beach, and the camping season runs May through October (508-283-8683). **Annisquam Campground** in Gloucester has only 35 sites so availability is more limited (508-283-2992). Sites start at around $15 at both campgrounds.

BEACHES

Cape Ann, with its excellent beaches, is an enjoyable place to unwind for a few days. **Crane's Beach**, off Route 133 in Ipswich, and **Good Harbor Beach**, off Route 127 in Gloucester, are two of my favorites. The parking lot at Good Harbor is for residents only, but sometimes you can find parking within walking distance. For a fee, anyone can park at Crane's. On hot summer days, especially weekends, the lot fills up quickly. The Crane Mansion at nearby Castle Hill (508-356-4070) was built with money made in bathroom fixtures and is now rented out for elegant parties; periodical concerts are open to the public. **Singing Beach**, while not the largest of Cape Ann beaches, is also lovely. Parking at the beach is for residents only, but the 10-minute walk from town is pleasant. Just be certain to park legally, for the law has no qualms about ticketing or towing your vehicle.

While Crane's, Good Harbor, and Singing Beach are good for a restful day at the ocean, **Salisbury Beach**, north of Newburyport is where people go on Cape Ann for amusement-park rides and honky-tonk. A roller coaster, carousel, miniature golf courses, and video arcades are among Salisbury's attractions.

NIGHTLIFE

A variety of musicals, celebrity concerts, and kid-oriented shows are performed at the **North Shore Music Theatre** in Beverly during its season, which runs from April through December. Call (508) 922-8500 for ticket and show information.

SIDE TRIPS - CAPE ANN

Sporting types may enjoy watching a polo match. Picnics and polo go hand-in-hand at the **Myopia Hunt Club**. The action usually starts around 3 p.m. on Sunday afternoons throughout the summer and early fall. The polo grounds are off Route 1A in Hamilton. Call (508) 468-7956 for information.

Summer whale-watching expeditions are a very popular Cape Ann pastime. The **Yankee Fleet** in Gloucester operates both whale-watching cruises and deep-sea fishing trips. Call (800) 942-5464 or (508) 283-0313 for prices and schedules. **Capt. Bill's Whale Watch**, also based in Gloucester, offers similar excursions (508-283-6995 or 800-339-4253). **Cape Ann Whale Watch** (508-283-5110 or 800-877-5110) in Gloucester operates its cruises in conjunction with the Whale Conservation Institute. Humpback, finback, and right whales are among the species you could see on your ocean cruise. (Most cruise operations guarantee that you will see whales, or you get a free trip on another day.) With **Gloucester Ocean Adventures** you can try your hand at lobstering, and one child can travel free with each adult ticket purchased (508-283-1979). **Essex River Cruises** (508-768-6981 or 800-748-3706) runs nature and bird-watching cruises on the Essex River. **Moby Duck Tours** (508-281-3825) offers a most unique way to tour Gloucester—by both land and sea in an amphibious vehicle. If you prefer a more traditional vessel for traveling on water, the **Rockport Schooner Company** cruises the coast in a 56-foot schooner (508-546-9876). All cruise operators recommend advance reservations.

If you're in the area in early October, a side trip to the **Topsfield Fair** might be in order. The annual event claims to be the oldest county fair in the country, and it certainly offers enjoyable entertainment for the entire family. Call (508-887-5000) for fair information.

Portsmith, N.H.: Although Portsmouth may not be well known outside New England, it is a gem of a city. In fact, even many New Englanders aren't aware of this port city's charms, but it is certainly worth a visit if you have time. In addition to an extensive selection of fine shops and restaurants—most notably, the **Blue Strawberry**, which serves fabulous six-course dinners (29 Ceres Street, overlooking the water; reservations are a must; 603-431-6420)—Portsmouth boasts an interesting and historic waterfront district.

Strawberry Banke Museum is in the heart of the waterfront district. The museum is really a preserved neighborhood originally settled in the 1630s and named for the profusion of strawberries that once grew there along the banks of the Piscataqua River. After existing as a thriving community for several centuries, the area gradually deteriorated and faced demolition in the 1950s. A group of concerned citizens stepped in and began creating the 45-building museum you see today.

Some have been decorated with period furnishings, some have costumed guides, some exhibit early American tools or building methods of the day, and a few can be viewed only from the exterior, as they are still awaiting restoration. The most interesting buildings at Strawberry Banke include the childhood home of Victorian writer Thomas Bailey Aldrich, the beautiful Goodwin Mansion, the Dinsmore Shop (where coopers make the wooden barrels once used extensively for transporting and storing goods), and the Drisco House. The latter, a two-family house built in 1795, is furnished on one side in the style of the 1790s and on the other as it would have appeared in the 1950s, an example of how a house's use can change over the years. Hours: Open daily 10 a.m. to 5 p.m. May through October. Admission is $10 for adults, $8 for seniors, $7 for children 6 to 17. Admission for families with two or more children is $25.

In addition to Strawberry Banke, a number of historic homes are open to the public throughout the city. The **Moffat-Ladd House and Gardens** was built around 1760. Hours: Mid-June through mid-October, Monday through Saturday 10 a.m. to 4 p.m., Sunday 2 to 5 p.m., admission $4 for adults, $1 for children 7 to 12. Address: 154 Market Street. The Georgian-style **Wentworth-Gardner House** was also built around 1760. Hours: Open late May through October 15, Tuesday through Sunday, 1 to 4 p.m.; admission: $4 for adults, $2 per child. A map and guide to the historic properties is available from the Chamber of Commerce—call (603) 436-1118. The **Portsmouth Heritage Museum** has exhibits of local history. Phone: (603) 431-2000.

Portsmouth also has a small **Children's Museum** with hands-on exhibits in the South Meeting House, built in 1865. Hours: Open Tuesday through Saturday from 10 a.m. to 5 p.m., Sunday 1 to 5 p.m. Also open on school holidays and on Mondays during summer. Address: 280 Marcy Street, just a few blocks from Strawberry Banke. Admission is $3.50 for adults and children, and $3 for seniors. Children under 1 are admitted free.

At Portsmouth's **Albacore Park**, visitors can tour a 1952 electric and diesel submarine. Hours: Open from 9:30 a.m. to 4:30 p.m. daily May through Columbus Day. Phone: Call (603) 436-3680 for winter hours. Admission is $4 for adults, $3 for seniors, $3 for children 7 to 17, and $10 for families.

As in many New England cities, harbor and whale-watching cruises leave from the port. **Portsmouth Harbor Cruises** (603-436-8084 or 800-776-0915) operates harbor cruises, and the **Isles of**

Shoals Steamship Company runs excursions to the Isles and whale-watch expeditions (603-431-5500 or 800-441-4620). To reach Portsmouth's historic district and waterfront, take Exit 7 off Interstate 95, about 20 miles north of the center of Newburyport. You'll see signs directing you to Strawberry Banke from downtown Portsmouth.

6

COASTAL MAINE

Maine bills itself as "Vacationland U.S.A." and often the heavily touristed areas in the state seem to be dedicated to the fine art of parting visitors from their cash. That's because tourism is one of the state's biggest industries, and many Maine natives make most of their annual income during the three summer months. The Atlantic coast of Maine continues to be the state's biggest draw for visitors, and with good reason. If you enjoy factory outlet shopping, Kittery and Freeport have become meccas for bargain-hunters. If you don't, it is possible to steer clear of them and enjoy the charm of quaint seacoast towns such as Camden and Wiscasset (the latter, reputedly "the prettiest town in Maine"), the coastal rocky shore, and the sweet smell of pine that permeates the air. Portland, Maine's largest city, is on the coast, along with such towns as Boothbay Harbor and Kennebunkport, where scenic coves, alluring shops, and art galleries await visitors. Flea-market buffs will find Route 1 in Searsport absolute heaven. ◣

COASTAL MAINE

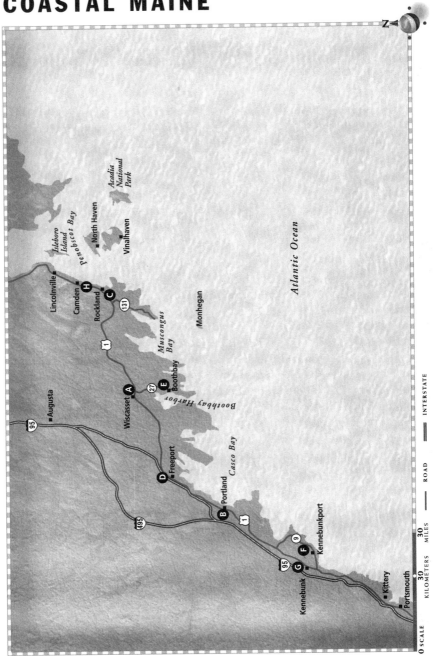

N

Atlantic Ocean

Acadia
National
Park

North Haven

Vinalhaven

*Isleboro
Island*

Penobscot Bay

Lincolnville

Camden

Rockland **H**

C

131

1

Monhegan

*Muscongus
Bay*

Boothbay

27 **E**

A Wiscasset

Boothbay Harbor

Augusta

95

Freeport **D**

Casco Bay

Portland **B**

1

495

9

Kennebunkport

F

95 **G**

Kennebunk

Kittery

Portsmouth

0 SCALE

30
KILOMETERS

30
MILES

——— ROAD

═══ INTERSTATE

Sights

- (A) Castle Tucker
- (B) Children's Museum of Maine
- (C) Farnsworth Art Museum
- (D) L.L. Bean
- (B) Old Port Exchange District
- (B) Portland Museum of Art
- (E) Railway Village
- (F) Seashore Trolley Museum
- (C) Shore Village Museum

Food

- (F) Allison's
- (H) The Belmont
- (G) The Kennebunk Inn
- (G) Squaretoes
- (F) The White Barn Inn
- (H) Whitehall Inn

Lodging

- (O) Abigail's
- (O) Blue Harbor House
- (F) Captain Lord Mansion
- (G) The Kennebunk Inn
- (O) Regency Hotel
- (O) Whitehall Inn

Camping

- (G) Yankeeland Campground

Note: Items with the same letter are located in the same town or area.

A PERFECT DAY ON THE MAINE COAST

I'd start my day visiting Kennebunkport's shops and galleries. Then I would head up the coast, stopping at the Portland Museum of Art, Boothbay Harbor, or the Farnsworth Museum in Rockland, depending upon my mood. I would aim for Camden late in the day, and end up there for dinner and lodging.

SIGHTSEEING HIGHLIGHTS

✵ **Castle Tucker** • In this striking home overlooking Wiscasset Harbor, visitors can see how well-to-do sea captains lived in the 1800s. The house dates back to 1807 and has a free-standing elliptical staircase. Hours: Open to the public Tuesday through Saturday, 11 a.m. to 4 p.m. during July and August. Admission is $3 for adults and 50 cents for children 6 to 12. (1 hour)

✵ **Children's Museum of Maine** • This might be a mandatory stop if you're traveling with small children. Located in a Victorian home, the museum's hands-on and interactive exhibits include a newsroom, science lab, and camera obscura. Hours: Generally open daily from 10 a.m. to 5 p.m., although on Tuesdays and Sundays the museum does not open until noon, and on Friday evenings it is open until 8 p.m. Address: 142 Free Street in Portland. Admission is $4 per person over the age of 1. (1 hour)

✵ **Farnsworth Art Museum** • Fans of artist Andrew Wyeth will approve of this Rockland museum. Collections include Wyeth paintings and works by other American Impressionists and landscape artists, as well as the Olson House, which appeared in many of Wyeth's paintings. Hours: During summer, open from 10 a.m. to 5 p.m. Monday through Saturday, and 1 to 5 p.m. Sunday. Address: 19 Elm Street in downtown Rockland. Phone: (207) 596-6457.

✵ **L.L. Bean** • It may seem odd to list a store as a sightseeing highlight, but L.L. Bean (open 24 hours) is a Maine institution, and a midnight shopping spree at the store is a rite of passage for any New England college student. Once a rather modest store, L.L. Bean's building has grown over the years, as has the town around it. The main street in Freeport is now lined with outlet stores to take advantage of the thousands of crusading shoppers that flock to town. (1 hour)

✤ **Old Port Exchange District** • Portland's waterfront district has been revitalized in recent years, and many visitors will enjoy spending time in the "Old Port's" enticing shops and restaurants. (2 hours)

✤ **Portland Museum of Art** • Located at Congress and High Streets in Portland, this museum has a wonderful collection of Winslow Homer paintings and is well respected in art circles. American artist Andrew Wyeth, who often painted in Maine, is also represented here, as are European masters Degas, Monet, Renoir, and Picasso. Hours: Open Tuesday through Saturday from 10 a.m. to 5 p.m., Sunday from noon to 5 p.m., and until 9 p.m. on Thursday. Admission is $6 for adults, $5 for seniors and students, $1 for children 6 to 12, and free on the first Saturday of the month and on Thursday nights. (2 hours)

✤ **Railway Village** • On Route 27 on the Boothbay Peninsula, you can ride a narrow-gauge steam train and view vintage autos. Hours: Open daily 9 a.m. to 5 p.m. from mid-June through mid-October; admission is $6 for adults, $3 for children. (1½ hours)

✤ **Seashore Trolley Museum** • The trolley as an early form of public transportation holds a certain romantic appeal to some. If you're one of those individuals, then this museum with its collection of over 200 trolleys is for you. Hours: Open daily May through mid-October. Address: On Log Cabin Road in Kennebunkport. Phone: Call (207) 967-2800 for current hours and admission prices. (1 hour)

✤ **Shore Village Museum** • In a state with more than 60 lighthouses, it is only natural that not only would Maine have a museum devoted to them, but also that museum would contain the largest collection of lighthouse paraphernalia in the entire United States. If you have a fascination with the inner workings of these often-mysterious coastal sentries, then a visit to the Shore Village Museum may be in order. Hours: Open daily from 10 a.m. to 4 p.m., June through mid-October. Address: On Limerock Street in Rockland. (1 hour)

FITNESS AND RECREATION

S now Bowl in Camden (207-236-3438) is a small mountain offering pleasant skiing for the whole family during the winter months.

FOOD

The White Barn Inn on Beach Street (207-967-2321) is reputedly where former President Bush dines when he wants a meal out while in Kennebunkport. For good pub food in a casual milieu, **Allison's** at Dock Square (207-967-4841) is a popular spot, especially on weekends when there's live entertainment. On Main Street in Kennebunk, **Squaretoes** (207-985-6636) offers traditional Italian, New England, and seafood dishes at reasonable prices, and also serves breakfast. **The Kennebunk Inn** across the street has fine dining. The menu changes fairly regularly, but New England specialties are the standard fare. Dinner entrées average $15 to $20.

In Camden, meals at the **Whitehall Inn**'s dining room are definitely "Down East" with lots of seafood dishes and goodies made with Maine blueberries. At **The Belmont**, at 6 Belmont Avenue, local seafood such as mussels are seasoned with spices more commonly found in Asia than New England, giving meals a slightly exotic flavor (207-236-8053). Boothbay also has a variety of eateries, and the Old Port District has the best selection of restaurants in Portland.

LODGING

There are many places to stay along the coast, and towns such as Camden, Kennebunkport, and Boothbay have high concentrations of bed and breakfast establishments. The Kennebunk area is a good place to put up for the night at the southern end of the coast. When deciding between Kennebunk or Kennebunkport, you should know that Kennebunkport gets more tourist traffic, which also means crowds and higher prices. Kennebunk is quieter and closer to the highway. **The Kennebunk Inn** on Main Street in Kennebunk center, built in 1799, is as comfortable and charming as anything you'll find in neighboring Kennebunkport, and less costly. Double rooms range from $85 to $139 during summer and start as low as $54 in winter. With the exception of Christmas Day, the inn is open year-round. There is also a good restaurant on the premises. Call (207) 985-3351 for reservations.

Should you decide to join the "Bush Watchers" in Kennebunkport (former President George Bush's summer home is here, and tourism in the town has increased since he was president), the Federal-style **Captain Lord Mansion**, listed on the National Register of Historic Places, is a good choice. During summer, doubles are $149–$199 per night, including a full breakfast (207-967-3141); rates are lower in the off-season.

In Camden, the **Whitehall Inn**, a 50-room country inn, and **Abigail's**, a smaller bed and breakfast, both are on the National Register of Historic Places and have had famous guests. The Whitehall was built in 1834 as a sea-captain's home, and antique furnishings are still sprinkled about the inn. Edna St. Vincent Millay is said to have recited her poem "Renascence" for the first time to inn guests back in 1912. Doubles including breakfast are about $100 per night for a room with a shared bath, and start at $120 per night for a room with a private bath in high season (207-236-3391 or 800-789-6565). The Whitehall is open for guests only from Memorial Day weekend through mid-October. Abigail's, in a Greek Revival home built in 1847, is run by welcoming hosts Donna and Ed Misner. Jefferson Davis was a frequent guest of the first owner, E.K. Smart, who was a member of the United States Congress. Today, guests sleep in four-poster beds and dine on souffles, quiches, or waffles in the morning. One suite has its own Jacuzzi, and Camden center is only a short walk away. Rates range from $65 to $125 including breakfast (207-236-2501 or 800-292-2501). The **Blue Harbor House** at 67 Elm Street is also convenient to the center of Camden. Rooms in the restored 1810 New England Cape home have antiques, canopy beds, and hand-sewn quilts. Suites in the carriage house have their own sitting rooms, private entrances, and whirlpool tubs. Breakfasts are a real treat at the inn with dishes such as lobster quiche, blueberry pancakes with blueberry butter, or the inn's special apples, baked with raisins and granola and topped with vanilla ice cream. If you don't want to leave for dinner, the inn offers candlelit dinners to guests by reservation only. Rates for two, including breakfast, range from $85 to $135 (207-236-3196 or 800-248-3196).

In the Old Port District of downtown Portland, the **Regency Hotel** offers comfortable hotel accommodations in what was originally a nineteenth-century armory. Guest amenities include evening turndown service, a morning newspaper, and a fitness center. Doubles run about $155 in the summer, and $110 during the winter. Weekend packages are also available during the winter months. Call (207) 774-4200 or (800) 727-3436 for reservations and information.

CAMPING

In Kennebunk, **Yankeeland Campground** is less than 3 miles from Interstate 95. Get off I-95 north at Exit 3; a right turn at the end of the exit ramp will take you in the opposite direction from Kennebunk. Drive straight for 2.7 miles. The campground entrance will be on your left. Hookups, hot showers, and complete recreational facilities (including swimming) are all available. Tent sites are about $13 per night, and RV sites start around $15. The campground is open from May through Columbus Day. For reservations, call (207) 985-7576.

SIDE TRIPS AROUND COASTAL MAINE

There are several islands off the Maine coast that make for enjoyable summer day excursions if your schedule allows. Because of its unspoiled beauty, Monhegan has long been an artists' retreat; you can visit this small rocky island by boat. The *Balmy Days II* leaves Boothbay Harbor from Pier 8 daily at 9:30 a.m. during the summer. Call (207) 633-2284 for reservations and ticket information. Bring a good pair of walking shoes, as cars are not allowed on the island.

Ferries travel to Vinalhaven and North Haven from Rockland several times a day year-round; trips take about 1¼ hours. Call (207) 596-2203 for departure and ticket information. The exclusive Islesboro is only a 20-minute ferry ride from Lincolnville Beach north of Camden and may be the best island destination if your time is limited. The Blue Heron (207-734-6611) restaurant is the island's most popular dining establishment if you decide against a beach picnic. Call (207) 789-5611 for ferry ticket information.

Many find the Maine coast most captivating from the sea, making windjammer cruises a favored pastime. Captains Ken and Ellen Barnes operate 6-day cruises out of Rockland aboard their beautiful and historic schooner the *Stephen Tabor*, which was originally launched back in 1871. The *Tabor* is the oldest documented sailing vessel in continuous service in the country, and is listed on the National Historic Register. Ellen doubles as the ship's chef, and her meals are so popular that she's written a cookbook. The 6-day cruise ranges from about $650 to $720 per person. Call (207) 236-3520 or (800) 999-7352 for reservation information; cruises book up quickly so be sure to call well in advance of your visit. **North End Shipyard** in Rockland has three schooners on which they run 3- and 6-day cruises. Three-day cruises range from $345 to $395 per person, and 6-day cruises are $585–$675 (800-648-4544). **Maine Windjammer Cruises** in Camden offers 3- and 6-day cruises with rates ranging from $330 to $655 per person (207-236-8873 or 800-282-9989). Bring lots of warm clothing if you opt for one of these scenic cruises. It can get very chilly on the water, even in mid-summer.

While in the Freeport area, if shopping is not your bag, the **Freeport Balloon Company** (207-865-1712) operates hot-air balloon rides that will take you far from the shopping mecca below.

For a change of scenery, travel inland to the Oxford Hills region in the western part of Maine that borders New Hampshire. With the beautiful freshwater lakes of Norway, Thompson, and Long; a mineral and gem-rich landscape; and numerous wooded trails, the area is a pleasant place for hikers, rock hounds, and fishermen to spend some extra time. Bethel is a good place from which to explore the surrounding countryside, and the **Bethel Inn** (207-824-2175) is the place to stay while you're there. The inn is open year-round, but during the summer months be sure to bring your golf clubs and tennis rackets, as the inn has good sports facilities. If your visit takes you to the area during winter, **Sunday River** in Bethel (207-824-2187) has 50 downhill ski trails and a 1,854-foot vertical drop.

HELPFUL HINTS

The State of Maine operates an excellent tourist information center in Kittery just a few miles over the state line. Accessible from the highway, it's a good place to pick up a state map and additional state tourist information from the helpful staff.

7

ACADIA NATIONAL PARK

Acadia National Park is the easternmost national park in the country. If you stand atop Cadillac Mountain at dawn, they say you can be the first person in the United States to see the sunrise. The park, which encompasses rocky coastline, sheltered coves, wooded mountain trails, freshwater lakes, and ocean vistas, was donated by conservation-minded individuals to create a national park. Today it is still easy to see why they felt the land should be preserved. Bar Harbor, which has been a thriving resort town for over 150 years now, is where most travelers establish their base when visiting Acadia.

With a multitude of souvenir shops and galleries (many of which stay open late during the summer months), and restaurants to suit every taste and budget, there is plenty to keep many-a-tourist engaged after exploring the national park. Those who prefer a quieter milieu will enjoy the less-hurried charm of Northeast Harbor on the eastern side of Mt. Desert Island. ◼

ACADIA

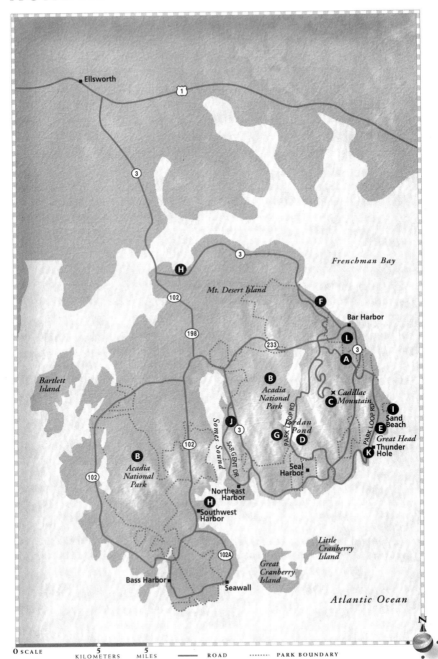

Ellsworth

1

3

3

H

102

Mt. Desert Island

198

233

Frenchman Bay

F

Bar Harbor

L

A

3

B

Acadia
National
Park

✕ *Cadillac
Mountain*

C

I

Sand
Beach

E

Great Head

J

3

G

*Jordan
Pond*

D

K

Thunder
Hole

Somes Sound

SARGENT DR

PARK LOOP RD

PARK LOOP RD

Seal
Harbor

*Bartlett
Island*

102

B

Acadia
National
Park

102

Northeast
Harbor

H

Southwest
Harbor

*Little
Cranberry
Island*

102A

Bass Harbor

Seawall

*Great
Cranberry
Island*

Atlantic Ocean

N

0 SCALE   **5**   **5**
KILOMETERS   MILES   ———— ROAD   ········· PARK BOUNDARY

Sights

A Abbe Museum

B Acadia National Park

C Cadillac Summit

D Gate House

E Great Head

F Oceanarium Bar Harbor

G Jordan Pond

H Mt. Desert Oceanarium

I Sand Beach

J Sargent Drive

K Thunder Hole

L Wild Garden

A PERFECT DAY IN ACADIA

First I would sit down to a hearty breakfast of blueberry pancakes at Jordan's restaurant. Then I would enter Acadia National Park and visit sights along the park loop road, such as the Wild Garden, Sand Beach, and Thunder Hole, trying to time my arrival at Jordan Pond for afternoon tea. After tea, I would drive to the top of Cadillac Mountain. Once I had my fill of the summit's grand views, I would head back down to Bar Harbor for shopping and dining.

SIGHTSEEING HIGHLIGHTS

✦✦✦ **Acadia National Park** • This park covers more than 35,000 acres. The largest portion of the park—and the most heavily touristed—is on Mount Desert Island, so named for its treeless top by French explorer Samuel de Champlain in the early 1600s. Frenchman's Bay, whose name also derives from the French Colonial era, lies between Mount Desert Island and the Schoodic Peninsula, where there is an extension of Acadia. Entrance to the park is $5 per car for a 7-day pass. Be sure to bring your binoculars, as seals and otters can often be seen playing on rocks just offshore.

The visitor information center near the Bar Harbor entrance is a good place to become familiar with the park. A 15-minute introductory film to Acadia is shown every half hour. Pick up a free map and a list of hiking trails if you wish to stray from the main road.

The **Wild Garden** is one of the first detours along the park loop. Plants you'll see in this garden of wildflowers are labeled, making them easier to identify when you spot them in their natural habitat elsewhere in the park. The **Abbe Museum**, at the same turnoff, is a small museum of tools and artifacts used by the Indians who were the island's first settlers. Hours: Open from mid-May through mid-October from 10 a.m. to 4 p.m., with extended hours to 9 a.m. to 5 p.m. during July and August. Admission is $2 for adults and 50 cents for children.

Back on the loop, you come to **Sand Beach**, unusual because most beaches you see on Mount Desert Island are rugged and rocky. Even on the hottest of summer days, this beach is kept cool by ocean breezes. The trail to **Great Head** starts at the far end of the beach. Farther along the park road is **Thunder Hole**, where wave erosion has created a hole in the rocks which resounds with a booming noise as the waves crash to the shore.

The restaurant at **Jordan Pond** serves a marvelous afternoon tea on the lawn with a splendid view of the pond and the "Bubbles"—two matching rounded mountains shaped by glaciers. If solitude is more your cup of tea, take a leisurely walk on the nature trail or on one of the flat paths alongside the pond. Find your own secluded rock and just soak up the scenery. The **Gate House** across the road from the restaurant is also worth a closer look because of its unique stone architecture.

The drive to **Cadillac Summit** is a high point of any visit to Acadia both figuratively and literally, as it is the highest point on the Atlantic coast. Though an uninterrupted climb by automobile takes only about 10 minutes, scores of breathtaking vistas will no doubt slow your progress. (The climb and descent will put a strain on your vehicle, so be sure to check the fluids and brakes before starting the ascent.) An arresting panorama awaits atop Cadillac Mountain. (Both the mountain and the luxury automobile were named after the same Frenchman.) From the summit you can see the harbors below, the Porcupine and Cranberry Islands dotting the foreground, and Winter Harbor, Ironbound, and Schoodic across Frenchman's Bay. The view is spectacular at sunrise or sunset, and the summit is also a popular star-gazing post. The road is closed from midnight until one hour before sunrise. (All day)

✹✹ **Sargent Drive** • This scenic drive takes you past some of the more exclusive residences in the area, and offers views of the majestic Somes Sound—the only natural fjord on the east coast. To get to the drive, follows the signs from the center of Northeast Harbor. Travel along Sargent Drive is limited to cars only.

✹ **Mt. Desert Oceanarium** • The Oceanarium has three separate locations on the island with different things to see at each locale. At the **Oceanarium Bar Harbor** on Route 3, about 4 miles north of the Bar Harbor Acadia entrance, you can tour a salt marsh, the Maine lobster museum, and watch harbor seals at play. The downtown Bar Harbor location is a lobster hatchery, and at the Southwest Harbor location a variety of aquatic creatures are on display in tanks. There's even a "touch tank" where you can find out what some of the more unusual ocean-life feel like—always a hit with children. Hours: The Oceanarium sites are open 9 a.m. to 5 p.m. Monday through Saturday mid-May through October, and combination tickets are available. Phone: (207) 244-7330.

FITNESS AND RECREATION

Many people choose to see Acadia from a bicycle rather than through a windshield. Except for the road to Cadillac Summit, which is demanding enough for a four-cylinder engine, two-wheeled transportation is a refreshing way to explore the park. Bicycles and mountain bikes can be rented in Bar Harbor from **Acadia Bike & Canoe** at 48 Cottage Street (207-288-9605 or 800-526-8615). (Acadia Bike & Canoe also operates sea-kayaking tours of Acadia.) **Bar Harbor Bicycle Shop** at 141 Cottage Street rents bikes for about $14 per day and multi-day rates are available (207-288-0342 or 207-288-3886). There are also more than 120 miles of trails within Acadia to tempt the hiker. Be sure to inquire about hiking trails while at the park's main visitor center if you wish to explore Acadia's backcountry on foot.

For those who are on a rigid exercise program and can't afford to take a day off from the gym, the **Mount Desert Island YMCA** on Mt. Desert Street in Bar Harbor rents daily passes to visitors. In addition to a gymnasium, weight room, and Nautilus equipment, the

Y also has a climbing wall. Call (207) 288-3511 for hours, fees, and program information during your visit.

FOOD

No trip to the Maine seacoast is complete without a lobster dinner, and **Abel's Lobster Pound** on Route 198 in Mount Desert won't disappoint you. Abel's is open for dinner only. Reservations are recommended; call (207) 276-5827.

The **Reading Room** at the **Bar Harbor Inn** (207-288-3351), at the base of Main Street, and the **Rinehart Dining Pavilion** (207-288-5663) on Eden Street in Bar Harbor both offer quality dining with arresting ocean views. While seafood dominates their menus, landlubbers will enjoy the Rinehart's Prime Rib. **George's** (207-288-4505), at 7 Stephen's Lane behind the First National Bank on Main Street, is not situated on the water, but its elegant ambience and unique presentation of traditional dishes warrant a visit. Dinner entrées start at about $15 in all three restaurants.

For more moderately priced meals, **Testa's** (207-288-3327) on Main Street has been a Bar Harbor institution for over 50 years, specializing in family-style Italian cuisine and seafood dishes. Dinner entrées are reasonably priced. **Jordan's Restaurant**, on Cottage Street at number 80, is *the* spot to go for breakfast. Jordan's is known for the best "blues" on the island, meaning blueberry muffins. Their blueberry pancakes are also tasty. They do a brisk business, so service is fast and curt (207-288-3586).

LODGING

Many of the lodgings in Bar Harbor are open during the summer months only, so be sure to call ahead if you are traveling during the off-season. For those on strict budgets, the **Mount Desert Island Hostel** on Kennebec Street has dormitory beds for about $10 per night. The hostel is open only during summer, and reservations are recommended (207-288-5587). The **Bar Harbor Inn**, in the heart of downtown right on the harbor, offers much fancier accommodations. Doubles range from $135 to $235 (207-288-3351 or 800-248-3351).

Mt. Desert Street, also convenient to downtown, has a whole string of inns. The half-timbered exterior of the Tudor style **Stratford House Inn** (207-288-5189 or 800-550-5189), built at the turn of the century, is striking; and guest sleep on four-poster or brass beds

($75–$150). **Holbrook House** (207-288-4970 or 800-695-1120) has wonderful porches, and all rooms have private baths. Rates including a full breakfast range from $110 to $225. The attractive Victorian **Primrose Inn** (207-288-4031 or 800-543-7842), built in 1878, is a pleasant establishment where rooms are priced from $90 to $185. Some of the rooms at the **Mira Monte** have fireplaces, and a continental buffet breakfast is included in the room rate (doubles are $115 to $145, suites with Jacuzzis are $170). The inn is on more than an acre of land, while guest rooms have antiques and private baths (207-288-4263 or 800-553-5109).

    The Ridgeway Inn, on nearby High Street, was originally built as a private home for J.P. Morgan's mistress around the turn of the century. Guest rooms—named for former summer cottages once owned by the well-to-do when Bar Harbor was in its heyday as a resort for the wealthy—have soothing touches such as down comforters and clawfoot tubs. The inn is open year-round and doubles including a gourmet breakfast start at $60 in low season, and range from $100 to $150 during the summer months (207-288-9682).

    There are countless motels and cottages along Route 3 as you approach Bar Harbor from Ellsworth. If you're not planning to visit during the month of August or on a holiday weekend, you can probably check into any of these without advance reservations. The Bar Harbor Chamber of Commerce will send you a free, useful brochure with detailed lodging listings. Write them at P.O. Box 158, Bar Harbor, ME 04609, or call (207) 288-5103, for your copy.

    Northeast Harbor, only 12 miles farther on Route 3 from Bar Harbor, can be a welcome alternative to Bar Harbor's summer throngs, and is equally convenient to Acadia. If your budget permits, the view of the harbor from **The Asticou** (207-276-3344) is first-rate and so is the service. It is best to book well in advance, particularly for August, and the oceanside rooms naturally fill up first. Double rooms are in the $220–$275 range and rates include a full dinner and breakfast. In the center of Northeast Harbor, **The Maison Suisse Inn** (207-276-5223, or 800-624-7668) provides attractive guest rooms complete with four-poster beds and cozy down comforters to take the nip out of the Maine night air. The inn is open seasonally from May through October. Double rooms start at $105 and suites at $175, breakfast included, in peak summer season.

ACADIA

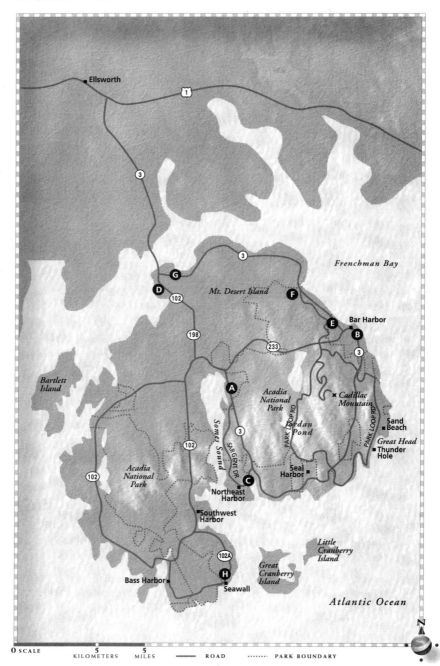

Ellsworth

1

3

3

Frenchman Bay

G

D
102

Mt. Desert Island

F

E Bar Harbor

B

198

233

3

Bartlett
Island

A

Acadia
National
Park

×Cadillac
Mountain

Somes Sound

PARK LOOP RD

Jordan
Pond

PARK LOOP RD

Sand
Beach

Great Head
Thunder
Hole

102

SARGENT DR

3

C

Northeast
Harbor

Seal
Harbor

Acadia
National
Park

102

Southwest
Harbor

102

Little
Cranberry
Island

102A

Bass Harbor

H

Seawall

Great
Cranberry
Island

Atlantic Ocean

N

0 SCALE   5   5
        KILOMETERS   MILES   ——— ROAD   ········ PARK BOUNDARY

Food

(A) Abel's Lobster Pound

(B) Bar Harbor Inn

(B) George's

(B) Jordan's Restaurant

(B) Rinehart Dining Pavilion

(B) Testa's

Lodging

(C) The Asticou

(B) Bar Harbor Inn

(B) Holbrook House

(C) The Maison Suisse Inn

(B) Mira Monte

(B) Mount Desert Island Hostel

(B) Primrose Inn

(B) Stratford House Inn

(B) The Ridgeway Inn

Camping

(D) Barcadia Campground

(E) Bar Harbor Campground

(F) Blackwoods Campground

(G) Mount Desert Narrows Camping Resort

(H) Seawall Campground

Note: Items with the same letter are located in the same town or area.

CAMPING

Blackwoods Campground, about 8 miles from Bar Harbor and 1 mile from Seal Harbor off Route 3, is the closest campground to Acadia's main loop road. Several miles from the Seal Harbor entrance to Acadia, it is operated by the National Park Service. The sites are more heavily wooded than in most private campgrounds in the area, and there's a path to the ocean. Reservations must be made through the Mistix reservation system up to eight weeks ahead; it's recommended that you reserve at least three weeks ahead. It may be possible to obtain a site on a space-available basis upon your arrival; generally, the earlier in the day you arrive, the better chance you'll have. There are bathrooms on the premises and a shower nearby. For provisions, there is a small store in Seal Harbor, and you'll find more substantial offerings at the Pine Tree Market on Main Street in Northeast Harbor about 4 miles away. Call (800) 365-2267 or write Mistix, P.O. Box 85705, San Diego, CA 92138, for reservations and current rate information. Major credit cards are accepted for reservations, and campsites run about $12 in the height of summer. **Seawall Campground** on Route 102A, 4 miles south of Southwest Harbor, is open from late May until late September, and sites ($10) are available on a first-come first-served basis.

Neither of the park service campgrounds have utility hook-ups, so you'll have to stay at one of the private campgrounds in the area if you need one. Several campgrounds are reasonably close to Bar Harbor on Route 3 between Bar Harbor and Ellsworth. **Bar Harbor Campground** (207-288-5185) is only 4 miles from the center of town and 3 miles from the main entrance to Acadia. It has modern facilities, including a heated pool. **Mount Desert Narrows Camping Resort** (207-288-4782), 8 miles from Bar Harbor, has RV hookups and ocean sites available ($20–$39 per night in high season). **Barcadia Campground** (207-288-3520) is about 10 miles from Bar Harbor on the water. Sites range from $16 for a non-ocean site in the off-season to $27.50 for an ocean site in high season.

JUST FOR KIDS

About 12 miles west of Bar Harbor on Route 3 are 3-miles of highway with enough mini-golf courses, ice-cream parlors, paddle boats, go-cart tracks, water slide parks—and even a small zoo—to bring any travel-weary child out of the doldrums.

SIDE TRIPS FROM BAR HARBOR

A sightseeing cruise on Frenchman Bay is an agreeable way to survey Acadia National Park and the islands of Frenchman Bay. **Frenchman Bay Boating Company**, next to the municipal pier in Bar Harbor, offers a variety of cruising options. Call (207) 288-3322 or (800) 508-1499 for more information. The ***Natalie Todd*** is a 129-foot, three-masted schooner that offers 2-hour cruises on the bay (207-546-4585).

Those with more time may wish to go on to Southwest and Bass Harbors, and to the western part of Acadia from Northeast Harbor. From Bass Harbor you can take a ferry to Swan's Island, and another ferry operates from Northeast Harbor to the Cranberry Islands. If you are so inclined and have the opportunity to stay a day or two longer, investigate some of them on your own.

Schoodic Peninsula, directly across Frenchman Bay from Bar Harbor, is also part of Acadia National Park. Because of its distance from the heart of Acadia, Schoodic is much less traveled but no less scenic. Take an extra day or two to traverse this more remote part of the park and the quiet fishing village of Winter Harbor. To get there, you'll need to take Route 3 back to Ellsworth and continue on U.S. 1 north to West Gouldsboro. From there, take Route 186 to Winter Harbor.

For those with lots of time on their hands, Nova Scotia is just a 6-hour ferry ride from Bar Harbor on the *Bluenose*. From mid-June through mid-September, the famous ferry departs daily for Yarmouth at 8 a.m. One-way passenger fare is about $40 for adults, $22 for children 5 to 12. Automobiles and mobile homes up to 20 feet cost in the $50 range one-way. The ferry runs on a reduced schedule the rest of the year, and fares are lower. Call (800) 341-7981 or (207) 288-3397 for further information and reservations. Gambling is allowed on board once the ship reaches international waters. In Nova Scotia, the most scenic routes are along the coasts. The Cabot Trail on Cape Breton, at the easternmost end of Nova Scotia, is generally considered to be the province's most beautiful region. From Caribou, Nova Scotia, you can take the ferry to sleepy Prince Edward Island where deserted white-sand beaches meet a surprisingly warm, blue sea.

Wilderness seekers will find what they are seeking in the Katahdin-Moosehead region of Maine several hours northwest of Bar Harbor. At more than 5,000 feet, Mt. Katahdin dominates the area—although at 40 miles long, Moosehead Lake is impressive in its own right. Baxter State Park, which surrounds Mt. Katahdin, is popular with hikers, especially since it is the northern end of the Appalachian Trail. There are 10 campgrounds within the park and reservations can be made by contacting the Reservation Clerk at Baxter State Park, 64 Balsam Drive, Millinocket, ME 04462. If you prefer to venture out into the wilderness from the comfort of an inn, the **Lodge at Moosehead Lake**, in Greenville at the southern end of the lake, has luxurious guests rooms with charming rustic touches such as totem pole bedposts, and wooden, carved-moose headboards. Rates, including a full breakfast, range from $135 to $185 during the summer (207-695-4400).

8
THE WHITE MOUNTAINS

The White Mountain National Forest is a 750,000-acre expanse in central New Hampshire that encompasses much of the Presidential Range, including 6,288-foot Mt. Washington, as well as a bounty of alpine lakes, streams, cascades, and hiking trails. Mt. Cranmore in North Conway is one of the oldest ski areas in the Northeast. Although rail service is no longer available, trains used to arrive from Boston on a regular basis, dropping off skiers right in the heart of the village. For this reason, the town has catered to tourists for many years, and the effects are beginning to show. In the past decade or so, factory outlets and the multitude of shoppers they bring have begun to crowd the town's charming core. Still, North Conway has its appeal, including the greatest variety of shops, restaurants, and lodging establishments in the Mt. Washington valley. It's a good base for your visit to the White Mountains. ◪

WHITE MOUNTAINS

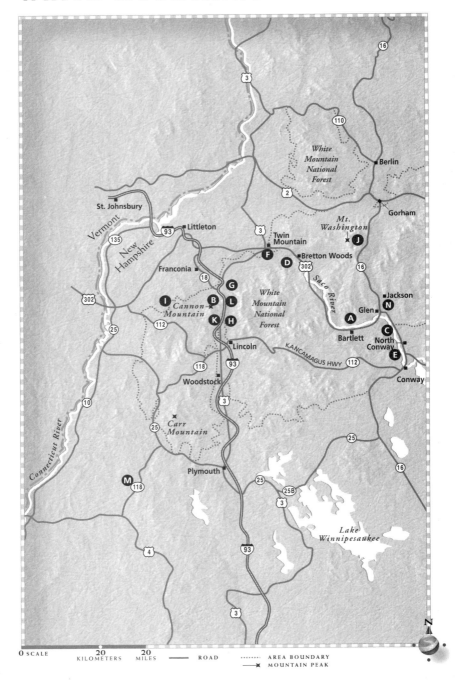

St. Johnsbury
Littleton
Franconia
Vermont
New Hampshire
Connecticut River
Cannon Mountain
Lincoln
Woodstock
Carr Mountain
Plymouth
Twin Mountain
Bretton Woods
White Mountain National Forest
Mt. Washington
Berlin
Gorham
Jackson
Glen
Bartlett
North Conway
Conway
KANCAMAGUS HWY
Lake Winnipesaukee

16
3
110
2
3
135
93
18
302
25
112
118
93
3
25
10
118
4
93
25
25B
3
16
302
302
16
112
25

White Mountain National Forest

A B C D E F G H I J K L M N

0 SCALE 20 20
KILOMETERS MILES ——— ROAD ·········· AREA BOUNDARY
—×— MOUNTAIN PEAK

N

Sights

Ⓐ Attitash Ski Area

Ⓑ Cannon Mountain Ski Area

Ⓒ Cathedral Ledge

Ⓓ Cog Railway

Ⓔ The Conway Scenic Railroad

Ⓕ Crawford Notch State Park

Ⓖ Echo Lake State Park

Ⓗ Flume Trail

Ⓘ Franconia Notch State Park

Ⓙ Gondola Skyride

Ⓙ Mt. Washington

Ⓚ New England Ski Museum

Ⓛ Old Man of the Mountain

Ⓛ Profile Lake

Ⓜ Ruggles Mine

Ⓝ Storyland

Note: Items with the same letter are located in the same town or area.

A PERFECT DAY IN THE WHITE MOUNTAINS

I would need an early start to accomplish everything I wanted to do in the White Mountains. First, I would drive through Crawford Notch State Park to the Cog Railway depot and take the train ride to the top of Mount Washington. I would then drive through Franconia Notch State Park, and hike the Flume trail. After the Flume, I would take the scenic Kancamagus heading east, and then on to North Conway or Jackson for a well-deserved dinner and night's rest.

SIGHTSEEING HIGHLIGHTS

★★★ **Franconia Notch State Park** • This park is in the heart of the White Mountain National Forest. Franconia Notch Parkway runs from **Cannon Mountain Ski Area** at the northern entrance to the park, south to Lincoln. Cannon operates an aerial tramway during nonskiing months ($8 for adults, $4 for children 6 to 12. While at Cannon, you can also visit the **New England Ski Museum** to learn more about the regional history of the sport through an audiovisual presentation. Hours: The museum is open from mid-May through mid-October, and again just after Christmas for the winter ski season, from noon to 5 p.m., closed on Wednesday. Admission is by donation.

The turnoff to **Old Man of the Mountain** is just after Cannon Mountain and Echo Lake. This portion of cliffs overlooking **Profile Lake** was so named because from certain angles, erosion has given the granite the appearance of an old man. Nathaniel Hawthorne wrote about the famous formation in his short story, *The Great Stone Face.* You will see the old man's profile on many of New Hampshire's highway route signs.

Other highlights of the park include **the Basin** and **the Flume.** Swirling with water, the Basin is a natural pothole formed by Ice Age glaciers and mountain cascades. There is wheelchair access. Swimming is prohibited. A well-maintained bike path runs through this section of the park, and hiking trails abound. You may wish to hike one of the trails that leave from the Basin area, which are free and likely to be less crowded than the **Flume Trail.**

The Flume is a narrow, moss-covered granite gorge discovered in 1808 by Jesse Guernsey, a 93-year-old woman who was hoping to find a prime fishing spot. After hiking the Flume, you can return to the visitors center or continue on the trail to view a waterfall and natural pool. Plan to spend about 1½ hours here if you decide to hike the entire loop. Although there are buses that can take you from the visitors center halfway to the Flume, much of the arduous walking still lies ahead, and there is no handicapped access. The trail is refreshingly cool on hot summer days, but on brisk autumn days you may want to bring an extra sweater or jacket along. Hours: The Flume is open from 9 a.m. to 4:30 p.m. daily (until 5 p.m. July 4 through Labor Day), June through October. Admission is $6 for adults, and $3 for children 6 to 12.

In contrast to the park's natural attractions, a small amusement park, Fantasy Farm, a waterslide park, and the Whale's Tail, are located on U.S. 3 just below the Flume.

★★★ **Mt. Washington** • At 6,288 feet, this is the highest peak in the Northeast, and on clear days the panoramas from the ascent and summit are unrivaled. On top are a weather station and complete tourist facilities. Even in July the peak's climate can be quite chilly, so be sure to bring warm clothing with you. The summit can be reached by the auto road in your own vehicle at a cost of $14 for car and driver, plus $5 for each additional adult, $3 for children 5 to 12. The auto road is open from mid-May to mid-October, weather permitting. However, you should not take those bumper stickers that read "This Car Climbed Mt. Washington" lightly; the climb to the top is not easy, even for an automobile in top-notch condition. Should you prefer not to put the wear and tear on your car, vans are available to take riders up the mountain: $18 for adults, $10 for children 5 to 12. After spending much of your vacation behind the wheel, you may find it a welcome relief to let a tour guide do the driving. There is also cog-railway service available from the other side of Mt. Washington at Bretton Woods. The round-trip by rail costs $35 for adults and takes 3 hours.

Of course, many hikers try their luck at climbing the mountain. Should you wish to do so, you'll need a whole day. The information center across from the entrance to the auto road can suggest trails that are right for your ability. It is fairly easy for weary hikers to get rides back down the mountain from people who have taken the auto road. Camping shelters along the trail provide sanctuary for hikers who get caught in bad weather or who just want to spend more time exploring the region.

For a different perspective of Mt. Washington, take the **Gondola Skyride** at Wildcat Ski Area, which faces the mountain. Hours: The ride operates on weekends Memorial Day through late June, and daily from July through Columbus Day from 10 a.m. to 4:30 p.m. Phone: (800) 255-6439. Tickets are $8 for adults, $4 for children 6 to 12.

✯✯ **Crawford Notch State Park** • As you travel west from Glen on Route 302 through the park, you'll pass two small waterfalls, the Silver and Flume Cascades, that slither rather than plunge down the mountainside. Both have parking areas. The better mountain view is from the Flume Cascade parking lot. The park's information center is located in a colorful train station near Twin Mountain.

As you near Twin Mountain, there is a striking view of the Mt. Washington Hotel at Bretton Woods. Built in 1902, the hotel was designed to entice the privileged set, and it still holds a commanding presence over the valley. In its heyday, visitors came by the trainload to visit the hotel. Today Bretton Woods is a thriving cross-country ski mecca. The entrance to the **Cog Railway** that climbs Mt. Washington is just beyond the hotel. Trains run every hour on the hour, and the 3-hour round-trip to the summit costs $35 for adults, $32 for seniors, $24 for children 6 to 12, children under 6 free. Hours: The train runs from early May to mid-October. The railway recommends advance ticket purchase. Phone: Call (800) 922-8825 or (603) 846-5404 for reservations.

✯ **Attitash Ski Area** • Four miles west of the junction of U.S. 302 and Route 16, this ski area in Bartlett operates an alpine slide, water park, a chairlift ride, and mountain bike trails during the summer. Phone: Call (603) 374-2368 for rates and information.

✯ **Cathedral Ledge** • Just a few minutes from the center of North Conway, the ledge draws throngs of rock climbers and spectators alike. You'll probably find this daring sport fascinating to watch if you've never witnessed it firsthand. Climbers can be observed from below, or you can drive up the road to the top of the ledge and congratulate the climbers as they reach their goal.

✯ **The Conway Scenic Railroad** • The railroad runs out of North Conway's picturesque depot, which was built in 1874. Three separate excursions are available—one travels south along the Saco River to Conway (55 minutes round-trip), the second travels west to Bartlett (1 hour and 40 minutes round-trip), and the third takes you all the way to the top of Crawford Notch and back (almost 5 hours round-trip). The trips are enjoyable for young and old alike. Hours: Trains depart daily from mid-May through October, weekends mid-April through mid-May, on Thanksgiving weekend, and on weekends November and

December through Christmas. In July and August there is also the Sunset Special, which leaves on Tuesday, Wednesday, Thursday, and Saturday nights at 6:30 p.m. Tickets for the Conway excursion are $7.50 for adults and $5 for children 4 to 12; tickets for the Bartlett run cost $12.50 for adults, $7.50 for children 4 to 12, and $3 for children under 4, and the round-trip to Crawford Notch is $29.95 for adults, $14.50 for children 4 to 12, and $3 for children under 4. First-class tickets in the "Gertrude Emma," a 92-year-old restored parlor car, are a couple of dollars more. Phone: (603) 356-5251 or (800) 232-5251.

✯ **Ruggles Mine** • Rock collectors may want to stop here. The mine first opened in 1803 and is known for its vast supply of mica. Visitors are allowed to take home mineral samples that they collect, probably accounting for the mine's steep admission charge ($10 for adults, $5 for children 4 to 11). Hours: The mine is open on weekends only from mid-May through mid-June, daily mid-June through mid-October 9 a.m. to 5 p.m. Address: Near Grafton off U.S. 4 between Interstate 93 and White River Junction. Phone: (603) 523-4275.

✯ **Storyland** • On Route 16 in Glen, this is an amusement park where storybook characters come to life, and is a favorite of youngsters. Open daily from Father's Day to Labor Day, and on weekends only Labor Day through Columbus Day. Admission to all rides and performances is $15 per person, children under 4 are free. Phone: (603) 383-4293.

FITNESS AND RECREATION

Adventurous travelers may find a river trip to their liking. **Saco Bound** in Conway, New Hampshire, operates a variety of river trips, including whitewater and flat-water, by raft or canoe, for several hours or several days. Contact them at (603) 447-2177 or Box 119, Center Conway, NH 03813, for more details. Many rock climbers test their skills at Cathedral Ledge just outside North Conway (see above). After climbing, you can cool off with a swim at neighboring **Echo Lake State Park**. There's also a mountain-stream swimming hole in nearby Jackson. Just follow the signs from Jackson toward the Eagle Mountain House. The swimming hole is about halfway up the hill on your right.

The White Mountains are heavily populated with ski areas. **Black Mountain** in Jackson (603-383-4490) and **Mt. Cranmore** in North Conway (603-356-5543) are good family mountains since they cater to

all levels of ability. Mt. Cranmore's skimobile tramway is a godsend to
those scared of chairlifts. **Attitash** in Bartlett (603-374-2368 or
800-862-1600), **Wildcat** opposite the Mt. Washington Auto Road
(603-466-3326 or 800-255-6439), **Cannon** in Franconia (603-823-5563
or 800-552-1234), and **Loon Mountain** in Lincoln (603-745-8111)
offer experienced skiers more of a challenge. Wildcat and Loon both
have gondolas, and Cannon operates an aerial tramway. **Bretton
Woods** near the cog railway to the top of Mt. Washington is best
known for its cross-country trails (603-278-5000). The town of Jackson
is also a major cross-country center; contact the Jackson Ski Touring
Foundation at (603) 383-9355 for information. **Tuckerman's Ravine**
at Pinkham Notch is only for the most adventurous and expert skiers.
There are no lifts so skiers must hike 2½ miles. Check with the White
Mountain National Forest Service before trying to tackle the ravine.
Because of avalanche danger in winter, only spring skiing is allowed in
the ravine (603-466-2725).

During summer, mountain bikers can take chairlifts up to trails at
Attitash, Bretton Woods, Loon, and Mt. Cranmore ski areas. Many
bicyclists enjoy riding through the National Forest, but check with a
ranger station before embarking on backcountry trails, as some are off-
limits to mountain bikes.

Mt. Cranmore's recreation center in North Conway has both
indoor and outdoor tennis, an indoor swimming pool, and a climbing
wall. Call (603) 356-5544 for information.

FOOD

There is fine dining on New England fare in Jackson at the **Eagle
Mountain House**. More-moderately priced meals can be had at
the **Thompson House Eatery** right in the center of Jackson
(603-383-9341); dinner entrées range from $5.95 to $16.95, and fresh
seafood specials are often available. Not too far from Jackson, the
Bernerhof Inn on U.S. 302 west in Glen, just 2 miles from the Route
16 intersection, serves appetizing European dishes with a German flair,
and also has accommodations for overnight guests (603-383-4414 or
800-548-8007).

In North Conway, just across from the railroad depot on Main
Street, **Horsefeathers'** menu ranges from deluxe burgers to pasta
and chicken entrées. The tavern atmosphere is lively, and prices are
reasonable at $5.95 to $13.95 (603-356-6862). Also in North
Conway's center, on Seavey Street 1 block up from Main Street,

Bellini's serves Italian specialties including homemade pastas prepared in delicious combinations. Try the fettucini with prosciutto, spinach, and mushrooms in a light cream sauce. If you have room, their desserts are also scrumptious. Dinner entrées start under $10. Call (603) 356-7000 for reservations.

LODGING

A covered bridge leads to the town of Jackson, which lies between North Conway and Mt. Washington. Although Jackson does have Black Mountain downhill ski area, the town is best known as a cross-country skiers' haven, so there are plenty of cozy bed and breakfasts around to take care of tired winter and summer visitors alike. It is central enough to be a good base for sightseeing in the White Mountains but tends to be a little quieter and less crowded than neighboring North Conway. The **Eagle Mountain House** in Jackson is a charming resort on a quiet country road with beautiful mountain views. The rooms in the restored hotel are comfortably elegant and start at $119 during the height of fall foliage season and $69 during early spring and late fall. Suites start at $155 during the summer and $110 in off-season. Tennis, golf, and swimming are all available at the resort as well. Follow signs up Carter Notch Road from the center of Jackson. Call (800) 966-5779 or (603) 383-9111 for reservations. The **Inn at Thorn Hill**, in a home designed by renowned architect Stanford White, is another lovely lodging option in Jackson village. Rooms are tastefully decorated with Victorian furnishings, and rates starting at $70 per person include lodging, a hearty breakfast, and gourmet evening meal (603-383-4242 or 800-289-8990).

The **Cranmore Inn**, only 1 block from the center of North Conway on Kearsarge Street, is more reasonably priced than many other inns in town yet offers the same services. A comfortable room for two costs from $39 to $85 per night (depending on the season), including an ample breakfast in the inn's sunny breakfast room. There are several sitting rooms and a swimming pool on the premises. Mt. Cranmore ski area is only 5 minutes away. Call (603) 356-5502 or (800) 526-5502 for reservations.

Route 16 in North Conway is lined with inns and motels, which can fill up at the height of fall foliage or for big ski weekends. If you're calling ahead, try the **Scottish Lion** (603-356-6381). The rooms are pleasant, meals have a Scottish slant, and there is a lively pub to unwind in after a long day of sightseeing or skiing. Rooms including a

WHITE MOUNTAINS

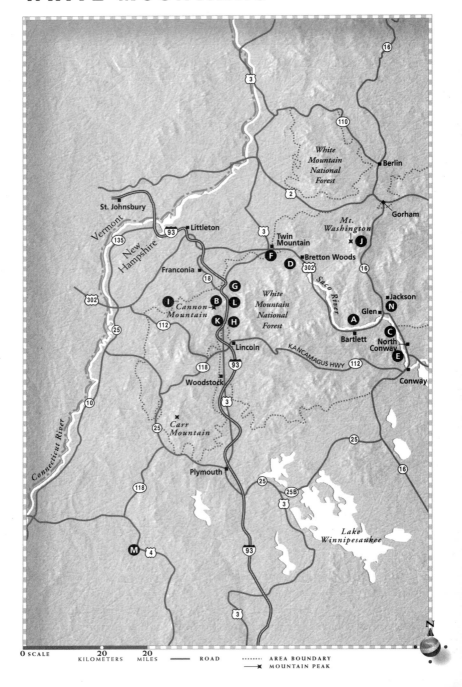

Food

- **A** Bellini's
- **B** Bernerhof Inn
- **C** Eagle Mountain House
- **A** Horsefeathers
- **C** Thompson House Eatery

Lodging

- **A** Cranmore Inn
- **C** Eagle Mountain House
- **C** Inn at Thorn Hill
- **A** Scottish Lion
- **A** White Trellis Motel

Camping

- **D** Dolly Copp Campground
- **E** Glen Ellis Family Campground

Note: Items with the same letter are located in the same town or area.

full breakfast start at $59. The inn also operates a Scottish import shop next door. The **White Trellis Motel**, which has pleasant mountain views, makes more of an effort than most to create an attractive atmosphere with flowering window boxes and ivy-covered trellises. Doubles start at $45 (603-356-2492). You might also want to try booking a room through **Mt. Washington Valley Chamber of Commerce Lodging Bureau** (603-356-3171 or 800-367-3364).

CAMPING

Dolly Copp Campground (named for an innkeeper who left her husband of 50 years by announcing at a party that "fifty years is long enough for any woman to live with one man") is a national forest campground with 176 sites near the base of Mt. Washington off Route 16, 6 miles south of Gorham. Reservations can be made by calling (800) 280-2267. If you arrive without a reservation, sites are assigned on a first-come, first-served basis. RVs are allowed, but hot showers and electrical hookups are not available. Sites cost about $12 per night. The campground is open from mid-May to late September.

Glen Ellis Family Campground, on U.S. 302 just west of the Route 16 junction, is convenient to Jackson, North Conway, and area travel routes. In case you are low on provisions, there is a supermarket next to the entrance. The campground itself has complete sanitary and recreational facilities. Sites start at $16 per night, and some are adjacent to the Saco River. The campground operates from Memorial Day to Columbus Day, July being the busiest month. Call (603) 383-4567 for information in season or (603) 539-2860 for inquiries during the winter.

PERFORMING ARTS

The Eastern Slope Playhouse next door to the Eastern Slope Inn on Main Street in North Conway presents professional musical productions during the summer months. Call (603) 356-5776 for schedule and ticket information.

SIDE TRIPS

The **Kancamagus Highway** (Route 112), which runs from Conway to Lincoln is a well-known scenic route in the White Mountains. While it doesn't offer as many things to get out and see as some of the other roads through the National Forest do, the route is a pretty drive if you have extra time in the area, especially during fall foliage.

For those wishing to explore New Hampshire further, the state's **Lakes Region** is worth visiting. New Hampshire's largest lakes are Squam (known for its beauty, loons, and the movie *On Golden Pond*) and Winnipesaukee. Weirs Beach is perhaps the most touristed spot on Winnipesaukee, complete with a honky-tonk boardwalk and the type of sandy beach normally found at seaside resorts. Despite its touristy nature, Weirs Beach does have beautiful views of the lake, and many excursion companies leave from there. **Mt. Washington Cruises** operates 3-hour boat cruises late May through late October and evening Moonlight Dinner/Dance Cruises at the height of the summer season. Day cruises cost about $14 for adults, $6 for children (kids under 4 are free with an adult). Dinner cruises are $27 to $32 per person. Call (603) 366-5531 for departure times and tickets.

The **Winnipesaukee Railroad** runs lakeside scenic railroad trips in restored historic railroad cars. Excursions leave from Weirs Beach and Meredith. Tickets that allow you to get on and off the train as many times as you'd like during the day are about $7.50 for adults, $5.50 for children 5 to 12. The railroad operates on weekends only from Memorial Day through late June, then daily through mid-October. Call (603) 279-5253 for information.

Other Lakes Region attractions include **Annalee's Doll Museum** (800-433-6557) in Meredith, **Castle in the Clouds** (800-729-2468) in Moultonboro, the **Polar Caves** (603-536-1888 or 800-273-1886) in Plymouth, and the slide and surf coaster at Weirs Beach. There are numerous accommodations and restaurants along Route 3 throughout the region.

9

NORTHERN VERMONT

A lmost more than any other northeastern state, Vermont embodies the spirit of New England that many travelers hope to discover when they visit this part of the world. Picture-perfect town greens, winding river valleys, and the beautiful Green Mountains that turn gentle pastel shades at sunset all seem unspoiled by modern development. Northern Vermont offers the visitor all this, as well as the appealing city of Burlington (Vermont's largest, although a small city by comparison to most), located on the shores of Lake Champlain, and home to the University of Vermont. Just south of Burlington is the Shelburne Museum—one of the nation's best American folk art museums.

Northern Vermont also has some of the most distinctive scenery in the state, ranging from the relatively low elevation of 95 feet above sea level at Lake Champlain, to the state's highest point of 4,393 feet atop Mt. Mansfield. Majestic Mt. Mansfield is the focal point of Stowe—Northern Vermont's premier ski resort and a charming town in its own right. ◼

NORTHERN VERMONT

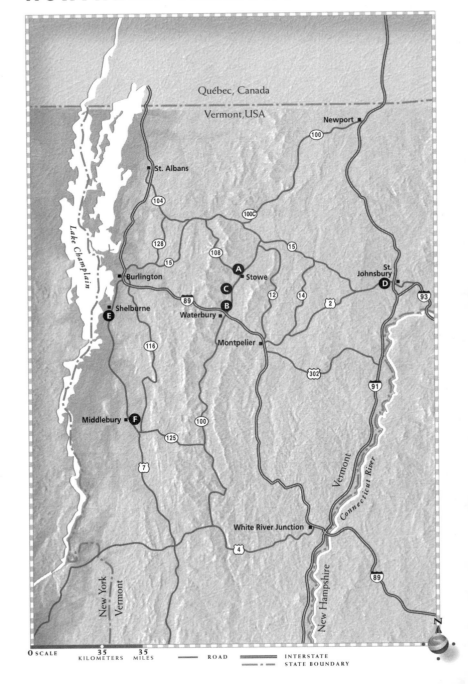

Québec, Canada

Vermont, USA

Newport ■

Lake Champlain

St. Albans ■

Burlington ■

Stowe ■

St. Johnsbury ■

Shelburne ■

Waterbury ■

Montpelier ■

Middlebury ■

White River Junction ■

New York
Vermont

New Hampshire

Connecticut River

Vermont

0 SCALE 35 KILOMETERS 35 MILES   ——— ROAD   ═══ INTERSTATE   —··— STATE BOUNDARY

N

Sights

A Alpine Slide

B Ben & Jerry's Ice Cream Factory

C Cold Hollow Cider Mill

A Gondola at Stowe

D Maple Grove Museum and Factory

A Mountain Auto Toll Road

E Shelburne House and Farms

E Shelburne Museum

A Stowe Mountain Resort

Food and Lodging

A Green Mountain Inn

E Inn at Shelburne Farms

F The Middlebury Inn

A Miguel's Stowe Away

F Otter Creek Bakery

A Trapp Family Lodge

A Whip Bar & Grill

Note: Items with the same letter are located in the same town or area.

A PERFECT DAY IN NORTHERN VERMONT

I really have two favorite but quite different days that I enjoy when I'm in northern Vermont. One is to spend the day in nature by hiking in the Stowe area, and perhaps sneaking off to the Ben & Jerry's factory for a tour and samples. The other is to visit the Shelburne Museum, and afterward, if there's time, take a boat ride on Lake Champlain or window shop in downtown Burlington.

SIGHTSEEING HIGHLIGHTS

★★★ **Shelburne Museum** • Generally considered to have one of the best collections of early American antiques and folk art, this delightful museum covers 45 acres and has 37 period homes housing its collection of art, china, silver, scrimshaw, Native American artifacts, carousel animals, decoys, weathervanes, ship figureheads, and antique toys and dolls. Some of the unique structures include a lighthouse, a round barn, a sidewheeler boat called the S.S. *Ticonderoga*, and a private railroad car. Built in the late 1800s, the latter has a plush interior of mahogany paneling, velvet upholstery, and modern bath and kitchen facilities.

Not to be missed is the Hat and Fragrance House, which contains much more than its name implies. Within its walls you'll find an especially fine assemblage of antique quilts, handwoven rugs, handmade lace, embroidered samplers, and costumes. The old-time country store, apothecary shop, and doctor's and dentist's offices in the general store building are fascinating; and the Electra Havemeyer Webb Memorial Building (built in memory of the woman philanthropist who founded the museum) has Degas, Manet, Rembrandt, and Monet originals. Hours: 10 a.m. to 5 p.m. daily from mid-May to mid-October. Address: In Shelburne a few miles south of Burlington. Admission (which will let you into the museum for two consecutive days) is $15 for adults, $6 for children 6 to 14. (½ day–full day)

After visiting the museum, you may wish to see nearby **Shelburne House and Farms** owned by Electra Havemeyer Webb's family. The estate, built in 1899, is stunningly set on Lake Champlain. Park architect Frederick Law Olmstead was consulted in the landscape design of the property. The estate now serves as an elegant inn.

★ **Ben & Jerry's Ice Cream Factory** • Outside of Waterbury on the road to Stowe, the tour of Ben & Jerry's main factory is fun for the whole family. Half of the nominal tour fee goes to charity, and the delectable ice-cream samples fresh off the production line are well worth the other portion. If the samples only whet your appetite for more, you can purchase cones when you're done with the tour, and naturally there's a gift shop selling logo products.

✿ **Stowe Mountain Resort** • When the ski slopes are not covered with snow, this resort operates an **Alpine Slide** on Little Spruce, an in-line skate park at the base of Spruce Peak, and the **Mountain Auto Toll Road** and **Gondola at Stowe** to the top of Mt. Mansfield for wonderful views and vistas. Phone: Call (802) 253-3000 for rates and hours of operation.

Cold Hollow Cider Mill • Cold Hollow does a lot of advertising, so you may find yourself stopping out of curiosity, but there really isn't much to see. The cider press and jelly kitchen aren't exactly exciting— but the cider samples are tasty, as are the other Vermont-made gourmet foods available for sampling and purchase. Cold Hollow is located on the road from Waterbury to Stowe.

Maple Grove Museum and Factory • If you happen to be as far east as St. Johnsbury and you're a maple syrup lover, you may want to visit this museum on U.S. 2. The museum is really just a small cottage where sugaring tools are displayed and a flat vat of syrup boils. Of more interest is the video on maple-syrup making that plays continuously in the gift shop, and the tour of the factory where maple candy is made. Hours: Visitors can tour the factory on weekdays year-round every 12 minutes from 8 a.m. to 11:45 a.m. and from 12:30 p.m. to 4:15 p.m., for a nominal admission charge.

FITNESS AND RECREATION

Stowe is one of the premier ski areas in New England, so if you're a downhill skier and you visit in winter, don't miss the opportunity to ski here. In warmer months hikers will find miles of trails to keep them busy in the Stowe/Mt. Mansfield area. If you take Route 108 from Stowe to Jeffersonville, you'll find plenty of entrances to hiking trails alongside the road and picnic areas as well. (At one point the road becomes very steep, narrow, and curvy, making driving tricky, but only for a short stretch.)

Stowe's in-town recreational path stretches 5 miles from the Village Church to the mountain foothills. If you're an active traveler but left your equipment at home, **Action Outfitters** can rent you anything from a mountain bike to a canoe to in-line skates (802-253-7975).

FOOD AND LODGING

Restaurants and accommodations are plentiful in Stowe—long a summer and winter resort—making it a good stopping place for a night or two. Perhaps the best-known hotel in Stowe is the **Trapp Family Lodge**, run by the Trapp family of *The Sound of Music* fame. With its chalet-style buildings bursting with flower boxes, and unrivaled views of Stowe below and the mountains beyond, the lodge easily lives up to its motto "a little of Austria . . . a lot of Vermont." As one might guess, entrées such as Wiener schnitzel in the Lodge's dining room have a distinctive Austrian flavor as well. During summer there are outdoor evening concerts in the Trapp Family Meadow. Doubles range from about $160 to $220 in high season (802-253-8511 or 800-826-7000).

The **Green Mountain Inn**, right in the heart of the village, is on the National Register of Historic Places. Built in 1833, it is centrally located and more affordably priced at $89 to $209 for a double room. Guests also have use of a health club (802-253-7301 or 800-445-6629). As its name suggests, the inn's **Whip Bar & Grill** specializes in grilled foods. The restaurant also has children's menu and a very affordably priced Sunday brunch.

For additional lodging choices in Stowe, there is an excellent reservation service (802-253-7321 or 800-247-8693) that can help book you a room in your price range. If you're dining out while in town, and crave something other than New England fare, try **Miguel's Stowe Away** for Mexican food. So popular are the restaurant's chips and salsa that they are packaged and sold in gourmet shops throughout the country. The restaurant is located on Mountain Road, and offers a children's menu as well as a "gringo menu" for those who can't handle spicy cuisine (802-253-7574).

In the Burlington area, one of the nicest inns can be found at the **Inn at Shelburne Farms**. Owned by the Webb family, who started the Shelburne Museum (see description above), the inn is truly worth a splurge and is open from late May through mid-October. Doubles range from $100 to $250 (802-985-8498 or 802-985-8686). Visitors can tour the farm daily beginning at 9:30 a.m., with the last tour leaving at 3:30 p.m., late May through mid-October. The farm makes its own delicious cheddar cheese that can be purchased at the farm store and visitor center. Proceeds go to the farm's nonprofit conservation education organization.

In addition to the Inn at Shelburne Farms, there are numerous motels along U.S. 7 between Shelburne and Burlington. If you have time, travel 1 hour south to Middlebury, a pleasant college town bisected by Otter Creek Falls. **The Middlebury Inn** is the popular place in town to stay (802-388-4961 or 800-842-4666). Doubles are $80 to $170. The **Otter Creek Bakery** at 1 College Street has terrific breakfast pastries, bread sticks, and picnic fixings.

SIDE TRIPS IN NORTHERN VERMONT

For a truly out-of-the-ordinary experience, how about a llama trek into the mountains? **Northern Vermont Llama Company** operates half-day and full-day treks (802-644-2257). The excursions leave from Smuggler's Notch, just over the mountain from Stowe.

Ferry rides across the lake to New York state are a pleasant way to see the lake and the Adirondack and Green Mountains that surround it. If you do venture out on the lake, be sure to keep an eye out for "Champ," Lake Champlain's own fabled creature—said to rival the Loch Ness monster. Ferries operate from Burlington late May through late October, and the crossing takes 1 hour each way. Call (802) 864-9804 for departure times and fares during your visit. (If you really want to extend your trip, Montreal, Canada, is only about 2 hours north of Burlington.)

10
CENTRAL VERMONT

Central Vermont is home to the popular ski areas of Killington and Pico, covered bridges, the Green Mountains, the Quechee Gorge, the city of Rutland, and Woodstock—a quintessential New England town. Woodstock appears to be the type of village that crime or hardship never touches, a model town with elegant Federal-style homes surrounding the Town Green. Even the grass seems perfectly groomed. Some of the bells in Woodstock's churches were made by Paul Revere himself. A tourist information booth right on the Green provides answers to visitors' questions, and the Town Crier Chalk Board in the center of the business district lists the goings-on for the day. In short, Woodstock is an ideal place to base yourself when visiting the surrounding region. ◥

CENTRAL VERMONT

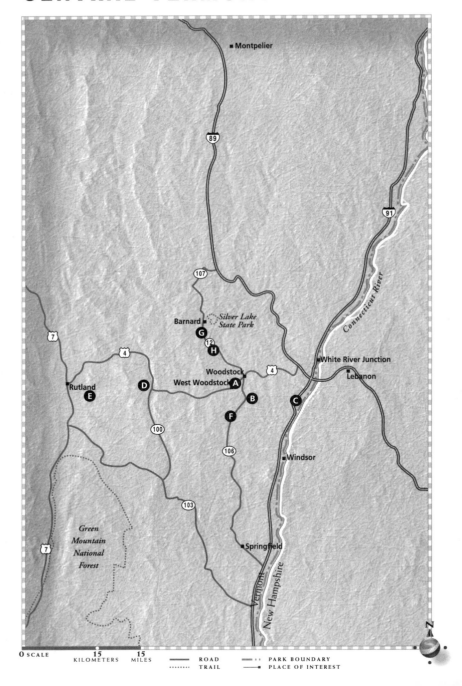

Montpelier

89

91

107

Connecticut River

Barnard ■ ·*Silver Lake State Park*

G

12
H

7

4

Woodstock
West Woodstock A

4

White River Junction ■
Lebanon ■

D

Rutland
E

B

C

F

100

106

Windsor ■

103

Green Mountain National Forest

7

Springfield ■

Vermont

New Hampshire

N

0 SCALE   15   15
KILOMETERS   MILES   —— ROAD   — · · PARK BOUNDARY
·········· TRAIL   —■ PLACE OF INTEREST

Sights

- Ⓐ **Billings Farm & Museum**
- Ⓑ **Dana House Museum**
- Ⓒ **Quechee Gorge**
- Ⓒ **Simon Pearce Glass**
- Ⓒ **Sugarbush Farm**
- Ⓑ **Vermont Raptor Center**

Food

- Ⓑ **Bentley's Restaurant**
- Ⓓ **Hemingway's**
- Ⓑ **Kedron Valley Inn**
- Ⓑ **The Prince and the Pauper**
- Ⓔ **Red Clover Inn**
- Ⓑ **Spooner's Restaurant**
- Ⓑ **Woodstock Inn and Resort**

Lodging

- Ⓑ **Braeside Motel**
- Ⓑ **Kedron Valley Inn**
- Ⓕ **Lincoln Inn at the Covered Bridge**
- Ⓖ **Maple Leaf Inn**
- Ⓔ **Red Clover Inn**
- Ⓑ **Woodstock Inn & Resort**

Camping

- Ⓒ **Quechee Recreation Area**
- Ⓗ **Silver Lake State Park**

Note: Items with the same letter are located in the same town or area.

A PERFECT DAY IN CENTRAL VERMONT

I'd begin my day in central Vermont dramatically, with a hike down into Quechee Gorge followed by a visit to Simon Pearce to watch the glass blowers and eat lunch in the old mill. Area agriculture would occupy my afternoon, visiting Sugarbush Maple Farm and the Billings Farm and Museum. Then I would hole up in a cozy country inn for my evening meal and night's accommodation.

SIGHTSEEING HIGHLIGHTS

★★ **Billings Farm & Museum** • The farm offers a look at rural Vermont life of a century ago. You can help hand-churn butter, see how cows were milked the old-fashioned way, and watch wood-carving demonstrations. Hours: May through October, daily 10 a.m. to 5 p.m.; on weekends during November and December 10 a.m. to 4 p.m. Address: Off Route 12 north of Woodstock. (2 hours)

★★ **Quechee Gorge** • In Quechee, Vermont, on U.S. 4, only a few miles from the Vermont/New Hampshire state line, a bridge crosses the dramatic 165-foot deep Quechee Gorge. Take the 1-mile hike to the bottom of the gorge, or just stretch your legs on the short (quarter-mile) hike to view the waterfall that empties into the river below. Picnic tables are adjacent to the gorge. (1 hour)

★ **Dana House Museum** • Woodstock artifacts, period furnishings, antique costumes, tools, and toys make up the majority of the exhibits at this small museum operated by the Woodstock Historical Society. Address: 26 Elm Street. Hours: Open May through October, Monday through Saturday 10 a.m. to 5 p.m., Sunday 2 p.m. to 5 p.m. (1 hour)

★ **Simon Pearce Glass** • A right-hand turn at the first blinking light after Quechee Gorge bridge will take you through one of New England's rustic covered bridges and into "downtown" Quechee. There, Simon Pearce has completely renovated the old mill so today you can watch glassblowers and potters at their crafts. You can also inspect the modern hydraulic power system that now fuels the ovens. The handmade glassware and pottery is sold in the gift shop along with natural fiber fabrics. Hours: The shop is open from 10 a.m. to 5 p.m., and you can watch glassblowing during those same hours, except from 1 to 2 p.m. when the craftsmen take their lunch. Admission is free. There is a fine restaurant on the premises as well. (½ hour)

★ **Sugarbush Farm** • At this maple farm you can visit a maple sugar-house to learn about processing the sweet syrup. Although the sugaring season is spring, the farm is open year-round and also makes tasty Vermont cheeses. To get there from Simon Pearce in Quechee, continue on River Road for several miles past lush green golf courses and farms, turn onto Hillside Road, and follow signs to the farm. Phone: Call (802) 457-1757 for hours of operation during your visit. (1 hour)

★ **Vermont Raptor Center** • Woodstock also boasts this unusual museum at Vermont's Institute of Natural Science on Church Hill Road about 1½ miles from the town green. At the outdoor museum, visitors can view more than 25 species of New England hawks, owls, and eagles, including bald eagles and the great horned owl. Hours: Daily from 10 a.m. to 4 p.m.; closed Sundays during the winter months. Admission is $4 for adults, $1 for children 5 to 15. (1 hour)

FITNESS AND RECREATION

There are three marked jogging trails in the village of Woodstock; pick up trail maps at the Woodstock Inn. The Woodstock Recreation Department has two outdoor pools (802-457-1502), and the Woodstock Sports Center has an indoor pool as well as fitness rooms (802-457-6656). Bikes can be rented in Woodstock from **Woodstock Sports** (802-457-1568), and **Silver Lake State Park** in nearby Barnard offers both swimming and boat rentals (802-234-9451). For downhill skiing, **Suicide Six** (802-457-1666) is only 3 miles from Woodstock, while **Killington** (802-773-1500) and **Pico** (802-775-4345), with their more extensive trail systems (Killington has more than 100 trails and a 3,081-foot vertical drop), are both less than 25 miles away. The **Woodstock Ski Touring Center** (802-457-6674) offers 37 miles of groomed trails and cross-country ski rentals and lessons.

FOOD

The **Woodstock Inn and Resort** has a fine-dining restaurant as well as the more casual Eagle Cafe. Savory herbs, light sauces, and fresh local ingredients combine to give meals at the **Kedron Valley Inn** in South Woodstock their distinguished reputation. **The Prince and the Pauper** on Elm Street in the center of Woodstock has a *prix fixe* menu that changes weekly, but dishes such as poached salmon and roast duckling are examples of the types of entrées you can expect to see offered. Call (802) 457-1818 for reservations.

Bentley's Restaurant, also in Woodstock center (802-457-3232), serves dishes ranging from veal to Szechuan to fresh salads. Dinner entrées average about $15. Families may want to try **Spooner's Restaurant** in Spooner Barn on U.S. 4 just east of Woodstock center. It has a children's menu, and specialties include western-style beef and traditional New England fare (802-457-4022). Prices are moderate.

Near Rutland, the **Red Clover Inn** serves tasty cuisine in three intimate, candlelit dining rooms. The menu changes daily. Appetizers are creative, the wine list is extensive (over 130 selections), and desserts are tempting. Entrées range from $15 to $24. On Route 4 in Killington, **Hemingway's** receives consistently high ratings for its food. Reservations are recommended (802-422-3886).

LODGING

For those seeking the comfort of a country inn combined with resort amenities such as golf, tennis, and swimming, the **Woodstock Inn & Resort** right on the village green has double rooms starting at $145 per night (802-457-1100 or 800-448-7900). The **Braeside Motel** on the east side of Woodstock offers doubles from $48 to $88 and has an outdoor swimming pool (802-457-1366).

The **Lincoln Inn at the Covered Bridge** (802-457-3312) on U.S. 4 in nearby West Woodstock is a 200-year-old farmhouse over-looking the Lincoln Covered Bridge and the Ottauquechee River. Double room rates including a full country breakfast run from $99 to $180. The **Kedron Valley Inn** on Route 106 in South Woodstock is known for its nouvelle cuisine (see Food, above) and has accommodations with canopy beds and country patchwork quilts. Rooms range from $114 to $189 including breakfast (802-457-1473). About 10 miles north of Woodstock, in Barnard near Silver Lake, the **Maple Leaf Inn** (802-234-5342 or 800-516-2753) welcomes guests in rooms with wood- burning fireplaces, stenciled walls, and handmade quilts. Doubles including a full breakfast range from $100 to $150.

About 5 miles east of Rutland and a half-mile from U.S. 4, the **Red Clover Inn** (802-775-2290 or 800-752-0571) has country-cozy rooms. Dinner in the inn's restaurant (see above) and a full breakfast are included in the rate-per-night for two ($120–$185; $170–$250 in fall foliage, ski season, and holiday weekends). As you travel toward Rutland, you'll find a number of reasonably priced motels.

CAMPING

The closest camping area to Woodstock is the state-operated **Quechee Recreation Area**, near the Quechee Gorge. A trail runs from the camping area to the bottom of the gorge. Both tent and camper sites are available (802-295-2990). Fifteen minutes north of Woodstock is a campground at **Silver Lake State Park** (802-234-9451).

11

SOUTHERN VERMONT

This area of New England is particularly well-traveled in autumn because of the abundant maple trees that turn brilliant orange and red as winter approaches. Southern Vermont's excellent ski resorts, beautiful mountain vistas, and charming towns with their tidy village greens are reason enough to visit the region in any season. All along U.S. 7 south from Rutland to Manchester Center are views of the Green Mountains. At Arlington, covered bridges sit on either side of the highway, and historic Manchester Village is 1 mile from Manchester Center on Route 7A. Farther to the south, Bennington was the site of a major Revolutionary War victory for the colonists in 1777, but today when you look at Old Bennington's graceful homes, it is hard to believe that a battle ever took place there. ◣

SOUTHERN VERMONT

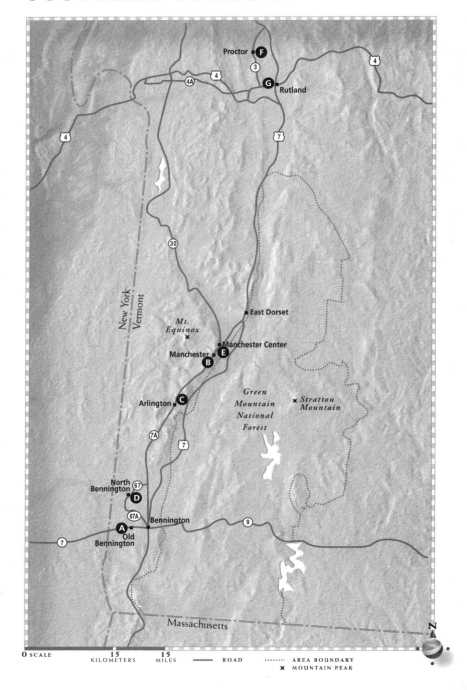

Proctor ● **F**
③
④ ④A ④
G Rutland
④
⑦
㉚
New York
Vermont
East Dorset
Mt.
Equinox
×
Manchester Center
Manchester ■ **E**
B
Green
Mountain × Stratton
Arlington ■ **C** National Mountain
Forest
⑦A
⑦
North 67
Bennington **D**
67A Bennington
A ⑨
⑦ Old
Bennington

Massachusetts

N

Sights

Ⓐ The Bennington Monument

Ⓐ The Bennington Museum

Ⓑ Hildene

Ⓒ Norman Rockwell Exhibition and Gift Shop

Ⓐ The Old First Church

Ⓓ Park-McCullough House

Ⓑ Sky Line Drive

Ⓔ Southern Vermont Art Center

Ⓕ Vermont Marble Exhibit

Ⓖ Wilson Castle

Note: Items with the same letter are located in the same town or area.

A PERFECT DAY IN SOUTHERN VERMONT

In the morning I would tour Wilson Castle, then head to Manchester Center for lunch and a bit of outlet shopping. After lunch I would visit the Lincoln family's lovely estate, Hildene, and then end the day with a drive up Mt. Equinox.

SIGHTSEEING HIGHLIGHTS

☆☆ **The Bennington Museum** • The primary reason for visiting this museum is its collection of works by famed American folk artist Grandma Moses, who started to paint in her 70s and continued to be productive well into her 90s. The collection also includes early American furniture, glassware, pottery, military artifacts, and household items such as pedal-operated sewing machines. Hours: Open daily from 9 a.m. to 5 p.m. The museum is closed the week of Christmas through New Year's Day. Also closed on Thanksgiving. Admission is $5 for adults, $4.50 for students and senior citizens, children under 12 are free. Address: Approximately ½-mile from the Bennington Monument on Route 9. (1½ hours)

✶✶ **Hildene** • The stucco Georgian revival mansion was built and owned by Robert Todd Lincoln, son of Abraham Lincoln. Hildene remained in the Lincoln family until 1975 and is now open to the public. The furnishings, including a 1,000-pipe player organ (complete with over 240 rolls of music) and a stovepipe hat worn by the president, belonged to the Lincolns. Beautifully set in the Manchester Valley, Hildene's expansive front lawn was used as a driving range by avid golfer Robert Todd Lincoln. The estate's formal English-style gardens were designed by his daughter, Jesse, after she returned from England. Many special events such as polo, symphony concerts, sleigh rides, and cross-country skiing take place on the estate's "meadowlands." Hours: Open for tours 9:30 a.m. to 5:30 p.m. from May through October. The last tour of the day leaves at 4 p.m. Admission to the house is $6 for adults, $2 for children 6 to 14, children under 6 are free. Address: Just south of Manchester Village on Route 7A. Phone: You may want to call (802) 362-1788 to see if there are any special goings-on, should your visit happen to fall in the off-season. Christmas candlelight tours are especially popular. (1½ hours)

✶✶ **Wilson Castle** • This nineteenth-century castle is set on 115 acres. Built by a Vermont doctor and his wealthy British wife, the castle is filled with an eclectic mix of European and Oriental pieces. Although the paint is peeling here and there, the hand-painted and hand-stenciled ceilings are unusual, and the colorful stained and etched glass windows throughout the house are quite beautiful. A Louis XV chair used by several popes, an ornate jewel case, an inlaid pool table, and a handsome curly maple fireplace in the master bedroom are a few of the other furnishings worth special note. Hours: Open daily for guided tours from mid-May through late October from 9 a.m. to 6 p.m. Admission is $6 for adults, $5.50 for seniors, $2 for children 6 to 12; children under 6 free. Address: On West Proctor Road off Business U.S. 4, west of Rutland about one-half mile from the Route 3 north turnoff. (1½ hours)

✶ **The Bennington Monument** • Completed in 1891, the monument commemorates the Battle of Bennington and is the centerpiece of lovely Old Bennington. It warrants a visit on any clear day for the view, and it is a must at the height of fall foliage season. You can see three states—Massachusetts, New York, and Vermont—from the observation deck. An elevator takes you to the top of the 306-foot structure, so there is no stair-climbing involved. A small admission fee is charged. The well-groomed houses that line the road leading to and from the monument are worth a look as well. Hours: Daily April through October from 9 a.m. to 5 p.m. Admission is $1 for adults, 50 cents for children. (½ hour)

✯ **Norman Rockwell Exhibition and Gift Shop** • More a gift shop than a museum, this place on Route 7A in Arlington has hundreds of Rockwell magazine covers on display but no original works. There is a film presentation on the artist. Admission is nominal. Hours: Open daily from 9 a.m. to 5 p.m. May through October, from 10 a.m. to 4 p.m. the rest of the year. I prefer the Rockwell Museum in Stockbridge, Massachusetts, which has many Rockwell originals, but if you don't plan to visit Stockbridge, and you're a Rockwell fan, then this may have to suffice. (½ hour)

✯ **The Old First Church** • Adjacent to the Town Green in Old Bennington, this is a lovely example of early nineteenth-century church architecture in New England. Perhaps more interesting, though, is its graveyard with headstones dating back to the Revolutionary War. Poet Robert Frost is buried here. (½ hour)

✯ **Park-McCullough House** • This lovely 35-room Victorian mansion was once home to two Vermont governors. The house is filled with family antiques, and beautiful details such as a stained-glass skylight and intricately patterned frosted-glass light fixtures. Hours: Open for tours from mid-May through October 10 a.m. to 4 p.m., with the last tour leaving at 3 p.m. Admission is $4 for adults and $3 for kids 12 to 17. Address: On the corner of Park and West Street in North Bennington. Phone: Call (802) 442-5441 for a schedule. Special "Victorian Christmas" tours are run during the holidays. (1 hour)

✯ **Sky Line Drive** • For better views of the Green Mountains, take the 5-mile-long Sky Line Drive (toll road) to the top of Mt. Equinox, the highest peak in the Taconic range. The drive is well worth taking on a clear day and is particularly dramatic at the height of fall foliage. There are a number of picnic areas and hiking trails on the way up and an inn at the 3,835-foot summit, but despite the view, you're better off opting for accommodations down in the village. Hours: The drive is open from 8 a.m. to 10 p.m. daily, May 1 to November 1. The toll is $6 per car. Address: Entrance to the auto road is on Route 7A south of Manchester Village. (1 hour)

SOUTHERN VERMONT

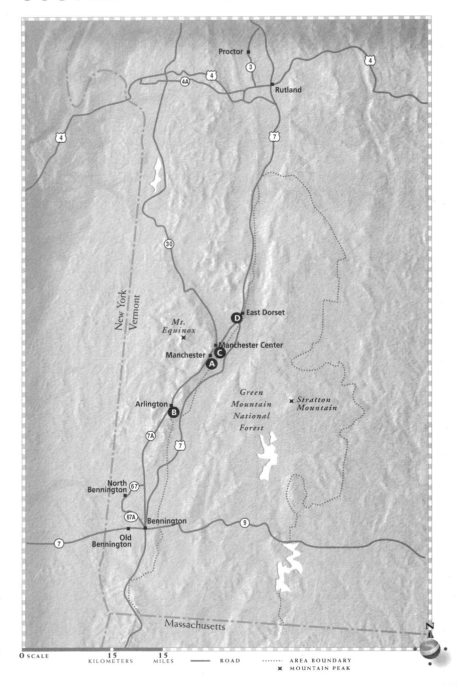

Proctor
Rutland
4A 4 3 4
4
7
30
New York
Vermont
Mt.
Equinox
East Dorset
D
Manchester Center
Manchester C
A
Green
Mountain
National
Forest
Stratton
Mountain
Arlington
B
7A
7
North
Bennington 67
67A Bennington
7 Old
Bennington
9

Massachusetts

0 SCALE   15   15
       KILOMETERS MILES   ——— ROAD   ········ AREA BOUNDARY
                                         ✕ MOUNTAIN PEAK

Food and Lodging

Ⓐ 1811 House

Ⓑ Arlington Inn

Ⓒ Ben & Jerry's

Ⓐ The Black Swan

Ⓒ Christo's

Ⓒ Cookie House

Ⓐ Equinox Hotel Resort and Spa

Ⓐ Inn at Manchester

Ⓐ Marsh Tavern

Ⓐ North Shire

Ⓒ Pancake House

Ⓒ Park Bench

Ⓐ Reluctant Panther

Ⓐ Seth Warner Inn

Ⓒ Up For Breakfast

Camping

Ⓑ Camping on the Battenkill

Ⓓ Emerald Lake State Park

Note: Items with the same letter are located in the same town or area.

✯ **Southern Vermont Art Center** • After viewing the changing exhibits by local artists, take a walk in the sculpture garden or on the botany trail, or have lunch in the attractive garden café where the menu changes daily. Hours: The center is open from mid-May through October, Tuesday through Saturday from 10 a.m. to 5 p.m., and noon to 5 p.m. on Sunday. Admission to the center is $3 for adults, 50 cents for students, free for children under 13. Address: Follow signs from Route 7A just south of Manchester Center.

✯ **Vermont Marble Exhibit** • Proctor, a small town about 8 miles from Rutland, calls itself the "marble capital of the world" because of the abundance of marble found in the area. At the Vermont Marble Exhibit on Main Street, visitors have the chance to see a marble sculptor at work. There is also a film explaining the natural forces that create marble and the steps taken to mold this stone for artistic and functional purposes. You will see examples of Vermont marble throughout Proctor, and in nearby Manchester Village the sidewalks are also made of marble. Hours: The exhibit is open daily, mid-May through late October, from 9 a.m. to 5:30 p.m. During winter, only the gift shop is open Monday through Saturday 9 a.m. to 4 p.m. There is an admission charge. Address: The town of Proctor is 5 miles beyond Wilson Castle (see directions above); once in Proctor follow, signs to the Marble Exhibit.

FITNESS AND RECREATION

Hikers will want to stop in at the U.S. Forest Service office on Route 30 just east of Manchester Center for local hiking suggestions. Skiers will be pleased to know that both **Stratton** (802-297-2200 or 800-787-2866) and **Bromley** (802-824-5522) mountains are convenient to the Manchester area. Bromley also operates an Alpine Ride during summer months for about $5 per person.

The Battenkill River, running from Manchester southwest through Arlington, is frequented by canoeists. **Battenkill Canoe Ltd.** at 1 River Road in Arlington can outfit you with the canoe trip of your choice. Contact them at (802) 362-2800 or (800) 421-5268 for additional information.

Battenkill Sports Bicycle Shop at the junction of Routes 7 and 30 in Manchester Center can fix you up with a mountain or touring bike for exploring the beautiful surrounding countryside. Call (802) 362-2734 or (800) 340-2734 for rental information.

FOOD AND LODGING

Reservations in southern Vermont—particularly for the Manchester area (which is the best place to stay)—are strongly advised, especially on weekends and during leaf-peeping season. At the Equinox, for example, rooms are often completely booked as much as six months in advance for peak foliage weekends. Some establishments have minimum stay requirements of two nights or more during high season, so be sure to check ahead of time. If the lodgings listed below are full during your visit, you may want to contact **Manchester and the Mountains Area Lodgings** (800-677-7829). They will try to locate a room for you in your price range, and there is no charge for the service.

The majestic **Equinox Hotel Resort and Spa** reigns supreme over historic Manchester Village. The historic hotel has been renovated in recent years, and now serves as a full-service resort and spa. The grand exterior appears to stretch endlessly, as do the marble sidewalks that surround the building. Carriage rides are available from the hotel's doorstep. Rooms in season will run over $150 per night for two, including breakfast. For extra pampering you may want to make use of the resort's spa facilities. Call (802) 362-4700 or (800) 362-4747 for reservations. Dinner entrées in the hotel's main dining room range from $16 to $24, with "lighter entrées" (really, expanded portions of appetizers) ranging from about $8 to $13. **Marsh Tavern** at the hotel has a buffet luncheon, dinner entrées from hamburgers to basil linguini ($9–$15), and evening entertainment.

The **Reluctant Panther** on West Road right in Manchester Village (802-362-2568 or 800-822-2331) has pleasant lodging and dining facilities. Room rates are based on a modified American Plan and range from $160 to $320. The inn's restaurant features hearty soups, stews, and pies in winter, and lighter fare such as seafood and grilled dishes during summer.

The **1811 House** (802-362-1811 or 800-432-1811), also in the village center, became an inn in 1811 but was built in the 1770s. Authentically furnished with fine antiques, the house is on the National Register of Historic Places and once belonged to Mary Lincoln Isham, President Lincoln's granddaughter. Doubles run from $110 to $200 including a full breakfast (a two-night minimum stay is required on weekends, during fall foliage, and on holidays). There is a pub on the premises (open from 5 p.m. to 7:30 p.m.). The **Inn at Manchester**, just down the street on Route 7A toward Manchester Center, is open all year and serves a complete breakfast. Rates range from $95 to $130.

Call (802) 362-1793 or (800) 273-1793 for reservations. The **Seth Warner Inn** (802-362-3830), also on Route 7A, has sunny rooms with country furnishings ($80 to $95 for two, including breakfast).

There are many motels in the vicinity of Manchester. Most of them are located on the outskirts of town on Routes 30, 7, and 7A. One of the nicest is the **North Shire**, on Route 7A on the south side of the village. Rooms are spacious and attractively furnished and have lovely mountain views. The outdoor pool is pleasant, as are the helpful hosts, who are more than willing to provide you with sightseeing and dining suggestions. Doubles are $75 to $80 per day including continental breakfast, and $5 higher per day during fall foliage (802-362-2336).

If your lodging establishment doesn't serve food, the Manchester area has plenty of restaurants to satisfy just about any food craving. For breakfast, try **Up For Breakfast** on Main Street in Manchester Center, where breakfast dishes are far from ordinary. Or indulge in pancakes at the **Pancake House** (802-362-3496) just south of the Route 7A/Route 30 junction. The **Park Bench** (802-362-2557), also on Route 7, is nearby and popular for lunch. **Christo's** (802-362-2408), next to Up for Breakfast, features pizza and pasta at moderate prices. For dessert, the aroma from the **Cookie House** is hard to resist, while Vermont's own **Ben & Jerry's** ice-cream shop just a couple of doors away will not do much to thin one's waistline either. **The Black Swan** (802-362-3807) on Route 7 between Manchester Center and the historic Village is renowned for its continental cuisine (entrées range from $11 to $22), and at the **Arlington Inn** (802-375-6532) on Route 7A in nearby Arlington you can enjoy fine dining by candlelight.

If you want to ship home some of Vermont's celebrated cheddar cheese, the Grand Union supermarket in Manchester Center is one of the best places in the area to purchase it. They have the cheese already packed for shipping, and their prices tend to be lower than elsewhere. The supermarket is also a good place to purchase Vermont maple syrup and prepared salads for picnicking.

CAMPING

Emerald Lake State Park, in East Dorset about 8 miles north of Manchester Center on U.S. 7, has camping, swimming, a nature trail, and boating on a beautiful green lake that lives up to its name. The camping area has 105 sites, no hookups, 35 lean-tos, bathrooms, and pay showers. Canoes and rowboats can be rented for an outing on the lake. Call (802) 362-1655 for reservations.

Camping on the Battenkill is a private campground with both tent and RV sites, plus swimming and fishing on the Battenkill River. The campground, located on Route 7A in Arlington, is open from mid-April through October. The rate is about $20 per campsite. Call (802) 375-6663 for reservations.

NIGHTLIFE

During June, July, and August, enjoy summer-stock productions at the **Dorset Playhouse** on Route 30, 5 miles north of Manchester Center. Call (802) 867-5777 for ticket information.

SHOPPING

Manchester Center has an array of tidy shops interspersed with Ralph Lauren and Liz Claiborne outlets, among others. The Northshire Bookstore at the intersection of U.S. 7 and Route 30 is one of the better bookstores in New England, and is definitely worth a visit. Orvis, the mail-order giant, has its flagship store on Route 7A in Manchester. The Equinox Valley Nursery on Route 7A is known for its colorful seasonal displays. The nursery's annual fall pumpkin patch is especially festive.

SIDE TRIPS

Lake George, New York, a very popular lake resort, is only 43 miles from Rutland. To get there, continue on U.S. 4 west from Rutland to Fort Ann. Then take Route 149 west to U.S. 9 and follow it north to the town of Lake George.

Fort Ticonderoga, about 50 miles northwest of Rutland at Ticonderoga, New York, is also a popular tourist destination. To get to the fort, continue on U.S. 4 west at Rutland to Whitehall, then take Route 22 north to Ticonderoga. The fort is open daily from mid-May through mid-October from 9 a.m. to 5 p.m., until 6 p.m. during July and August. Admission is charged.

Horse-racing fans visiting the area in August may want to take a 35-mile detour from Arlington, Vermont, to Saratoga Springs, New York. In addition to being recognized for thoroughbred horse-racing and natural springs, Saratoga also has fine homes in its favor. The **National Museum of Racing and Thoroughbred Hall of Fame** is in Saratoga, as well as the unusual **Petrified Sea Gardens**.

12

THE BERKSHIRES

The Berkshires offer the visitor much in the way of outdoor recreation, such as golf, skiing, and hiking, and in cultural events such as the Boston Symphony Orchestra at Tanglewood. With the picturesque villages of Stockbridge and Lenox and the beauty of the Berkshire hills themselves, it's no wonder the area has remained a popular resort for more than 100 years. Considering the Berkshires are only 3 hours from both New York City and Boston, it's amazing that the area is not overrun with souvenir shops, factory outlets, and T-shirt shops designed to take advantage of the tourist dollar. Thanks to careful planning, though, most towns remain much as they were when Norman Rockwell painted here in the 1950s, and many have changed little in the last century.

In Williamstown, the quintessential college town, Williams College dominates almost every aspect of town life, providing the residents of the sleepy Berkshire community with a wealth of cultural activities other rural communities lack, including two outstanding art museums. ◣

THE BERKSHIRES

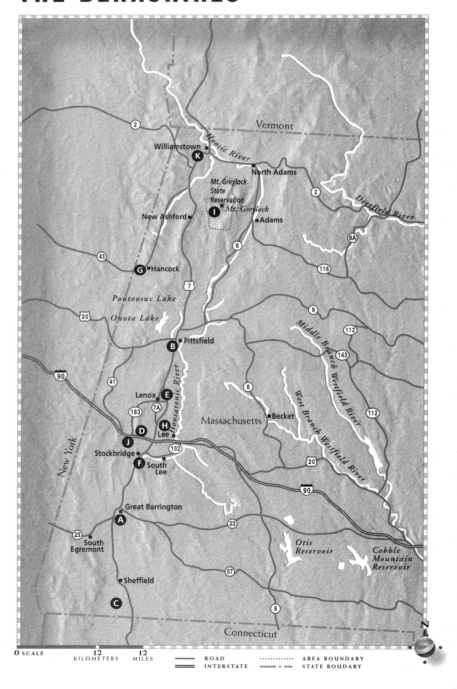

Vermont

Williamstown
North Adams

Mt. Greylock
State
Reservation
× Mt. Greylock

New Ashford
Adams

Hoosic River

Deerfield River

New Ashford

Hancock

Pontoosuc Lake

Onota Lake

Pittsfield

Lenox

Becket

Massachusetts

Middle Branch Westfield River

West Branch Westfield River

Housatonic River

Lee

Stockbridge

South
Lee

New York

Great Barrington

Otis
Reservoir

Cobble
Mountain
Reservoir

South
Egremont

Sheffield

Connecticut

N

0 SCALE   12   12
KILOMETERS   MILES   ———— ROAD   ·········· AREA BOUNDARY
                      ═════ INTERSTATE   ═══ ═ ═ STATE BOUDARY

Sights

(A)   Albert Schweitzer Center

(B)   Arrowhead

(C)   Bartholomew's Cobble

(D)   The Berkshire Botanical Garden

(B)   The Berkshire Museum

(E)   Berkshire Scenic Railway Museum

(F)   Chesterwood

(G)   Hancock Shaker Village

(F)   Merwin House

(F)   Mission House Museum

(H)   The Mount

(I)   Mt. Greylock

(F)   Naumkeag

(J)   The Norman Rockwell Museum

(G)   Sterling & Francine Clark Art Institute

(K)   Williams College Art Museum

Note: Items with the same letter are located in the same town or area.

A PERFECT DAY IN THE BERKSHIRES

I'd either spend a leisurely morning at Hancock Shaker Village, picnicking on the grounds at lunch, or I'd enjoy the works of Impressionists masters at the Clark Art Institute. In the afternoon I would visit Chesterwood, followed by window shopping in Stockbridge in the late afternoon. Dinner would be determined by my evening plans. If the weather was good, I'd opt for a picnic dinner on "the lawn" at Tanglewood and stay to watch a concert. If rain threatened, I'd dine at the Red Lion Inn and then head to Jacob's Pillow for a dance performance.

SIGHTSEEING HIGHLIGHTS

★★★ **Hancock Shaker Village** • Allow at least 2 hours to explore this village, one of the best examples of the everyday life of an unusual religious sect called the Shakers. There are live demonstrations of Shaker crafts such as broom making and basket weaving. The descriptive panels in each room describe different aspects of Shaker life. Don't miss the unique round barn. Hours: The village is open daily from 9:30 a.m. to 5 p.m. April through November. Two 60-minute tours daily at 10:30 a.m. and 2 p.m. take you through part of the village. If you are unable to time your visit for a guided tour, you are free to tour the complex on your own. Entrance fees are $10 for adults, $8 for students and seniors, $4.50 for children 6 to 12, and $25 for families. For a truly uncommon evening, visit the village for a candlelight Shaker dinner and tour. You'll tour the village and then dine on traditional Shaker dishes while seated communal style at one of the long tables in the "Believers Room." The dinner events usually begin at 5 p.m. on Saturday evenings during summer and early fall, and run about $35 per person. Address: The village is located at the junction of Routes 41 and 20 in Hancock. There are picnic tables outside the visitor center. Phone: Call (413) 443-0188 for reservations. (2 hours–half day)

★★★ **Sterling & Francine Clark Art Institute** • The museum has room after room of stunning French Impressionist paintings, including Renoirs and Monets, and works by noted American painters such as Homer, Cassatt, and Sargent. The fine collection also includes English silver and works dating back to the fifteenth century. Hours: Open 10 a.m. to 5 p.m. Tuesday through Sunday. Closed on Thanksgiving, Christmas, and New Year's Day. The museum is open Memorial, Labor, and Columbus Days. Admission is free. (1½ hours)

✮✮ **Chesterwood** • This was the summer home of sculptor Daniel Chester French, who is known for the Lincoln Memorial in Washington and the *Minute Man* statue in Concord, Massachusetts, as well as many other works that adorn governmental buildings. Plaster castings of his works are displayed in his barn, home, and studio. Many of his works were so large he had to transport them out of his studio on railroad tracks just to see how they'd look in the sunlight. Each summer, usually beginning July 4th weekend, contemporary sculpture from local artists is on exhibit throughout the 12-acre grounds and along the nature trail. Other annual events include an antique show in May, a flower show in July, and Christmas at Chesterwood. Hours: Operated by the National Trust, the museum is open daily May through October from 10 a.m. to 5 p.m. Admission is $6 for adults, $3 for children 13 to 18, and $1 for children 6 to 12. Address: Off Route 183 in Stockbridge. There is a picnic area next to the parking lot. (1½ hours)

✮✮ **The Norman Rockwell Museum** • In 1993 the museum moved from its previous quarters in the quaint "Old Corner House" on Main Street in downtown Stockbridge to this $4.4-million facility on Route 183 just west of town. Now the museum can display up to one-third of its more than 500 Rockwell works at a time, and exhibits also include the venerated artist's studio. Devoted Rockwell fans will enjoy this choice collection, and those previously indifferent to Rockwell will become converts when they witness firsthand the clarity and vitality of his oils. Hours: Open daily from 10 a.m. to 5 p.m., May through October. November through April the museum is open Monday through Friday from 11 a.m. to 4 p.m., and on Saturday and Sunday from 10 a.m. to 5 p.m. It is closed on Christmas, Thanksgiving, and New Year's Day. Admission is $8 for adults, $6 for students, $2 for children 6 to 18, and $20 for families. (1 hour)

✮✮ **Williams College Art Museum** • The museum's collection ranges from ancient Greek vases to Andy Warhol pop art. A gallery is devoted to the artist brothers, Maurice and Charles Prendergast. Hours: Open 10 a.m. to 5 p.m. Tuesday through Saturday, and Sunday from 1 to 5 p.m. The museum is closed for Thanksgiving, Christmas, and New Year's Day. Admission is free. (1 hour)

✮ **Arrowhead** • Author Herman Melville made his home here for 13 years during the mid-1800s. See the room where Melville penned *Moby Dick* and several other novels. Hours: 10 a.m. to 4:30 p.m. Monday through Saturday, and Sunday from 11 a.m. to 3:30 p.m. After Labor Day, the museum is closed on Tuesday and Wednesday. Arrowhead is open for guided tours Memorial Day through October. Admission is $3.50 for adults, $3 for seniors, and $2 for children 6 to 16. Address: On Holmes Road in Pittsfield. (1 hour)

✸ **The Berkshire Botanical Garden** • This 15-acre botanic garden off Route 102, just before you come to the intersection with Route 183, is a nice spot for a picnic lunch between visits to Hancock Shaker Village and Chesterwood. Hours: Daily from 10 a.m. to 5 p.m. The greenhouses are open year-round, while the gardens may be toured mid-May through October, and admission is charged during those months (somewhat pricey for a botanic garden of this size, the garden is run by a non-profit organization). Admission is $5 for adults, $4 for seniors, $1 for children 6 to 12, and $10 for a family. (½ hour–1 hour)

✸ **The Berkshire Museum** • The museum is a combination art and natural history museum. Its collections include everything from gem-stones to boa constrictors to a fine selection of landscapes by artists of the Hudson River School. Hours: Open Tuesday through Saturday from 10 a.m. to 5 p.m., and Sunday from 1 p.m. to 5 p.m. During July and August, it is also open on Monday from 10 a.m. to 5 p.m. Admission is $3 for adults, $2 for students and seniors, and $1 for children 12 to 18. Address: 39 South Street, on U.S. 7 in Pittsfield. (1 hour)

✸ **The Mount** • This was the summer estate of American novelist Edith Wharton. *Ethan Frome*, perhaps her most famous novel, was set in Lenox. Hours: Visitors can tour the property during summer months. Admission is $4.50 for adults, $4 for seniors, and $2.50 for children 13 to 18. Plays based on the author's works are presented here during July and August. Tickets to the matinee performances include afternoon tea. Address: Off U.S. 7 between Lenox and Stockbridge. Phone: Call (413) 637-1899 for complete details. (1 hour)

✸ **Mt. Greylock** • In fair weather the scenic drive over Mt. Greylock offers extraordinary views of the Berkshire mountains. The entrance to the visitors center is off U.S. 7 just south of New Ashford.

✸ **Naumkeag** • A stately brick and shingle home designed by Stanford White, its formal gardens are open from 10 a.m. to 5 p.m. during sum-mer. The house may be toured Tuesday through Sunday beginning at

10 a.m. with the last tour leaving at 4:15 p.m. Open daily Memorial Day through Labor Day, on weekends and holidays from Labor Day through Columbus Day. Admission to the house and gardens is $6, admission to the house or garden alone is $4. Address: One-half mile from the Red Lion Inn on Prospect Hill Road. (1½ hours)

Albert Schweitzer Center • At 50 Hurlburt Road in Great Barrington, this museum and library are dedicated to Dr. Schweitzer. There is a wildlife sanctuary on the grounds. Hours: The center is open Tuesday through Saturday from 10 a.m. to 4 p.m., and Sunday from noon to 4 p.m. during summer, and on weekends from 11 a.m. to 4 p.m. during winter months. Donations are requested.

Bartholomew's Cobble • This delightful 277-acre nature preserve off Route 7A south of Sheffield is worth a visit if you're a nature-lover.

Berkshire Scenic Railway Museum • This model train museum in a restored 1902 train station should appeal to railroad buffs. Hours: Open from 10 a.m. to 3 p.m. weekends and holidays June through October. Admission is free. Address: On Willow Creek Road in Lenox. Phone: Call (413) 637-2210 for ticket and schedule information if you're interested in taking the short train ride along the Housatonic River.

Merwin House • A Federal-style home (circa 1825). Hours: Can be toured June 1 through October 15 on Tuesday, Thursday, Saturday, and Sunday from noon to 5 p.m. Admission is $4 for adults and $2 for children. Address: West Main Street in Stockbridge.

Mission House Museum • Diagonally across the street from Merwin House, Mission House was built in 1739 for the Reverend John Sargeant, the first Christian missionary to the Stockbridge Indians. The house originally stood on the hill overlooking town but was moved to its present location in 1926. Hours: Tours of the house and garden run Tuesday through Sunday from 11 a.m. to 4 p.m. Memorial Day weekend through Columbus Day. Admission is $4 for adults, $1 for children 6 to 12.

FITNESS AND RECREATION

Butternut Basin in Great Barrington (413-528-2000), **Catamount** in South Egremont (413-528-1262 or 800-342-1840), **Jiminy Peak** in Hancock (413-738-5500), and **Brodie Mountain** in New Ashford (413-443-4752) are all in the Berkshire region and provide skiing terrain for all levels of ability. Brodie has the greatest vertical drop at 1,250 feet, while Catamount straddles the Massachusetts and New York border. Brodie and Butternut both have cross-country trails as well.

FOOD AND LODGING

You can find comfortable lodging at the **Williams Inn** (413-458-9371) on the village green in Williamstown if you plan to stay for a performance at the playhouse. Doubles range from about $100 to $150. If you're not attending the theater, I suggest basing your Berkshires stay in either Stockbridge or Lenox, as they are better jumping-off points for area activities. **The Red Lion Inn** in Stockbridge is one of the best-known inns in the area and deservedly so; the focal point of the town, it has been treating its guests regally for over 200 years. Double rooms at the inn start around $100 in peak season (May through October). Singles and two-room suites are also available. Call (413) 298-5545 for reservations. If you are unable to book a room here, at least partake of a traditional New England meal such as prime rib, stuffed lobster, or scrod in the main dining room; or people-watch while sipping cocktails on the inn's front porch. The **Lion's Den** downstairs has pub fare and entertainment in the evenings.

There are two pleasant inns in the quiet town of South Lee, once a mill town, about 1½ miles from Stockbridge. The historic **Merrell Inn**, built in 1794, has the only remaining colonial circular bar in America. Rooms are furnished with antiques, and the property borders on the Housatonic River. Double rooms, including an ample breakfast, range from $85 to $155 per night in high season (413-243-1794 or 800-243-1794). Just across the street, the **Federal House**, known locally for its fine European cuisine, also rents rooms to overnight guests. Call (413) 243-1824 for dining or lodging reservations.

Lovely Lenox has its share of attractive inns right in the center of town on Walker Street. Each guest room in the **Walker House** is named after a famous composer and is furnished accordingly. Guests are welcome to use the inn's delightful porches or watch movies in the library. The hosts are warm and friendly, and breakfast and afternoon tea are included in the high-season room rates of $70 to $180 (413-637-1271). The **Gables Inn** just down the street was once the home of Edith Wharton. Rooms here are also thematic—the Shakespeare Room, the Show Business Room, and the Presidential

Room with pictures and memorabilia of past presidents. Rates, including continental breakfast at an elegantly set table, are $75 to $195 per night depending on the season and type of room. There's also a pool on the premises. Call (413) 637-3416.

Two other inns on Walker Street have restaurants and overnight accommodations. **Gateways Inn and Restaurant** has four large suites with private baths, fireplaces, and curly maple furniture for $100 to $295 (413-637-2532). *Prix fixe* dinners feature dishes such as breast of chicken topped with crawfish, truffle and crèpes served in a honey liqueur sauce, and medallions of monkfish stuffed with Norwegian salmon and topped with a fresh basil sauce. The menu at the **Candlelight Inn** changes seasonally but is primarily continental and American in focus. Dinner entrées range from $18 to $25, and lunch generally runs anywhere from $5 to $15. Try the Chocolate Chippie for dessert. Upstairs rooms range from $90 to $155 per night in season and $65 to $120 per night in the off-season (413-637-1555).

Outside Lenox, a turreted estate has been turned into one of the most elegant lodging establishments around. Set on 85 acres, and restored by the owners of the Red Lion Inn, **Blantyre** is truly a feast for the eyes. You'll have to have a deep pocketbook to stay at Blantyre, however, as rooms average about $250 per night—tennis and continental breakfast included. Call (413) 637-3556 for reservations.

Somewhat more affordable are the motels on U.S. 7 between Pittsfield and Lenox, including the **Susse Chalet**, where a double room goes for $50 to $90 a night (413-637-3560 or 800-524-2538). More motels can also be found on U.S. 7 between Stockbridge and Great Barrington. The area abounds with country inns, but accommodations do fill up quickly on weekends, so you may want to call the **Berkshire Visitor's Bureau** at (413) 443-9186 for a complete lodging list.

For less-formal dining options, **Michael's** (413-298-3530) on Elm Street in Stockbridge serves a variety of American dishes, and dinner prices are moderate. **20 Railroad Street** in Great Barrington has tasty tavern-style food in a pleasant and comfortable milieu. Exposed brick walls add charm, and prices are reasonable (413-528-9345).

CAMPING

The **Pittsfield State Forest** (413-442-8992) has 31 campsites (about $10 per site), and the **October Mountain State Forest** (413-243-1778) in Lee has 50. The October Mountain campground is more convenient for sightseeing, so reservations are strongly

THE BERKSHIRES

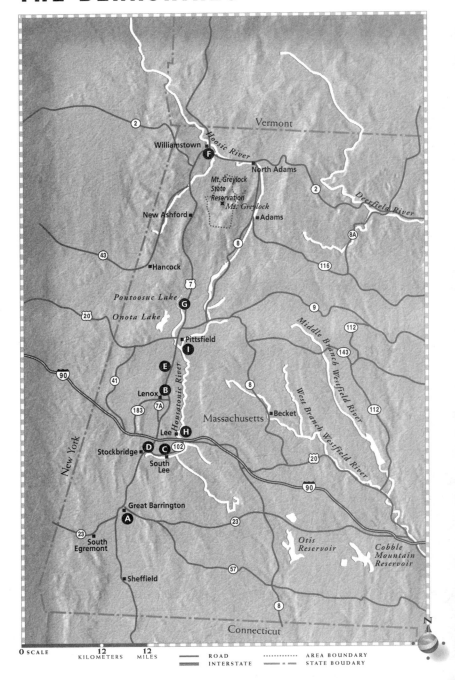

Vermont

Williamstown **F**
Hoosic River
North Adams

Mt. Greylock
State
Reservation
× Mt. Greylock
New Ashford ■
■ Adams
Deerfield River

2
8A
116

Hancock

Pontoosuc Lake **G**
Onota Lake

9

Middle Branch Westfield River
112
143
112

■ Pittsfield **I**

E

Lenox ■ **B**

183
7A

Housatonic River

8

Becket ■

Massachusetts

West Branch Westfield River

Lee ■ **H**

New York

D **C** 102
Stockbridge ■
South
Lee

20

90

Great Barrington
A

23
South
Egremont

23

Otis
Reservoir

Cobble
Mountain
Reservoir

■ Sheffield

57

90

8

Connecticut

N

O SCALE
12 KILOMETERS
12 MILES

ROAD
INTERSTATE
AREA BOUNDARY
STATE BOUDARY

Food and Lodging

A 20 Railroad Street

B Blantyre

B Candlelight Inn

C Federal House

B Gables Inn

B Gateways Inn and Restaurant

D Lion's Den

C Merrell Inn

D Michael's

D The Red Lion Inn

E Susse Chalet

B Walker House

F Williams Inn

Camping

G Bonnie Brae Cabins and Campsites

H October Mountain State Forest

I Pittsfield State Forest

Note: Items with the same letter are located in the same town or area.

recommended. Sites are about $12 per night. Both campgrounds have bathrooms with wheelchair access and are open seasonally. **Bonnie Brae Cabins and Campsites** at Pontoosuc Lake, just off U.S. 7 several miles north of downtown Pittsfield, might also be an economical alternative to staying in a country inn. Open May through mid-October, Bonnie Brae has cabins that rent for $40 to $65 per night, and campsites start at $23 per night. Call (413) 442-3754 for information.

PERFORMING ARTS

The **Williamstown Theatre Festival** is widely known for its high-quality summer productions. Many popular actors got their start here, and some return on occasion to hone their stage skills. Call (413) 597-3400 for performance and ticket information.

A visit to **Tanglewood**, the Boston Symphony Orchestra's summer home in Lenox, is the favorite form of nighttime entertainment in the Berkshires. The BSO performs in the "Shed" on lovely wooded grounds, while smaller-scale concerts are given in the new concert hall. Tickets are available for seating in the Shed, but on clear nights Beethoven is best heard with a champagne picnic on the lawn. Bring your own blanket and dress warmly. Early birds can catch afternoon rehearsal performances at bargain prices. Call the box office at (413) 637-1940 for information during summer months. In the off-season, you'll need to contact the BSO's office in Boston, (617) 266-1492, for details. Tanglewood is located off Route 183 about 2 miles south of Lenox Center.

Jacob's Pillow is also a popular summer cultural event. The dance festival features various well-known and talented traveling dance troupes. The Pillow is located in Becket on U.S. 20 about 8 miles from Lee. Call (413) 243-0745 for schedule and tickets.

Other cultural events in the area include the **Berkshire Theatre Festival** in Stockbridge (413-298-5576), the **Berkshire Ballet** in Pittsfield (413-442-1307), the **Berkshire Opera Company** (413-243-1343), and the **Berkshire Public Theatre** in Pittsfield (413-445-4634).

The **Berkshire Ticket Booth** at the Chamber Office (in the Lenox Academy building, 75 Main Street, Lenox) sells tickets to area events. The booth is open Monday through Saturday from 1:00 to 5:00 p.m.; it sells same-day discounted tickets whenever they are available.

SIDE TRIPS FROM THE BERKSHIRES

From the Berkshires, it is only a 2-hour drive to the Catskill Mountains in New York state. The Catskills are somewhat less traveled during fall foliage than most of New England, but the scenery is no less spectacular. To get there, take U.S. 7 south to Great Barrington, then follow Route 23 west to Hudson, New York. At Hudson, cross the Rip Van Winkle Bridge to Catskill, New York.

Deerfield, about 35 miles southeast of Williamstown, Massachusetts, is one of the most perfectly preserved historic towns in New England. While many of the buildings are privately owned by either individuals or Deerfield Academy, 12 of them are open to the public and can be toured with one admission ticket. Guided tours of the houses last 30 minutes each, so you'll need a full day if you want to visit them all. Tickets are $10 for adults, $5 for children 6 to 17, and can be purchased at the information center on the village's main street (called The Street). The buildings, which range in age from the early 1700s to the late 1800s, are open daily from 9:30 a.m. to 4:30 p.m. except Thanksgiving, Christmas Eve, and Christmas.

The **Memorial Hall Museum** on Memorial Street in the center of Deerfield has period rooms including a Victorian bedroom and a colonial kitchen. Indian artifacts and pottery, handmade quilts, and nineteenth-century clothing are also on display. The museum is open May through October from 10 a.m. to 4:30 p.m. on Saturday and Sunday. Admission is $5 for adults, $3 for students, $1 for children 6 to 12. The grounds of Deerfield Academy are also worth strolling through.

If you do plan to stay in Deerfield for a day, there are picnic tables behind the information center. The **Deerfield Inn**, right across the street from the information center, is a fine lodging and dining establishment. Lunch entrées range from $8.75 to $10.25, while pheasant, veal with wild mushrooms, and venison dishes are just a sampling of the varied dinner menu which changes seasonally and is priced from $17 to $23. Overnight accommodations including breakfast start at $65 per person. Call (413) 774-5587 or (800) 926-3865 for reservations.

13

THE HEART OF CONNECTICUT

Connecticut wears many faces—from the serene Litchfield Hills in the northeastern corner of the state to industrial cities such as New Haven, Bridgeport, and Waterbury. From the winding Connecticut River Valley and its sleepy towns, to the state's Atlantic coast—Connecticut has many distinct personalities.

Litchfield is a showplace for exquisite eighteenth-century estates. The Congregational church on Litchfield's village green is widely noted for its classic New England architecture. In central Connecticut, the state capitol of Hartford was once home to Mark Twain and Harriet Beecher Stowe. Essex, located on the Connecticut River, is an attractive town whose past and present have been shaped by nautical endeavors. In 1814, during the War of 1812, the British raided Essex and burned many of the town's ships, causing great hardship to the townspeople. Today, well-kept houses are discreetly tucked away on the waterfront, while the marina is filled with pleasure craft. The importance of the sea in Connecticut's history also comes to life in Mystic Seaport's re-creation of a nineteenth-century maritime village. ◾

CONNECTICUT

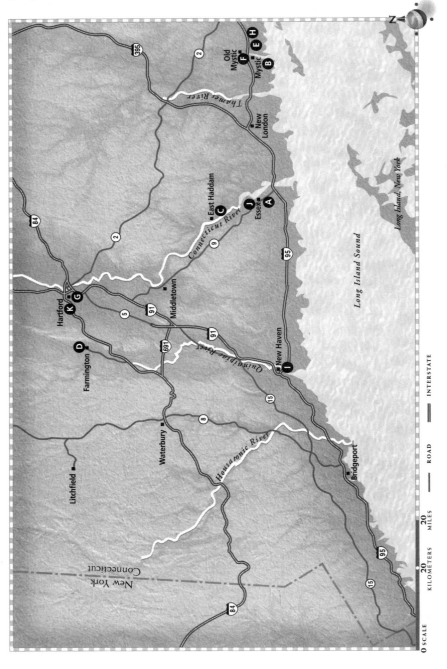

N

Long Island Sound

Long Island, New York

Old Mystic
Mystic
F
E H
B

2

395

Thames River

New London

East Haddam
C
J
A
Essex

Connecticut River

9

95

Middletown

91

5

Hartford
K G

91

D
Farmington

691

New Haven
I

Quinnipiac River

15

8

Waterbury

Housatonic River

Litchfield

Bridgeport

95

New York
Connecticut

84

15

84

2

0 SCALE

20
KILOMETERS

20
MILES

ROAD

INTERSTATE

Sights

Ⓐ Connecticut River Museum

Ⓑ Denison Pequotsepos Nature Center

Ⓒ Gillette's Castle

Ⓓ Hill-Stead Museum

Ⓔ Mystic Marinelife Aquarium

Ⓕ Mystic Seaport Museum

Ⓖ Nook Farm

Ⓗ Olde Mystic Village

Ⓘ Peabody Museum of Natural History

Ⓙ Steam Train and Riverboat Ride

Ⓚ Wadsworth Athenaeum

Ⓛ Yale Center for British Art

Ⓛ Yale Collection of Musical Instruments

Ⓛ Yale University

Ⓛ Yale University Art Gallery

Note: Items with the same letter are located in the same town or area.

A PERFECT DAY IN CONNECTICUT

I would start my day catching up on literary history by visiting the homes of Harriet Beecher Stowe and Mark Twain at Hartford's Nook Farm. From there I would travel down the Connecticut River to have a late picnic lunch on the grounds of Gillette's Castle, followed by a tour of the home itself. Afterwards, I would travel to Essex for window shopping and a traditional New England dinner at the Griswold Inn.

SIGHTSEEING HIGHLIGHTS

✯✯✯ **Mystic Seaport Museum** • You'll need the better part of a day to explore the museum grounds fully. Climb aboard a whaling vessel to see the cramped quarters of deckhands and where whale blubber was processed; visit seaport shops typical of those that would have served a fishing community 100 years ago; watch boatbuilders at work; in the planetarium, learn how fishermen navigated by the stars; and in a special tribute to the America's Cup, see how sailing, once a necessary skill, has become a modern sport. For a fast-food lunch of clam cakes, burgers, or hot dogs, there is a snack bar in the village. For more refined dining, try the Seaman's Inne next to the complex. Hours: The museum is open daily in spring and fall from 9 a.m. to 5 p.m., in summer from 9 a.m. to 8 p.m., winter from 9 a.m. to 4 p.m., and closed Christmas Day. General admission to the village—$15 for adults and $7.50 for children 6 to 15—is rather expensive, but due to the vast number of exhibits the Seaport has to offer, it's worth it. Separate tickets must be purchased if you wish to take one of the steamboat cruises that leave from the village or to visit the museum's planetarium. Address: Entrance to the village is on Route 27, less than 1 mile east from I-95. (½ day–full day)

✯✯✯ **Nook Farm** • Only a handful of houses remain from this nineteenth-century community for the literary elite of Hartford. Two are open to the public and worth seeing: the homes of Harriet Beecher Stowe and Mark Twain. The Beecher Stowe house exemplifies a conventional upper-middle-class Victorian home, whereas the more pretentious Twain house is a monument to his eccentricities. In both cases, many of the writers' personal effects have been preserved, among them Stowe's original paintings, Twain's bed, and the dining room chair from which the author told fantastic tales to his guests and family. Tour guides recount humorous details from the authors' everyday lives. The guided tour of both homes takes approximately 1¼ hours. Hours: Open

Memorial Day 1 through Columbus Day, and the month of December, Monday through Saturday from 9:30 a.m. to 5 p.m., Sunday from noon to 5 p.m., and closed Tuesdays the rest of the year. The last tour of the day leaves at 4 p.m. Admission is charged. Combination tickets are available, or you can tour each house separately. (1½ hours)

✯✯ **Gillette's Castle** • They say a man's home is his castle, and in actor William Gillette's case, that statement can be taken literally. Best known for his portrayal of Sherlock Holmes, Gillette built his castle overlooking the Connecticut River in East Haddam. The jagged stone exterior is striking, but except for several intricately carved wooden doors, the interior is fairly modest. Children will no doubt enjoy exploring the castle, and theater buffs will appreciate the Broadway memorabilia on display. The castle grounds are a Connecticut state park, so there are picnic tables available as well as a souvenir shop and refreshment stand. Skip the wooded trail unless you are in the mood to stretch your legs. Hours: The castle is open daily from Memorial Day through Columbus Day 11 a.m. to 5 p.m. and on weekends only, Columbus Day through mid-December from 10 a.m. to 5 p.m. The grounds are open throughout the year. Admission is $4 for adults and $2 for children 6 to 11. (1 hour)

✯✯ **Hill-Stead Museum** • Hill-Stead was originally designed as a private home by architect Stanford White. The house is now filled with choice furnishings and Impressionist paintings, and the gardens and grounds are lovely. Hours: Closed from mid-January to mid-February. Admission is $6 for adults, $5 for seniors and students, and $3 for children 6 to 12. Address: Located in Farmington. Phone: Call (203) 677-4787 for hours of operation. (1 hour)

✯✯ **Wadsworth Athenaeum** • One of the nation's oldest art museums, its collections include African-American art, contemporary works, Impressionist paintings, and a fine assemblage of oils by Hudson River School painters. Hours: Tuesday through Sunday from 10 a.m. to 5 p.m. Closed on major holidays. Admission is $5 for adults, $2 for students and seniors, and free to children under 13. Entrance is free all day on Thursdays, and on Saturday mornings before noon. Address: 600 Main Street in Hartford. (2 hours)

✯✯ **Yale University** • A prestigious member of the Ivy League and rival to Harvard, its northern cousin, this university is located in New

Haven. Hours: Hour-long walking tours of the campus are given at
10:30 a.m. and 2 p.m. during the week, and on weekends at 1:30 p.m.
Phone: (203) 432-2300.

Yale also has a number of museums worth a visit. The **Yale
University Art Gallery** has works by Degas, Monet, Van Gogh,
Picasso, and respected American painters, as well as decorative arts.
Hours: Tuesday through Saturday 10 a.m. to 5 p.m., and Sunday from
2 p.m. to 5 p.m. September through July, and admission is free.
Address: 1111 Chapel Street.

The **Yale Center for British Art**, with artwork dating back to
the Elizabethan era and some 1,300 paintings, 17,000 drawings, 30,000
prints, and 22,000 rare books, has one of the most respected collections
of British art in this country. Hours: Tuesday through Saturday from
10 a.m. to 5 p.m., Sunday from noon to 5 p.m., and admission is free.
Address: 1080 Chapel Street.

Yale also has its own **Peabody Museum of Natural History**,
which is open the same hours as the Center for British Art, but admission to the Peabody is $4 for adults, $3 for seniors, and $2.50 for chil-
dren 3 to 15, except during free hours, which are 3 p.m. to 5 p.m.
weekday afternoons. Address: 170 Whitney Avenue.

For music-lovers, the university even has the **Yale Collection of
Musical Instruments**. The museum at has more than 800 instruments
(some of sixteenth-century vintage), including a large bell collection.
Address: 15 Hillhouse Avenue. Phone: Call (203) 432-0822 for information as hours are limited (unfortunately for the many travelers who
visit the school during summer, the museum is closed during July and
August). Donations are requested.

✯ **Connecticut River Museum** • On the waterfront at the end of
Main Street in Essex, the museum's exhibits pertain to river history. Of
special interest is the replica of America's first submarine—called the
Turtle, it was originally constructed in 1775. Hours: Tuesday through
Sunday from 10 a.m. to 5 p.m. Admission is $4 for adults, $2 for chil-
dren 9 to 12, and kids under 8 are admitted free. (1 hour)

✯ **Mystic Marinelife Aquarium** • This is a worthwhile stop if you
didn't make it to the New England Aquarium in Boston and have extra
time after visiting the Seaport. Hours: Open daily from 9 a.m. to
5:30 p.m. July 1 through Labor Day and 9 a.m. to 4:30 p.m. the rest of
the year. It is closed Thanksgiving, Christmas, New Year's Day, and
the last week in January. Entrance fees are $9.50 for adults, $8.50 for

seniors, $6 for children 5 to 12. Address: Just off I-95 at the Mystic Exit. (1½ hours)

✯ **Steam Train and Riverboat Ride** • This excursion offers a good alternative way to see the Connecticut River and sights such as Gillette's Castle and Goodspeed's Opera House if you're tired of driving, or if you fancy steam-powered locomotives. All trains connect with a riverboat cruise, except the last one of the day. Tickets cost $14 for adults, $7 for children 2 to 11, children under 2 free, for the combined train and riverboat trip, less for the train ride only. The combined trip takes over 2 hours; separate tickets are not sold for the riverboat cruise. Hours: Call ahead for departure times; they vary from day to day and season to season. The service operates May through October. Address: On Railroad Avenue in Essex. Phone: (203) 767-0103. (2½ hours)

Denison Pequotsepos Nature Center • The 125-acre center, on Pequotsepos Road in Mystic, is comprised of self-guided nature trails and a small natural-history museum. One trail is designed especially for blind visitors. Hours: Open May through Christmas Tuesday through Saturday 9 a.m. to 5 p.m., Sunday noon to 5 p.m. Admission is $3 for adults, $1 for children over 6.

Olde Mystic Village • Probably best to pass on this group of souvenir shops and informal eating establishments adjacent to Mystic's aquarium—unless you have plenty of time to kill.

FOOD AND LODGING

The **Griswold Inn** in lovely Essex is always one of my favorite stops while in Connecticut. The restaurant serves sandwiches and burgers for lunch, and traditional New England fare for dinner, in a lively atmosphere. A fine collection of firearms, maritime, oils, and Currier and Ives prints graces the walls of the Griswold's several dining rooms. Lunch is about $12 per person, and dinner entrées run from $12 to $30. Servings are hearty. The inn also has 25 guest rooms ($100–$196 per night). Reservations are strongly recommended for overnight lodging or weekend dinners. Call (203) 767-1776.

Mystic is a good place to base yourself for Connecticut sightseeing because it not only is within a couple of hours from most attractions in the state, but also has a helpful Tourist Information Center at the

CONNECTICUT

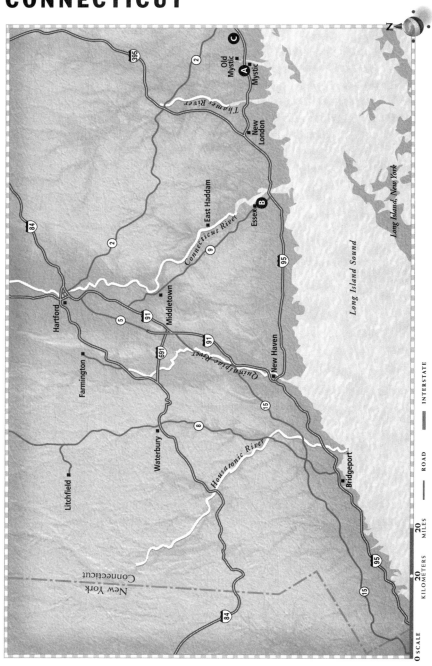

Long Island Sound

Long Island, New York

New York
Connecticut

Thames River

Old Mystic

Mystic

New London

East Haddam

Essex

Connecticut River

Middletown

New Haven

Quinnipiac River

Housatonic River

Hartford

Farmington

Waterbury

Litchfield

Bridgeport

84
2
395
9
91
5
691
8
95
15
2

N

0 SCALE

20 KILOMETERS
20 MILES

INTERSTATE
ROAD

Food and Lodging

Ⓐ 2 Sisters Deli

Ⓐ Bee Bee Dairy

Ⓐ The Draw Bridge Inne

Ⓑ The Griswold Inn

Ⓐ Inn at Mystic

Ⓐ Seaman's Inne

Ⓐ The Whaler's Inn

Camping

Ⓒ Seaport Campground

Note: Items with the same letter are located in the same town or area.

Mystic exit of I-95 that will help you find appropriate lodging in the area. A board lists nearby accommodations, their rates, and driving distances. The center's helpful personnel will even call ahead to secure your room. While there, be sure to peruse the menus from area restaurants and pick out the ones that best suit your tastes and budget. The tourist center is also a great source of area sightseeing information.

The **Inn at Mystic**, at the junction of Route 27 and U.S. 1, has accommodations ranging from motor court rooms to comfortable rooms in a traditional country inn. There are gardens, a tennis court, a restaurant, a pool, and a hot tub on the premises. Rooms in the motor court are $95 to $145 during the summer and $75 to $95 off-season. Inn rooms go for $165 to $225 per night. Call (800) 237-2415 or (203) 536-9604 for reservations.

If you wish to stay within walking distance of Mystic's downtown shops and restaurants, **The Whaler's Inn**, offering simple, motel-like accommodations and senior citizen discounts, is your only lodging choice in Mystic center. Doubles range from $65 to $125 per night. Call (203) 536-1506 or (800) 243-2588.

The Mystic area has a number of reasonably priced restaurants and fast-food establishments in and around Olde Mystick Village, just off I-95. The **Seaman's Inne** (203-536-9649), next to Mystic Seaport, specializes in seafood and prime-rib dinners. In downtown Mystic, locals recommend **The Draw Bridge Inne**, a half-block from the drawbridge on Main Street, offering specialties for seafarers and landlubbers alike. Dinner entrées are $13 and up (203-536-9653). For a simple but filling meal, try an overstuffed sandwich at **2 Sisters Deli** (203-536-1244) on Pearl Street just off Main. For breakfast, try **Bee Bee Dairy**, a family-style restaurant on Main Street (203-536-4577).

In Hartford, the best selection of restaurants is found along Main Street, and national lodging chains such as Holiday Inn, Sheraton, and Ramada have hotels in downtown Hartford.

CAMPING

Seaport Campground, 3 miles from Mystic Seaport Museum, is the closest campground to Mystic's attractions. From Exit 90 on Interstate 95, take Route 27 north for 1¼ miles to Route 184. Follow that east for about ½-mile and watch for the campground on your left. RV hookups and tent sites are available, as well as complete recreational facilities, including swimming, on the premises. Open mid-April through late October. Call (203) 536-4044 for reservations.

PERFORMING ARTS

Goodspeed's Opera House is an attractive building on the banks of the Connecticut River in East Haddam, and is a regional landmark. Should you decide to stay in the area awhile, the opera house hosts evening performances of popular musicals April through December. You can picnic on the river's edge prior to a show, or dine next door at the **Gelston House**. Call (203) 873-8668 for schedule and ticket information.

ENTERTAINMENT

Foxwoods Casino in Mashantucket southeast of Norwich gets a lot of press, and even more business, because it is the only casino in New England. Operated by the Pequot Indians, the casino has brought a financial boon to the once all-but-extinct tribal nation, and perhaps if you're lucky a visit to the casino will be a financial boon to you as well. Restaurants and accommodations are conveniently located at the resort casino complex. Call (800) 752-9244 for details.

SIDE TRIP TO LONG ISLAND

Those who wish to extend their New England vacation southward to explore the exclusive Hamptons or sand dunes at Montauk can take the ferry from New London, Connecticut (several miles south of Mystic), to Orient Point on Long Island, New York. The ferry costs over $20 one-way for most automobiles including the driver, and you really do need to bring your car across to do any sightseeing. The ferry operates year-round except for Christmas Day. Sailing time is approximately 1½ hours. Call (203) 443-5281 for schedule and reservation information. To visit the Hamptons from Orient Point, take Route 25 west to Riverhead where you pick up Route 24. Follow Route 24 until it intersects with Route 27. Drive east on Route 27 to the Hamptons, then continue all the way out to the lighthouse at Montauk Point.

14
NEWPORT

Newport, on Aquidneck Island, is a city of contrasts ranging from the wealthy in their turn-of-the-century mansions, to military personnel stationed at the naval base, to the yachting crowd that invades Newport each summer. Somehow this city manages to satisfy all of these groups in their varied pursuits, and quite competently at that. It is also this diversity that makes Newport such an appealing place to visit. One can wander through a topiary garden, then visit the oldest synagogue in the United States; tour a lavish oceanfront mansion such as the Vanderbilt's Breakers, then stroll past more modest colonial homes in the center of the city; shop for souvenirs in the Brick Marketplace, then admire handsome ships docked at the waterfront; and dine overlooking the grass tennis courts at Newport Casino or opt for a traditional New England clambake on a sandy beach. The choices abound. ◤

NEWPORT

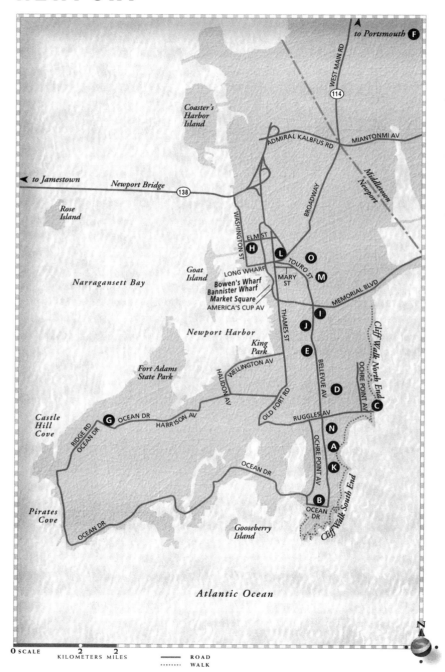

to Portsmouth **F**

WEST MAIN RD

114

Coaster's
Harbor
Island

ADMIRAL KALBFUS RD

MIANTONMI AV

BROADWAY

Middletown
Newport

to Jamestown

Newport Bridge

138

Rose
Island

WASHINGTON ST

ELM ST

H

L

TOURO ST

O

M

Goat
Island

LONG WHARF

Bowen's Wharf
Bannister Wharf
Market Square

MARY
ST

MEMORIAL BLVD

Narragansett Bay

AMERICA'S CUP AV

I

Cliff Walk North End

THAMES ST

J

E

Newport Harbor

King
Park

BELLEVUE AV

OCHRE POINT AV

Fort Adams
State Park

WELLINGTON AV

D

C

HALIDON AV

OLD FORT RD

RUGGLES AV

Castle
Hill
Cove

RIDGE RD

OCEAN DR

G OCEAN DR

HARRISON AV

N

A

OCHRE POINT AV

K

OCEAN DR

B

OCEAN
DR

Pirates
Cove

OCEAN DR

Gooseberry
Island

Cliff Walk South End

Atlantic Ocean

N

0 SCALE   2   2
KILOMETERS MILES   ———— ROAD
                          ········· WALK

Sights

(A) Beechwood

(B) Bellecourt Castle

(C) The Breakers

(D) Château-Sur-Mer

(E) The Elms

(F) The Green Animals

(G) Hammersmith Farms

(H) Hunter House

(I) International Tennis Hall of Fame

(J) Kingscote

(K) Marble House

(L) Museum of Newport History

(M) Newport Art Museum

(N) Rosecliff

(O) Touro Synagogue

A PERFECT DAY IN NEWPORT

I would begin my day touring Marble House and then stroll along the Cliff Walk, a 3-mile promenade that skirts the great lawns of many of Newport's finest homes as well as the ocean some 30 feet below. I'd have a picnic lunch at Brenton Point State Park followed by the pièce de résistance—a tour of the sumptuous Breakers Mansion. Afterwards, I'd head downtown for an ice-cream cone at Newport Creamery and shopping along Thames Street and the Wharf area. I'd end the day with a seafood dinner at either the Cooke House or the livelier Black Pearl restaurant next door.

SIGHTSEEING HIGHLIGHTS

★★★ **Newport Mansions** • The Preservation Society of Newport operates six exquisite mansions (or "cottages," as they were called by their original owners), one historic home, and a topiary garden. You will probably have time to visit only two properties in one day unless you're very energetic. Take your pick—you won't be disappointed. Hours: Marble House, the Elms, and Château-Sur-Mer are open throughout the winter from 10 a.m. to 4 p.m. on weekends and are beautifully decorated for Christmas. Most of the remaining mansions are open weekends starting in April, and all are open daily through-out the summer from 10 a.m. to 5 p.m. The Breakers is open from 9:30 a.m. to 6 p.m. July through Labor Day. Since the hours do vary from mansion to mansion and season to season, it is best to check with the Preservation Society for hours during your visit. Admission to most of the mansions is at least $7.50 for adults and about $4 for children 6 to 11. Reduced rates are available when you purchase combination tickets to more than one mansion. The combination tickets range from $12.50 for any two mansions to $35.50 if you wish to visit them all. Phone: (401) 847-1000

The Breakers, on Ochre Point Avenue off Bellevue, is the most extravagant of all the mansions and the most popular with tourists. Designed by architect Richard Morris Hunt, who also designed the extraordinary Biltmore House in North Carolina, the Breakers was built in an Italian Renaissance style for Cornelius Vanderbilt in 1895. This stately home, with an abundance of gold leaf and marble through-out its interior, is almost overwhelmingly opulent and not to be missed by first-time visitors to Newport. Children will enjoy the "Children's Cottage" on the grounds.

Château-Sur-Mer ("House by the Sea") and **Rosecliff** (on Bellevue Avenue) are situated on the ocean as well. Château-Sur-Mer has a Chinese Moon Gate on its grounds. Rosecliff was designed by well-known architect Stanford White, and has the largest private ball-room in Newport. Robert Redford and Mia Farrow waltzed in this ballroom in the movie version of *The Great Gatsby*.

Marble House on Bellevue Avenue is my personal favorite. Appropriately named for the beautiful and rare marble throughout, the "cottage" was built for William K. Vanderbilt in 1892. A Chinese tea-house on the grounds exemplifies the fascination of the moneyed class with the Orient at the turn of the century.

Also on Bellevue Avenue are **The Elms** and **Kingscote**. The Elms, modeled after a French château, is known for its array of trees and shrubbery. Kingscote, built in 1839, is one of the oldest mansions open to the public. Incorporating elements of both Victorian and Gothic architecture, the estate was named after William Henry King, who acquired the property in 1864.

The **Hunter House** at 54 Washington Street is much smaller in scale than the grand "cottages," reflecting its mid-eighteenth-century time period. It was the headquarters for French naval forces during the Revolutionary War, and is a National Historic Landmark.

The Green Animals topiary gardens are located on Cory's Lane off Route 114 north in Portsmouth. An elephant, a giraffe, and a camel are just a few of the animal-shaped shrubs that are bound to amuse children and adults alike.

Several other stately homes, not operated by the Preservation Society, are also open to the public. **Hammersmith Farms**, near Fort Adams, is often considered the most "livable" of the Newport mansions. The wedding reception for John F. and Jacqueline Kennedy was held here. Its colorful gardens were designed by Frederick Law Olmstead. Hours: Open weekends in March and November, daily April through October from 10 a.m. to 5 p.m. At the height of the summer season, hours are extended to 7 p.m. Admission is charged to tour the estate.

Bellecourt Castle on Bellevue Avenue is still owned and occupied by the Tinney family. The house is open for high tea and guided tours by attendants in period costume. A gold coronation coach and art treasures from all over the world are among the items on display. Hours: Open daily from 9 a.m. to 5 p.m. during summer and closed during January. Admission is charged. Phone: Call (401) 846-0669 for castle hours if you plan to visit during spring or fall.

Beechwood, also on Bellevue Avenue, was built for the Astors. Although the home is not as lavish or well kept as the Preservation Society mansions, the tour can be quite entertaining: actors playing members of the Astor household greet you as a dinner guest and treat you to family gossip of the day. Hours: The house is open from 10 a.m. to 4 p.m. on weekends February through mid-May, from 10 a.m. to 5 p.m. daily mid-May through December. Closed during the month of January. A "calling card" is about $8 for adults, $6 for children and senior citizens, and $30 for a family.

The grand mansions of Newport are not the only homes that

merit a look while you're here. There are many beautifully restored colonial homes in and around Queen Anne Square 1 block from Thames Street. Explore these streets on your own or take an organized walking tour with the Newport Historical Society. Hours: Tours usually begin at 10 a.m. in the summer. Address: The Society is at 82 Touro Street. Phone: (401) 846-0813 for schedules and cost.

✯ **International Tennis Hall of Fame** • The museum is adjacent to the emerald green grass courts of the Newport Casino. The shingled casino was designed by the renowned architecture firm of McKim, Mead & White, and was constructed in 1880. Professional tennis tournaments are still held there today. Tennis buffs will no doubt want to visit the museum to see its collection of trophies, costumes, and equipment, but those who don't play will probably be content to poke around the outside of the building. Hours: The museum is open from 10 a.m. to 5 p.m. June through September and 11 a.m. to 4 p.m. the rest of the year. Museum admission is $6 for adults, $2.50 for youths under 16. Senior citizen discounts are available. Address: 194 Bellevue Avenue.

✯ **Museum of Newport History** • Those wanting to delve deeper into Newport's history should visit this museum, created by the Newport Historical Society. Hours: Monday through Saturday (with the exception of Tuesday) from 10 a.m. to 5 p.m., and from 1 p.m. to 5 p.m. on Sunday. The museum stays open on weekend evenings during summer, but is closed on Tuesday. Admission is $5 for adults, $3 for children 6 to 12, and family rates are available. Address: Located at the Brick Marketplace.

✯ **Newport Art Museum** • Exhibits of American art change regularly in this museum, housed in the Griswold Mansion that was built in 1864. Hours: Monday through Saturday from 10 a.m. to 4 p.m., and Sunday from noon to 4 p.m. September through May, and until 5 p.m. each day during the summer months. Address: 76 Bellevue Avenue. Phone: Call (401) 848-8200 to find out what's on display during your visit.

✯ **Touro Synagogue** • Built in 1763, the oldest synagogue in the country is now a National Historic Site. Hours: In summer, from 10 a.m. to 5 p.m. Sunday through Thursday, and from 10 a.m. to

3 p.m. on Friday. Phone: Winter visitors should call (401) 847-4794 for an appointment.

FITNESS AND RECREATION

Should you wish a two-wheeled view of the island, you can rent bicycles from **Ten Speed Spokes** at the corner of Elm and America's Cup Avenue (401-847-5609). At **Adventure Sports Rentals and Tours** at Bowen's Landing, you can rent everything from a mountain bike to a waverunner to a sailboat. They also offer fishing trips, kayaking, and parasailing (401-849-4820).

You can take a horseback ride along the beach with **Newport Equestrian Center** (401-848-5440), or if you prefer to lie on the sand rather than ride on it there are three popular public beaches in the area. **First Beach** is located in Newport at the end of the Cliff Walk and has a parking lot and bathhouse. **Second** and **Third Beaches** have better sand than First Beach, but they are located in nearby Middletown, less convenient to the center of Newport.

FOOD

The **Black Pearl** (401-846-5264) on Bannister's Wharf is a very popular Newport restaurant, as evidenced by the throngs of hungry diners in line to be seated. Because of its reputation, the restaurant can be crowded and the service slow. Next door at the **Cooke House** (401-849-2900), you'll find truly elegant dining upstairs for dinner, and a more casual atmosphere downstairs at the **Candy Store**. For dining in unique settings, try the **La Forge Restaurant** (401-847-0418) overlooking the grass courts at the Newport Casino, which serves veal and chicken dinner entrées that run about $15; or the **White Horse Tavern**, the oldest operating tavern in the United States (401-849-3600).

Numerous restaurants along Thames Street offer cheaper alternatives for eating out. **Cafe Zelda** at 528 Thames has a varied menu with everything from burgers to lobster, and prices are easy on the pocketbook (401-849-4002). For Italian and Mediterranean specialties, try **Pronto** at 464 Thames. Prices are reasonable and the mood is romantic (401-847-5251). For dessert, visit any one of the **Newport Creamery**'s several locations for a traditional ice-cream cone. **Poor Richard's** at 254 Thames Street is the place to get breakfast.

NEWPORT

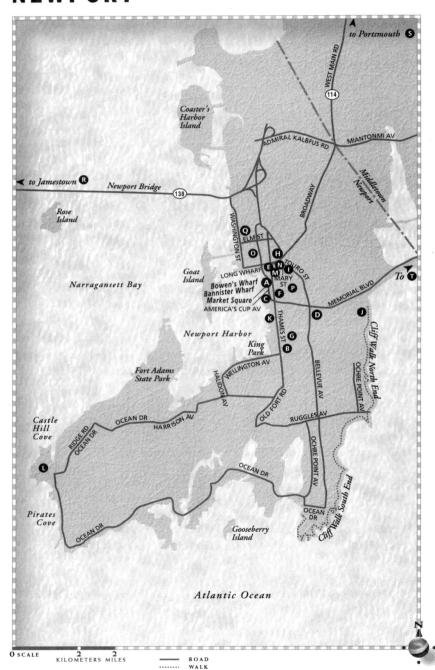

to Portsmouth **S**

WEST MAIN RD

114

Coaster's
Harbor
Island

ADMIRAL KALBFUS RD   MIANTONMI AV

BROADWAY

Middletown Newport

to Jamestown **R**   Newport Bridge   **138**

Rose
Island

WASHINGTON ST

Goat
Island

ELM ST   **Q**

O

H   TOURO ST

E   **N**   **I**

M   MARY ST

Long Wharf   **A**   **P**

Bowen's Wharf   **C**   **F**

Bannister Wharf

Market Square

AMERICA'S CUP AV

MEMORIAL BLVD

To **T**

Narragansett Bay

Newport Harbor

K   **D**   **J**

THAMES ST

G   Cliff Walk North End

King   **B**

Park

OCHRE POINT AV

Fort Adams
State Park

WELLINGTON AV

BELLEVUE AV

HALIDON AV

OLD FORT RD

Castle
Hill
Cove

RIDGE RD   OCEAN DR

OCEAN DR   HARRISON AV

RUGGLES AV

OCEAN DR   OCHRE POINT AV

L

OCEAN DR

Pirates
Cove

OCEAN DR

Gooseberry
Island

OCEAN
DR

Cliff Walk South End

Atlantic Ocean

N

0 SCALE   **2**   **2**

KILOMETERS MILES   ——— ROAD

········· WALK

Food

A The Black Pearl

B Cafe Zelda

C Candy Store

C Cooke House

D La Forge Restaurant

E Newport Creamery

F Poor Richard's

G Pronto

H White Horse Tavern

Lodging

I Admiral Farragut

J Cliffside Inn

K Francis Malbone House

L Inn at Castle Hill

M Inntowne

N Jailhouse Inn

O Marriott

P Melville House

Q Willows of Newport

Camping

R Fort Getty Recreation Area

S Melville Ponds Campground

T Middletown Campground

LODGING

S tay in the heart of things at the **Inntowne** at Thames and Mary Streets, where many of Newport's shops and restaurants are at your doorstep. Rates range from $95 to $250, depending on the season and type of accommodation. Call (401) 846-9200 or (800) 457-7803 for reservations. Rooms at the **Francis Malbone House** at 392 Thames are elegantly furnished with attractive colonial reproduction furniture. The 1760 colonial mansion is listed on the National Register of Historic Places and a full gourmet breakfast is included in the room rate, ranging from $160 to $295 in season and $95 to $175 off-season (401-846-0392 or 800-846-0392).

The **Marriott** on the waterfront is also convenient to Newport center. Nine of the Marriott's rooms are specially equipped for handicapped guests. Doubles run from about $110 to $235. Call Marriott's toll-free number, (800) 458-3066, or the hotel directly at (401) 849-1000.

If you like to be centrally located, there are two comfortable bed and breakfast establishments on quiet Clarke Street. The **Admiral Farragut** (401-846-4256 or 800-343-2863) at 31 Clarke was built in 1650. Their doubles range from $115 to $145 during the summer and start at $60 during the winter. The **Melville House** (401-847-0640) at 39 Clarke Street, built in 1750, is listed on the National Register of Historic Places. Doubles are $60 to $85 in winter and $85 to $125 in summer, including breakfast and afternoon tea. In winter, one suite has a working fireplace.

For an out-of-the ordinary night's sleep, try the **Jailhouse Inn** (401-847-4638) where bars on the windows and black-and-white-striped bedspreads are not just for show—the inn was once a jail. It is at 13 Marlborough Street, just around the corner from the Brick Marketplace, and doubles with continental breakfast range from $95 to $165 in the summer months, less in the off-season. At the **Willows of Newport**, about a 5-minute walk from the Brick Marketplace, guests are served breakfast in bed by attendants in black-tie on bone china and a silver tea service. Hostess Pattie Murphy, a long-time resident of Newport, is happy to share her knowledge of Newport's diverse history with her guests. Doubles range from $88 to $185. Call (401) 846-5486 for reservations. If you prefer to be adjacent to the Cliff Walk rather than downtown, the **Cliffside Inn** (401-847-1811 or 800-845-1811) at 2 Seaview Avenue might be a good choice for you. The lovely Victorian home is furnished with antiques, and a full breakfast and afternoon hors d'oeuvres are included in the rates ($145 to $325).

For a splurge you won't soon forget, stay at the **Inn at Castle Hill**, off Ocean Drive. With a room overlooking the ocean, you'll feel almost like a Vanderbilt. Doubles with a private bath and water view are $190 during the summer, significantly less during the winter months. The inn's restaurant is also well worth a try (401-849-3800).

Bed & Breakfast of Rhode Island (401-849-1298 or 800-828-0000) can also help you locate accommodations. Their service is free of charge.

CAMPING

There are several municipal campgrounds near Newport, the closest being **Middletown Campground** on Second Beach in neighboring Middletown. Since there are only 44 campsites, reservations are strongly recommended. Call (401) 846-5781. Open May through early October. Facilities include toilets, showers, and sewer hookups.

On the far side of the island, **Melville Ponds Campground** off Route 114 in Portsmouth has tent sites, RV sites with hookups, and recreational facilities. Open April 1 through October 31. Call (401) 849-8212.

If all campgrounds on the island are filled, try the one in Jamestown at **Fort Getty Recreation Area**. You can fish at the campground, but you will have to cross the toll bridge to sightsee in Newport. Open during the summer months on a first-come, first-served basis. Tent sites are about $17 per night, and RV hookups are $22 per night. Call (401) 423-7211 for directions and additional information.

SHOPPING

The Brick Marketplace on Thames Street and Bannisters and Bowen wharves off America's Cup Avenue comprise Newport's main shopping district. Not to be missed by nautical buffs is the **Armchair Sailor Bookstore** on Lee's Wharf, which has one of the most comprehensive selections anywhere of maritime publications.

NIGHTLIFE

Jai alai is considered to be the fastest game on two feet, and you may wish to view a match or two at **Newport Jai Alai**, 150 Admiral Kalbfus Road. Rhode Island is one of the few states that allows parimutuel wagering on the sport. Admission is nominal to encourage betting, which some find similar to playing the horses. Call (800) 451-2500 or (401) 849-5000 for schedule and information.

Many of Newport's bars and restaurants offer musical entertainment in the evenings. Try **The Pelham** on Thames Street for jazz. **Club Thames** on America's Cup Avenue is the place to go for dancing to a contemporary beat.

SIDE TRIPS FROM NEWPORT

Need a break from vigorous sightseeing? Need a break from the world in general? Then a trip to Block Island may just be the antidote. Only 12 miles off the coast of Rhode Island, Block Island was originally settled in 1661. The island offers visitors all of the quiet beauty, miles of beach, and dramatic cliffs of Martha's Vineyard, without the commercialism.

If you enjoy cycling past sand dunes, beach roses, lily ponds, and old stone walls; exploring wildlife refuges and lighthouses; or just lounging on the beach, Block Island will be a welcome retreat. But if you're looking for art museums, chic shops, and active nightlife, then this is not the place for you. There is only one town on the island, consisting primarily of one main street lined with Victorian-era hotels and a handful of restaurants and souvenir shops.

Ferries to the island operate from Point Judith, Rhode Island, year-round, though a winter visit is not recommended. Service is more frequent during the summer, and ferries even run from Newport during the summer months. The trip from Point Judith takes a little over an hour. One-way fares are $6.60 for adults, $3.15 for children, and $10.50 and $5, respectively, for a same-day round-trip. Passenger cars cost $20.25 one way, motorcycles are $11.85, and bicycles are $1.75. Call (401) 783-4613 for reservations and a current ferry schedule. If you're lucky enough to get a legal parking spot along the street, parking is free. Otherwise it will cost you about $5 per day.

Once on the island, just about every service you'll need is within a block of the ferry dock. The tourist booth in the dock parking lot can provide you with a map of the island for $1 (some bike rental places will give you an island map for free with a rental). It will guide you to the unusual gray granite lighthouse at Sandy Point, Crescent Beach, the Clayhead Nature Trail, or the wildlife refuge at Rodman's Hollow. The map and your sense of direction are about all you'll need to find your way around this small island.

Across the street from the dock area you can rent a bike or moped, then shop for picnic foods at the market next door (one of the few places on the island to get provisions). While bringing your car over to the island may be cheaper than renting bikes for a family (about $10 per day per bicycle) or mopeds (about $60 per day for two), these two-wheeled vehicles bring you closer to the island's charm.

Most of the island's accommodations are right along Old Harbor's main street. (Some have limited seasons, so be sure to call ahead if you plan to stay overnight.) The **National Hotel**, built in 1888, is the most prominent. You can't miss it as the ferry pulls into the harbor. The hotel's restaurant has pleasant outdoor dining and an excellent appetizer menu. Double rooms at the hotel go for $79 to $219, depending on the season and type of view. Call (401) 466-2901 or 800-225-2449 for reservations. The **Harborside Inn** (401-466-5504), with doubles including continental breakfast ranging from $69 to $195 (some rooms have shared baths), is another Victorian inn right in the town's center. The **Hotel Manisses** and the **1661 Inn**, both on the edge of town, are jointly managed. Guests staying at either can enjoy a small animal farm behind the Manisses Hotel, buffet breakfasts, and dinner at the hotel. The hotel has one of the most interesting menus on the island; dinner entrées are priced from $15. Room rates range from $65 to $325 (401-466-2421 or 800-626-4773). **Finn's Seafood Restaurant** is the place to go for lobster (401-466-2475).

New Bedford: Just over the Rhode Island/Massachusetts border, bargain-hunters with time to spare may profit from prospecting the New Bedford/Fall River area factory outlet stores. These stores are factory outlets in the truest sense since they are generally located on the factory premises. A guide to the outlets can be picked up at the New Bedford visitor center.

Once a bustling whaling center, New Bedford experienced a great decline during the twentieth century. Recently, efforts have been made to restore the city to its past glory. You can see the handsome result of those efforts by rambling through the 16-block cobblestone area that comprises the historic district, originally built up in the 1760s. New Bedford's visitor center, on Second Street in the historic district, is open Monday through Saturday 9 a.m. to 5 p.m., Sunday 11 a.m. to 5 p.m.

At New Bedford's **Whaling Museum** you can see exhibits ranging from model vessels and ship's logs to artwork depicting whaling expeditions, including scrimshaw. A visit to the museum at 18 Johnny Cake Hill will give you a fascinating look at an industry and an era that have long since died out.

After visiting the whaling museum, you may want to see the **Seaman's Bethel** across the street: it was the whalemen's chapel referred to in Herman Melville's *Moby Dick*. If you like period homes, the **Rotch-Jones-Duff House & Garden Museum** should be on your itinerary while in New Bedford. Built in what is now New Bedford's County Street Historic District, this 1834 Greek Revival home is a fine example of the "brave houses and flowery gardens" Melville described in *Moby Dick*. The museum is open from 10 a.m. to 4 p.m. Tuesday through Saturday, and on Sundays from 1 p.m. to 4 p.m. On some summer evenings, the museum offers concerts under the stars. Call (508) 977-1401 for more information. New Bedford also has the **Buttonwood Park Zoo**, on 13 acres surrounded by a 90-acre park designed by Frederick Law Olmstead of Boston Public Gardens fame. The zoo is open daily from 10 a.m. to 5 p.m., and a small admission fee is charged.

If you plan to dine in New Bedford, **Freestone's Restaurant & Bar** (508-993-7477) is located in an attractive building on the corner of Williams and Second Streets. It serves seafood-melt sandwiches, and the like at reasonable prices; entrées are more expensive (around $12 apiece). **Jimmy Connor's Irish Pub**, on the corner of Acushnet and Union Streets, is a good place to stop for a casual burger and draft beer at a modest price (508-997-2808). **The Last Laugh** at 784 Purchase is a bar and deli just north of the historic district, where you can sample sandwiches named for famous comedians such as Jackie Gleason (508-999-9812).

Fall River: The world's largest exhibit of historic fighting ships can be found in Fall River's **Battleship Cove**. Visitors can tour the *USS Joseph P. Kennedy Jr.* destroyer, a 35,000-ton battleship called "Big Mamie" that saw action in WWII, a WWII attack sub, and PT boats. The cove is open daily from 9 a.m. to 5 p.m., and admission is $8 for adults, $6 for seniors, and $4 for children 6 to 14. The **Marine Museum** nearby has ship models, a Titanic exhibit, and other marine collections. The museum is open 9 a.m. to 5 p.m. Monday through Friday, noon to 4 p.m. on weekends and holidays May through October. (Call 508-674-3533 for winter hours.) Admission is $3 for adults, $2.50 for seniors, $2 for children under 14.

Providence: Providence is Rhode Island's capital, and the Ocean State's largest city. In Providence you can visit the lovely campus of **Brown University**, several historic homes, and the **Roger Williams Park Zoo**.

MARTHA'S VINEYARD

Although Martha's Vineyard is only seven miles from Cape Cod and the mainland, once you get there it doesn't take long to relax and leave the rest of the world behind. The island is 20 miles long by 10 miles wide at its widest point, and its population swells from around 12,000 year-round residents to almost 62,000 during the summer. Even so, if you venture out of the main towns, you almost always can find a quiet spot to call your own.

Martha's Vineyard was named for an early settler's daughter and for the abundance of grapes that used to cover the island. Now the island is comprised of three main towns, Vineyard Haven, Oak Bluffs, and Edgartown, with stretches of white sand beach and sand dunes in between. Edgartown, the most elegant of the three, is another example of the prosperity that the whaling trade brought to nineteenth-century New England communities. Vineyard Haven is the quietest of the three, while Oak Bluffs, with its colorful Victorian "gingerbread" houses and active nightlife, is the most flamboyant. ◪

MARTHA'S VINEYARD

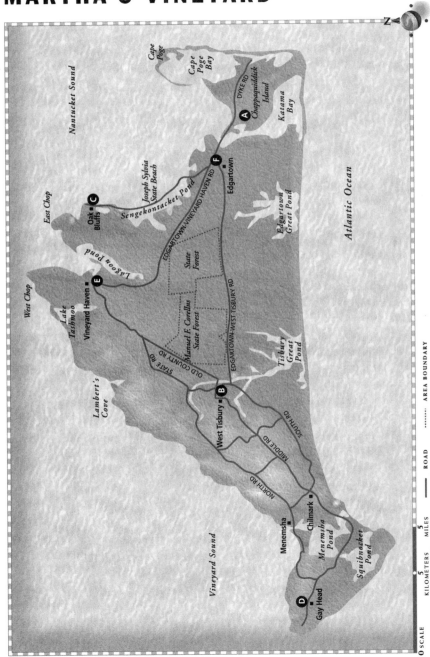

Sights

Ⓐ Chappaquiddick Island

Ⓑ Chicana Vineyards

Ⓒ Flying Horses Carousel

Ⓓ Gay Head

Ⓔ Jirah Luce House

Ⓔ Old Schoolhouse Museum

Ⓕ Vineyard Museum

Note: Items with the same letter are located in the same town or area.

GETTING TO MARTHA'S VINEYARD

Boats to Martha's Vineyard leave from either Woods Hole or Hyannis on Cape Cod, but if you wish to bring your car over to the Vineyard, then you must take the ferry from Woods Hole. Hy-line (508-778-2600) boats take passengers only to the Vineyard from Hyannis, and although the trip is longer and more expensive than from Woods Hole, it may be more convenient depending upon where you are staying on the cape. The first ferry to the Vineyard from Woods Hole usually leaves around 7 a.m. in summer, and sailing time is approximately 45 minutes. Boats leaving from Woods Hole arrive in either Oak Bluffs or Vineyard Haven, only a few miles apart.

Passenger fares one-way from Woods Hole to Martha's Vineyard are about $5 for adults, $2.50 for children 5 to 12. Automobiles cost about $40 one-way from mid-May through mid-October, and are somewhat less expensive during winter months. Reservations for automobiles are *strongly* recommended during summer months. Although it may seem expensive to bring a car over, when you consider that moped rentals are at least $50 a day, it may be worth the fare, particularly if you decide to stay more than one day or if there are more than two people in your party. Call the Steamship Authority in Woods Hole (508-548-3788) for the ferry schedule and reservation information.

TRANSPORTATION ON MARTHA'S VINEYARD

Mopeds are one of the easiest ways to get around the island. You don't have to worry about finding a parking space when you discover that deserted stretch of beach, and you can travel much faster than on a bicycle. There are clearly marked and well-maintained bicycle paths on the island. Moped and bicycle rental places abound in Vineyard Haven, Edgartown, and particularly Oak Bluffs. Many operations claim they have the lowest rates on the island. You may want to shop around, but my experience has been that rates tend to be fairly consistent from one place to the next and that your time is better spent sightseeing than looking for a bargain-priced moped rental. Daily rentals cost at least $50 in season for a moped that seats two fairly comfortably. Bicycle rentals run about $15 per day. Numerous taxi services and sightseeing operators will greet you right at the boat and take you around the island, if you don't want to get around on your own steam.

A PERFECT DAY ON MARTHA'S VINEYARD

I'd pack a picnic lunch, rent a moped, and set out to explore the island with Gay Head as my ultimate destination. After visiting Gay Head, I'd look for a quiet stretch of beach and soak up the sun for a few hours. Later in the afternoon, I would head to Edgartown for window shopping and a good meal.

SIGHTSEEING HIGHLIGHTS

✯✯ **Gay Head** • The jagged cliffs at Gay Head offer the most dramatic scenery on the island. Gay Head which also has a lighthouse, is at the opposite end of the island from the towns of Oak Bluffs, Edgartown, and Vineyard Haven.

✯ **Chappaquiddick Island** • Many visitors to Martha's Vineyard enjoy an excursion to Chappaquiddick. A ferry runs from the waterfront in Edgartown to the island from 7:30 a.m. to midnight during summer. Fares are nominal and prices are even quoted for horses and cattle in case you brought yours along. The ferry runs as needed and must be one of the shortest ferry crossings you'll ever experience.

✯ **Vineyard Museum** • Most people don't come to Martha's Vineyard to spend their time in museums, but if inclement weather forces you indoors, this museum and library are dedicated to preserving island history through exhibits of maritime artifacts, scrimshaw, and antique clothing. Hours: Daily 10 a.m. to 4:30 p.m. July 4 through Labor Day. Admission is $5 for adults, $3 for children 12 to 17. Phone: For hours in the off-season call (508) 627-4441.

Chicana Vineyards • In keeping with the island's origins, Martha's Vineyard now has this active vineyard. Hours: Open to visitors during the summer months from 11 a.m. to 5 p.m. Monday through Saturday, and from 1 p.m. to 5 p.m. on Sunday. Address: Located on Stoney Hill Road in West Tisbury. Phone: (508) 693-0309.

Flying Horses Carousel • If you're traveling with kids, a visit to this carousel at the bottom of Circuit Avenue in Oak Bluffs might be a must on your Vineyard itinerary. It is the oldest working carousel in the United States.

Jirah Luce House • Displays here include a collection of Victorian dolls, as well as nautical and other artifacts representing nineteenth-century island life. Hours: Tuesday through Saturday 10 a.m. to 4:30 p.m. from mid-June through mid-September. A small admission fee is charged. Address: Beach Street in Vineyard Haven.

Old Schoolhouse Museum • On Main Street in Vineyard Haven, this small museum is run by the Historical Preservation Society. Hours: Monday through Friday 10 a.m. to 2 p.m. from mid-June through mid-September. Admission is by donation.

FITNESS AND RECREATION

If you like to swim, the beaches on the Vineyard are lovely. Perhaps the most accessible beach to the public is the **Joseph Silvia State Beach**, which runs along the road between Edgartown and Oak Bluffs. Just park your vehicle on the side of the road, hop over the dunes, and stretch out. Warning: as tempting as it may be, overnight camping is not allowed.

Bicycling is one of the most popular activities on the island. Renting a bicycle has already been discussed in the transportation section of this chapter. If you brought your own bicycle over on the ferry, you'll find there are clearly marked and well-maintained bike paths all over the island.

FOOD

During the summer, the visitor has plenty of dining choices on the island. In Edgartown, the **Navigator Restaurant and Boathouse Bar** (508-627-4320) at the foot of Main Street and the **Wharf Restaurant** (508-627-9966) across the street both serve seafood. The Navigator overlooks the water, and lunches go for about $7.95, while dinner entrées are around $18.95. In summer, the Navigator also has a light dinner menu which is in the $10 range. If your appetite runs to dishes such as roast rack of lamb Dijon, veal scaloppini, and prime rib, try the **Shiretown Inn & Restaurant** (508-627-3353). Dinner entrées start around $20, and there is a pub on the premises. **O'Brien's Restaurant** (508-627-5850) on Upper Main Street features both seafood and pasta dishes in an elegant but comfortable setting. For the cheapest oceanfront table in town, get a burger or fried clams to go from **The Quarterdeck** stand near the Chappaquiddick ferry, and sit on the docks.

In Oak Bluffs, meals are usually casual, and on Circuit Avenue, you can get anything from steak and seafood to subs, pasta, and pizza at one of the many eateries there. **Seasons** restaurant, is pleasant and informal, and serves good pub style food at reasonable prices. **Two Fabulous Guys** (508-696-6494) on Circuit is an unpretentious establishment that serves all three meals, but it's a great place to start off your day with a breakfast burrito.

The **Black Dog Tavern**, in Vineyard Haven, is one of the most popular establishments on the island (508-693-9223) Even President Clinton ate here when he visited the island. But don't let the word "tavern" mislead you—Vineyard Haven is a dry town, so no liquor can be served. Prices at the Black Dog are at the high end, and some feel that the restaurant is beginning to ride on its reputation and that the quality of the food is not what it once was.

If you travel to Gay Head and forgot to pack a picnic, there are several fast-food establishments there where you can get fried clam platters and the like.

LODGING

For sumptuous accommodations in Edgartown, the **Charlotte Inn** on South Summer Street fits the bill while providing country inn comfort in restored nineteenth-century homes that originally belonged to sea captains. Doubles start at $250, and suites run as much as $550 during the high season (508-627-4751). The lovely **Victorian Inn** on South Water Street was once a whaling captain's home as well, and is now listed in the National Register of Historic Places. Prices are $125 to $265 in high season, and start at $65 in the off-season. Breakfast is included (508-627-4784). The **Daggett House** at 59 North Water Street (508-627-4600) was built in 1660, has a secret stairway, and is a country inn on the water in Edgartown. Doubles are $85 to $285 during the winter months, and $150 to $400 in summer. The **Governor Bradford Inn**, at 128 Main Street (508-627-9510), is also a handsome home originally built for a sea captain. Doubles range from $60 to $155 in low season, and $95 to $210 in summer. Rates include a continental breakfast, year-round, and in winter months an afternoon tea is also served.

The **Oak Bluffs Inn**, at the corner of Circuit Avenue and Pequot Avenue in Oak Bluffs, is painted flamboyantly in pink to exemplify the lighter side of Victorian architecture. Rates range from $115 to $140 during the summer, and start as low as $80 in the off season. Call

MARTHA'S VINEYARD

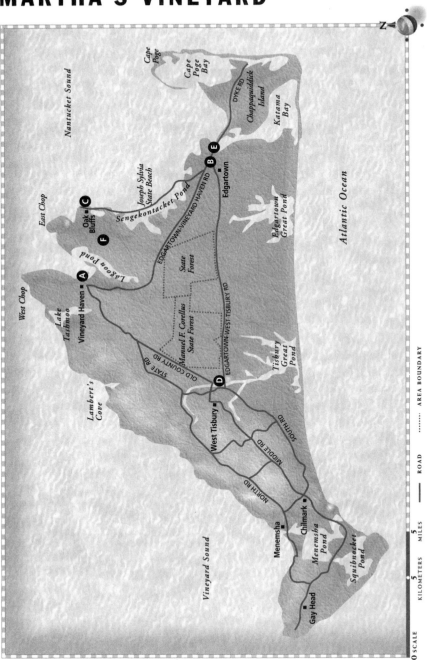

Food

Ⓐ Black Dog Tavern

Ⓑ Navigator Restaurant and Boathouse Bar

Ⓑ O'Brien's Restaurant

Ⓑ The Quarterdeck

Ⓒ Seasons

Ⓑ Shiretown Inn & Restaurant

Ⓒ Two Fabulous Guys

Ⓑ Wharf Restaurant

Lodging

Ⓑ Charlotte Inn

Ⓑ Daggett House

Ⓑ Governor Bradford Inn

Ⓓ Manter Memorial AYH Hostel

Ⓒ Oak Bluffs Inn

Ⓑ Victorian Inn

Ⓒ Wesley Hotel

Camping

Ⓔ Martha's Vineyard Family Campground

Ⓕ Webb's Camping Area

Note: Items with the same letter are located in the same town or area.

(508) 693-7171 or (800) 955-6235 for reservations. The **Wesley Hotel** on Lake Avenue overlooking Oak Bluffs Harbor has been restored, and is typical of many turn-of-the-century seaside hotels. In high season, double rooms with shared baths are $65, doubles with private baths are $125 to $165 (505-693-6611 or 800-638-9027).

Perhaps the least expensive lodging on the island can be found at the **Manter Memorial AYH Hostel** on the Edgartown-West Tisbury Road 3 miles west of the airport. Dormitory-style accommodations cost $12 per night per person for AYH members and $15 for non-members. The hostel is open from April through November; call (508) 693-2665 for further information.

CAMPING

There are two campgrounds on Martha's Vineyard: **Webb's Camping Area** on Barnes Road several miles southwest of Oak Bluffs (508-693-0233) and **Martha's Vineyard Family Campground** on the Edgartown-Vineyard Haven road a little over a mile from the ferry dock (508-693-3772). Martha's Vineyard Family Campground is open mid-May through mid-October, and nightly rates start at $25. Webb's Camping Area is open mid-May through mid-September, with nightly rates starting at $22. Both campgrounds have facilities for RV and tent campers.

NIGHTLIFE

Of the three main towns, Oak Bluffs has the most active nightlife on the Vineyard. The **Atlantic Connection Nightclub** (508-693-7129) as well as some of the neighboring bars on Circuit Avenue can be jam-packed during summer months. Many of the patrons are college students working on the island during school break.

16
NANTUCKET

Thirty miles from the Massachusetts coast, Nantucket Island is a sparkling oasis in the Atlantic. Evidence of the island's onetime whaling prominence can be seen in the facades of graceful Federal, Greek Revival, and Georgian-style homes that border Nantucket town's cobblestone streets. Shingled cottages in Siasconset on the other side of the island are more modest, yet no less respectable, reminders of the seafaring life. In between are miles of low-lying moors and soft sand beaches.

For visitors, Nantucket is a delightful getaway. Fine galleries, boutiques, and restaurants abound in handsome Nantucket town, while historic sights such as the Old Mill, the Fire Hose Cart House, and the Old Gaol serve as reminders of the island's past. For some, finding a deserted stretch on one of Nantucket's glorious beaches is all the retreat they need to make the 2-hour boat trip from the mainland worthwhile. ◨

NANTUCKET ISLAND

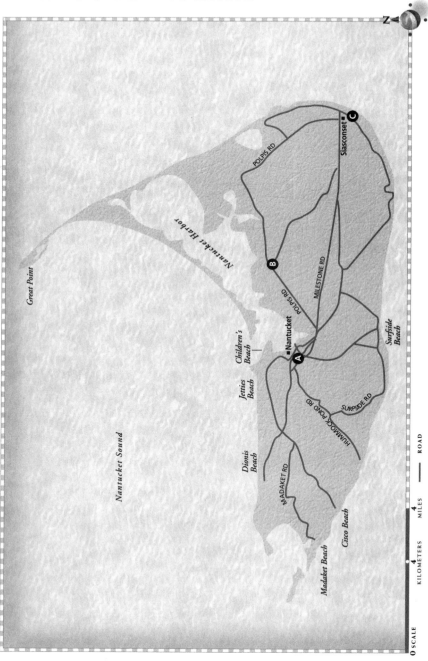

Great Point

Nantucket Sound

Nantucket Harbor

POLPIS RD

B

Children's
Beach

■Nantucket

Jetties
Beach

Dionis
Beach

MADAKET RD

Madaket Beach

Cisco Beach

HUMMOCK POND RD

SURFSIDE RD

Surfside
Beach

MILESTONE RD

POLPIS RD

Siasconset ■

C

Z

0 SCALE   4   4
KILOMETERS   MILES

—— ROAD

Sights

Ⓐ Fair Street Museum

Ⓐ Fire Hose Cart House

Ⓐ The Hawden House

Ⓐ Thomas Macy-Christian House

Ⓐ Maria Mitchell Science Center

Ⓑ Nantucket Life-Saving Museum

Ⓐ Old Gaol

Ⓐ The Oldest House

Ⓐ The Old Mill

Ⓐ Peter Fougler Museum and Research Center

Ⓐ Quaker Meeting House

Ⓒ Siasconset

Ⓐ Thomas Macy Warehouse

Ⓐ Whaling Museum

Note: Items with the same letter are located in the same town or area.

A PERFECT DAY ON NANTUCKET

After breakfast at the Downyflake, I would browse through Nantucket's shops in the morning, and perhaps visit one or two Nantucket Historical Association sites. I'd lunch at the Rose & Crown, and then bicycle to Sconset where I would wander down inviting residential lanes, relax on the beach, or travel out to the lighthouse. If I was in the mood for an elegant dinner, I'd dine at the Chanticleer, or at the less formal Sconset Café. If the weather was especially nice, I might opt for a picnic dinner on the beach instead.

GETTING TO NANTUCKET

To get to Nantucket, Steamship Authority boats leave from South Street in Hyannis, while Hy-Line Boats leave from Ocean Street, which intersects with South Street. Because of their proximity to one another, and because fares from Nantucket (around $11 for adults and $5.50 for children 5 and over) are about the same on both lines, it is possible to take the Hy-Line out to the island and return by the Steamship Authority, or vice versa, giving you more departure times to choose from. Sailing time from Hyannis is roughly 2 hours to Nantucket, although some of the Hy-Line boats can do the trip in 1 hour and 45 minutes. Cars can travel on Steamship Authority (508-771-4000) ferries only, at a rate of $90 each way. Since Nantucket is such a small island, it really makes more sense to leave your car on the mainland and travel by other means once on the island.

Hy-Line (508-778-2600) also operates an inter–island ferry from Oak Bluffs, Martha's Vineyard, to Nantucket from mid-June to September 15. The ferry takes passengers only. It departs Oak Bluffs three times a day and costs $11 for adults, $5.50 for children 5 and older. Bikes are $4.50.

GETTING AROUND THE ISLAND

Nantucket is small and flat enough so that you can get around rather easily by bicycle. Rentals cost about $10 to $15 per day, and you should have no trouble locating the rental shops as you come off the boat. Moped rentals are much more expensive—at least $50 per day for a two-person vehicle. However, if you can afford it, renting one may make sense since they allow you to cover much more ground in a short period of time. Most bike rental establishments also offer mopeds.

Barrett's Tours at 20 Federal Street operates both a shuttle service to Siasconset, Jetties, Surfside, and Madaket beaches in the summer, as well as guided tours of the island. Call (508) 228-0174 or 800-773-0174 for information.

SIGHTSEEING HIGHLIGHTS

★★ The Nantucket Historical Association (508-228-1894) operates a number of period homes, museums, and monuments, representing four centuries of Nantucket history. The sights are located throughout the town of Nantucket, so you should pick up the "Historic Nantucket" brochure, which maps out the route, from the tourist office on the corner of Chestnut Street, just one block from Main Street.

The tour begins at the Thomas Macy Warehouse on Straight Wharf, then continues to the Whaling Museum on Broad Street near Steamboat Wharf. Just next door is the Peter Fougler Museum and Research Center building where genealogical charts and ship's logs are on display. The period homes include The Oldest House, built in 1686 and considered to be the oldest house still standing on the island; The Hadwen House, a stately Greek Revival built in 1845 at the height of the whaling era; and Thomas Macy-Christian House. You can also visit the Old Gaol, or old jail, built in 1805; the Old Mill, built in 1746 and still operational today; the Quaker Meeting House, dating to 1838; the Fair Street Museum next door, containing Nantucket decorative arts exhibits; and the Fire Hose Cart House, which contains nineteenth-century firefighting equipment and was built in 1866. Hours: The buildings close at 5 p.m. Admission charges to the various buildings range from $2 to $5, or you can buy a visitor's pass that will admit you to all of them: $8 for adults, $4 for children 5 to 14. (half day–full day)

★★ Siasconset • In Siasconset (affectionately called Sconset by locals), about 7½ miles from Nantucket's main town, there are no official sights to see, but the town's often-deserted beach, quiet seaside lanes, and charming weathered cottages are enough to warrant the trip from Nantucket center. One of my favorite walks is along the footpath that runs between some of Sconset's most beautiful homes and the beach's plum-covered sand dunes that serve as a protective barrier between the houses and the sea. To reach the footpath, proceed straight from the market in the town's center to the row of houses overlooking the beach. When you come to the end of the row, at a house named "Casa

10 Travel◆Smart Trip Planner

Marina" turn right (just to the left of the house) on what looks like a driveway. Where the driveway veers back to the main road, continue straight ahead onto the lawn. This is the beginning of the footpath, which will lead you across people's lawns—this is legal, but of course one must be considerate of property. The path runs from the village out to Sankaty Head Lighthouse.

✶ **Maria Mitchell Science Center** • Dedicated to the nation's first prominent woman astronomer, the center operates a science library, a small natural science museum, an aquarium, an observatory, and the astronomer's birthplace built in 1790. Hours: Open from 10 a.m. to 4 p.m. Tuesday through Saturday during the summer. Admission to the birthplace is $3 for adults and $1 for children under 14, and a combination ticket which will admit you to the birthplace and aquarium is $5 for adults, and $2 for children. Stop in at the library at 2 Vestal Street. Phone: (508) 228-9198.

Nantucket Life-Saving Museum • On Polpis Road outside of town, this claims to be the only museum of its kind in the world. Hours: Mid-June through mid-September from 10 a.m. to 4:30 p.m. Tuesday through Saturday. Admission is charged.

FITNESS AND RECREATION

Those with time to beachcomb may want to visit **Children's Beach**, **Jetties Beach**, and **South Beach**, all within walking distance from downtown Nantucket. **Dionis Beach**, 3 miles south of town, has still-water swimming, while more adventurous swimmers will enjoy the surf at **Madaket**, **Surfside**, and **Siasconset**. Serious surfers find **Cisco Beach** to their liking.

There are bike paths to Siasconset, Madaket, and Surfside beaches. Another bike trail runs along Cliff Road, and the bike path across the island's central moors is for mountain bikes only. If you didn't bring a bicycle with you, see the above "getting around the island" section for information on bike rentals.

FOOD

The **Sconset Café** (508-257-4008), in Siasconset Center, serves both lunch and dinner in addition to selling its own cookbook. With entrées such as Indonesian grilled shrimp and shrimp stuffed artichokes, the café offers an interesting twist to its seafood dishes that one doesn't come across in too many New England restaurants. Lunch entrées run about $7 to $13, dinner entrées begin at $17.50. The café is only open during the summer, as is the market around the corner where you can pick up fresh sandwiches and pasta or potato salad to take down to the beach with you.

The **Chanticleer Inn** (508-257-6231), also in Siasconset, special-izes in French gourmet fare and is considered by many to be the best restaurant on the island. Festive flowers and a brightly painted carousel horse greet diners in the restaurant's garden courtyard, making outdoor dining a must in good weather. The atmosphere, cuisine, and service will cost you, however, as lunch entrées start around $15, it would be hard to sit down to dinner for less than $40 per person.

In downtown Nantucket on South Water Street, the **Atlantic Cafe** (508-228-0570) and the **Rose & Crown** (508-228-2595), several doors down, both offer satisfying meals in a pub atmosphere ($6.95–$19.95). For casual fare, there are numerous fast-food joints on the road leading to the Steamship Authority boat dock. One of them, **Henry's Sandwiches** on Steamboat Wharf (508-228-0123), makes great subs. For a hearty, down-home traditional breakfast, try the **Downyflake** on South Water Street (508-228-4533). They have ter-rific homemade doughnuts.

LODGING

In Sconset, your lodging choices are limited to **Wade Cottages** (508-257-6308), which has a three-night minimum, and the **Summer House Inn** (508-257-9976), which has a restaurant. Both overlook the ocean and offer pleasant accommodations. Wade Cottages opens in late May and operates through September. A room with a private bath is $475 for three nights. Lodging at the Summer House includes private sitting rooms and marble Jacuzzis. Rates start at $275 in high season, and are less off-peak. The inn closes for the season at the end of September.

The **Jared Coffin House** at 29 Broad Street in downtown Nantucket, one of the better-known inns on the island, is open all year. Guest rooms are spread out among six dwellings, the oldest dating to the 1700s. The inn also operates a respectable restaurant, with courtyard dining in the summertime, and a cozy bar. Dining prices are moderate, while doubles go for $145 to $185 (508-228-2405). The **Nesbitt Inn**, just down the block at 21 Broad Street in a large, friendly

NANTUCKET ISLAND

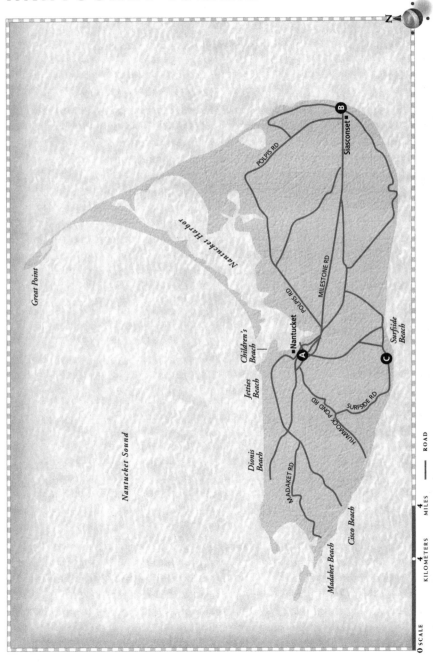

Food

Ⓐ Atlantic Cafe

Ⓑ Chanticleer Inn

Ⓐ Downyflake

Ⓐ Henry's Sandwiches

Ⓐ Rose & Crown

Ⓑ Sconset Café

Lodging

Ⓐ 18 Gardner Street

Ⓐ Brass Lantern Inn

Ⓐ Centre Street Inn

Ⓐ Jared Coffin House

Ⓐ Nesbitt Inn

Ⓐ Periwinkle Guesthouse

Ⓐ Sherburne Inn

Ⓒ Star of the Sea AYH Hostel

Ⓑ Summer House Inn

Ⓑ Wade Cottages

Note: Items with the same letter are located in the same town or area.

Victorian, is reasonably priced at $65 to $100 per night for a double (508-228-0156).

The town of Nantucket has a seemingly endless list of bed and breakfasts, yet remarkably they fill up quickly during the height of summer. **Nantucket Accommodations** (508-228-9559) is a reservation service that can help you find a room; or you can try the **Sherburne Inn** where rooms are decorated with four-poster and canopy beds. Originally built as a silk factory in 1835, the Sherburne is rumored to have a ghost. Doubles range from $125 to $160 in high season, and start at $75 per night in the off-season (508-228-4425). Lodgers will not be disappointed with the quality and comfort of **18 Gardner Street** (508-228-1155) where double rooms rent for $110 to $300 per night.

There is also a string of guest houses on North Water Street convenient to the town center, among them, the **Brass Lantern Inn** (508-228-4064 or 800-377-6609) and the **Periwinkle Guesthouse** (508-228-9267 or 800-992-2899). Room rates run from $115 to $180 at the Brass Lantern, from $95 to $195 at the Periwinkle during the summer. On nearby Centre Street, the **Centre Street Inn** is decorated with English pine antiques, white wicker furniture, and Laura Ashley and Ralph Lauren fabrics. Cranberry sour cream coffee cake is a specialty at breakfast which is included in the room rate of $55 to $110 for a double with a shared bath, or $85 to $145 for a double with a private bath. A single room with a shared bath is also available ($35–$65), as is a suite with its own sitting room and fireplace ($95–$125).

CAMPING

There are no campgrounds on Nantucket, but **Star of the Sea AYH Hostel** in Surfside does give budget travelers a lodging option. Dormitory-style beds rent for $12 per night for members, and $15 per night for non-members. The hostel is 3½ miles from the ferry. The hostel is on the National Register of Historic Places, and its oceanside location is appealing. Reservations are essential (508-228-0433). It is open April 1 through the end of October.

17

CAPE COD

C ape Cod juts out into the ocean from the Massachusetts mainland like an arm flexing its biceps. At the base of the arm is the town of Sandwich—a quintessential Cape Cod village, with neat shingled houses, gentle tidal marshes, and many sights to occupy the out-of-town visitor. In 1987 the town of Sandwich celebrated its 350th birthday. If you follow scenic Route 6A from Sandwich down the arm of the Cape, you'll pass through other quaint towns such as Barnstable and Yarmouth. Some of the cape's most beautiful homes are at the Cape's elbow in the lovely town of Chatham. Chatham also has a lighthouse on Shore Road off Route 28. The pristine beaches of the Cape Cod National Seashore border the Atlantic as you travel up the forearm. Provincetown, forming Cape Cod's hand, feels as if it should be remote. Yet somehow, the latest trends in food, fashion, and art still manage to find their way out to the town at the tip. Once, Provincetown was the pilgrims' first stopover in the new land. Today, the art, tourist, and gay communities all vie for space along Provincetown's harbor, making the town a busy place during the summer months. ◣

CAPE COD

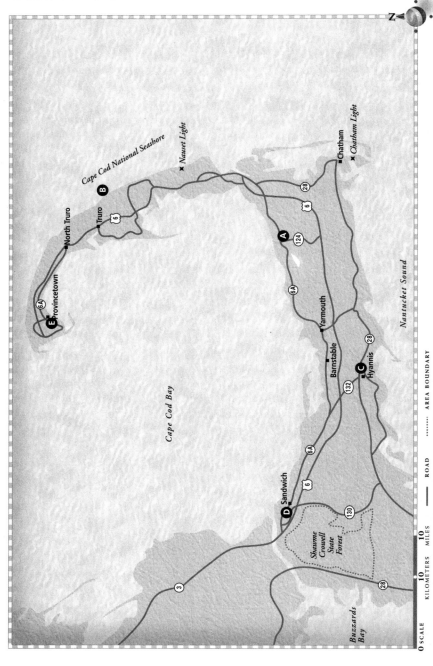

N

Cape Cod Bay

Cape Cod National Seashore

× Nauset Light

B

North Truro

Truro (6)

Provincetown (6A)

E

(6A)

Yarmouth

Barnstable

Hyannis

C

(132)

(28)

(28)

(6)

Chatham × Chatham Light

A (124)

(6A)

Sandwich

D

(6) (6A)

(130)

Shawme Crowell State Forest

(3)

(28)

Buzzards Bay

Nantucket Sound

0 SCALE 10 KILOMETERS 10 MILES

ROAD ······· AREA BOUNDARY

Sights

Ⓐ Cape Cod Museum of Natural History

Ⓑ The Cape Cod National Seashore

Ⓒ Cape Cod Potato Chip Factory

Ⓓ Green Briar Nature Center and Jam Kitchen

Ⓓ Heritage Plantation

Ⓓ Historic Homes of Sandwich

Ⓐ New England Fire and History Museum

Ⓔ Pilgrim Monument and Provincetown Museum

Ⓔ Provincetown Art Association and Museum

Ⓔ Provincetown Heritage Museum

Ⓓ Sandwich Glass Museum

Ⓓ Thornton Burgess Museum

Ⓓ Yesteryears Doll Museum

Note: Items with the same letter are located in the same town or area.

A PERFECT DAY ON CAPE COD

In good weather, I'd pack a picnic lunch and head to the National Seashore, spending part of the day hiking, and the rest of the day stretched out on a beach towel. If mother nature was not cooperating, I'd spend the day in the Sandwich area between Heritage Plantation and the Sandwich Glass Museum, dine at the Sagamore Inn, saving room for an ice-cream cone at O'Brien's for dessert.

SIGHTSEEING HIGHLIGHTS

★★★ **The Cape Cod National Seashore** • The National Seashore stretches from the eastern half of the cape's elbow all the way out to its fingertips at Provincetown, offering the visitor miles of nature trails, beaches, and wind-sculpted sand dunes peppered with beach grass. You won't be able to cover all 27,000 acres of the seashore in an afternoon, but a ranger at the Salt Pond Visitor Center (off U.S. 6 in Eastham) can send you off in the direction of Nauset Lighthouse, a good hiking trail, or a remote beach. There's a marsh trail right behind the visitor center, as well as a nature trail especially designed for the blind. You can park at Nauset Beach for $5 a day, and there is a bathhouse facility available in season. From the nearby Coast Guard Station you can see the place where Henry Beston's "Outermost House" once stood before it was washed away with the extreme tides created by the blizzard of 1978. The seashore is open to the public year-round.

★★ **Heritage Plantation** • The plantation is on Grove and Pine Streets in Sandwich. The prettiest time to visit the plantation is in early June when the rhododendrons are in full bloom, but the beautifully land-scaped 76-acre grounds are handsome in any season. American folk art, Currier & Ives lithographs, antique firearms, and early automobiles are among the plantation's other attractions. The antique cars, housed in a replica of the Shaker Round Barn at Hancock, include a vibrant green and yellow Duesenberg designed for Gary Cooper which will delight auto buffs. The art museum houses a carousel to entertain the children while you view the Currier & Ives collection. Buses run at regular intervals between the museums. Hours: Daily mid-May through late October from 10 a.m. to 5 p.m., although tickets are not sold after 4:15 p.m. Picnicking on the grounds is not allowed. Admission is $7 for adults, $6 for seniors, $3.50 for children 6 to 18, and there is no charge for children 5 and under. Address: Turn left onto Grove Street next to the town hall in Sandwich Center. The parking lot will be on your left approximately one half mile from the center.

✵ **Provincetown Art Association and Museum** • Changing exhibits include works by respected American artists such as Milton Avery, as well as promising newcomers to the art scene. Hours: Daily from noon to 5 p.m., and from 7 p.m. to 10 p.m. during summer months. Admission is $3 for adults, $1 for children, students, and seniors. Address: 460 Commercial Street. Phone: Call (508) 487-1750 for off-season hours.

✵ **Provincetown Heritage Museum** • Artifacts pertaining to the sea make up the majority of the museum's exhibits, the focal point being the 64-foot-long half-scale model of the *Rose Dorothea*, a turn-of-the-century fishing vessel. It is the largest indoor boat model in the world. Hours: The museum is open from 10 a.m. to 6 p.m. during summer. Admission to the museum is $3 for adults, free for children under 12. Address: At the corner of Commercial and Center Streets.

✵ **Pilgrim Monument and Provincetown Museum** • You will have no trouble locating the monument because, at 255 feet, it is the tallest all-granite structure in the United States. It affords marvelous views of the cape and South Shore on clear days. Museum exhibits spotlight outer Cape Cod history. Unfortunately, handicapped access is limited as there is no elevator to the top of the monument. Visitors must use ramps and stairs to climb to the top. Hours: Open daily 9 a.m. to 5 p.m. except during the summer months when it is open until 7 p.m. Admission is $5 for adults and $3 for children ages 4 to 12.

✵ **Sandwich Glass Museum** • Across from Town Hall Square in Sandwich Center, the museum houses a fine collection of glassware made in the 1800s by the Boston & Sandwich Glass Company and the Cape Cod Glass Works. Exhibits include an explanation of glass manu-facturing procedures and a chronology of the Sandwich operation. Hours: Daily from 9:30 a.m. to 4:30 p.m. April through October, closed during January, and open the remaining months Wednesday through Sunday from 9:30 a.m. to 4 p.m. Admission is $3 for adults, 50 cents for children over 5.

Historic Homes of Sandwich • In Sandwich, you can also visit a number of historic homes, all within a 3-block radius of Town Hall

Square. There's a water-operated stone mill, **Dexter's Grist Mill**, and **Hoxie House**, the oldest house on Cape Cod. Hoxie House was originally built in the 1600s and restored in 1960. Hours: Monday through Saturday from 10 a.m. to 5 p.m. (last tour 4:15 p.m.), and Sundays from 1 p.m. to 5 p.m. June through September. Admission is $1.50 for adults, 75 cents for children. Combination tickets to both sites are $2.50 for adults, $1 for children. Admission to the mill is $1.50 for adults, 75 cents for children 12 to 16. Address: 130 Water Street.

Yesteryears Doll Museum • This doll museum, in the Pilgrim's First Parish Meetinghouse on Main Street in Sandwich, has a collection of rare and antique dolls and dollhouses. Hours: Monday through Saturday from 10 a.m. to 4 p.m. mid-May through October. Admission is $3 for adults, $2.50 for seniors, and $2 for children.

Thornton Burgess Museum • This was the home of the children's books author, and some first editions of his books and his original artwork are on display here. Admission is by donation. Address: 4 Water Street, just up from the mill in Sandwich.

Green Briar Nature Center and Jam Kitchen • If you're traveling with small fans of Peter Rabbit and the famous briar patch, then you may want to visit Green Briar Nature Center and Jam Kitchen. You can watch homemade jams bubbling away in the kitchen, visit "Peter Rabbit," then take the nature trail around the "old briar patch" that served as an inspiration for Burgess's marvelous children's tales. Hours: Both the museum and the jam kitchen are open Monday through Saturday 10 a.m. to 4 p.m., Sunday from 1 p.m. to 4 p.m. During July and August, there is storytelling at the museum. Address: On Discovery Hill Road off Route 6A east of Sandwich between Sandwich center and Quaker Meeting House Road.

New England Fire and History Museum • This small Brewster museum has antique fire-fighting equipment, a replica of Ben Franklin's firehouse, and a diorama of Chicago's great fire. Hours: Monday through Friday 10 a.m. to 4 p.m., Saturday and Sunday from noon to 4 p.m., mid-May through mid-October, or by appointment throughout the rest of the year. Admission is $4.50 for adults, $4 for seniors, and $2.50 for children 5 to 12.

Cape Cod Museum of Natural History • Features exhibits highlighting the flora and fauna of Cape Cod located in Brewster. Hours: Monday-Saturday from 9:30 a.m. to 4:30 p.m. and Sunday from 12:30 p.m. to 4:30 p.m. May through mid-October, closed Monday during the rest of the year. Admission is $4 for adults, $2 for children over 6.

Cape Cod Potato Chip Factory • If you're a potato chip lover, you may want to tour this factory in Hyannis on Breeds Hill Road in Independence Park off Route 132 opposite the Cape Cod Mall. The tour is self-guided, free, and you even get a complimentary bag of chips at the end of the tour. Hours: Open for tours Monday through Friday from 10 a.m. to 4 p.m. Phone: (508) 775-7253.

FITNESS AND RECREATION

The **Cape Cod Rail Trail** is a bike path that runs up the center of the Cape along an old railway line. **Rail Trail Bike Shop** adjacent to the trail in Brewster rents bicycles, and even has baby seats, and tagalong trailers for those traveling with children that are too young to ride on their own (508-896-8200).

FOOD

If you're staying in the Sandwich area, the dining room at the **Dan'l Webster Inn** has a fine reputation—serving such favorites as filet mignon ($21.95) and baked scrod in lobster sauce ($17.50). If those prices are too steep for your budget, a little west of Sandwich Center on 6A is the **Sagamore Inn** (508-888-9707), a favorite with locals. Pressed tin ceilings amplify the sound of diners, and crowded tables create an atmosphere that is always animated, while the fare includes fresh seafood, New England-style dinners, and Italian specialties. **The Beehive** (508-833-1184), a sunny yellow, tavern-style eatery on Route 6A east of Sandwich Center, serves seafood and tasty sandwiches. **O'Brien's** on 6A in East Sandwich is the place to go for homemade ice-cream—there's always a tempting array of flavors to choose from, and the scoops are generous. If your lodging does not provide breakfast, try the casual **Marshland Restaurant** (508-888-9824) on 6A near Sandwich Center. Portions are large, but the prices are not. If you like micro-breweries, **Cape Cod Brew House** at 720 Main Street in

CAPE COD

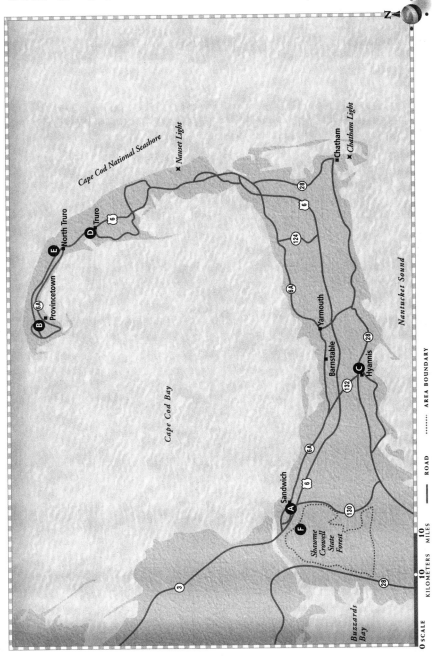

Cape Cod National Seashore

× Nauset Light

Truro
6

North Turo
6A

E

Provincetown
6A

B

D

Cape Cod Bay

■ Chatham
× Chatham Light

28

6

124

6A

Yarmouth

Barnstable ■

20

132

G Hyannis

Nantucket Sound

6A

Sandwich
6

A

130

F

Shawme
Crowell
State
Forest

3

28

Buzzards
Bay

N

O SCALE
10
KILOMETERS
10
MILES

ROAD   ⋯⋯⋯ AREA BOUNDARY

Food

- Ⓐ The Beehive
- Ⓑ Cafe Blase
- Ⓒ Cape Cod Brew House
- Ⓑ Ciro & Sals
- Ⓐ Dan'l Webster Inn
- Ⓐ Marshland Restaurant
- Ⓑ The Mew's
- Ⓐ O'Brien's
- Ⓑ Old Reliable Fish House
- Ⓑ Pepe's
- Ⓐ Sagamore Inn
- Ⓑ Vorelli's

Lodging

- Ⓐ Captain Ezra Nye Guesthouse
- Ⓐ Dan'l Webster Inn
- Ⓐ Earl of Sandwich Motor Manor
- Ⓒ HyLand Youth Hostel
- Ⓐ Isaiah Jones Homestead
- Ⓓ Little America Hostel
- Ⓑ Somerset Guesthouse
- Ⓐ Spring Garden Motel
- Ⓑ Victorian Anchor Inn
- Ⓑ White Wind Inn
- Ⓐ Wingscorton Farm Inn

Camping

- Ⓑ Coastal Acres Camping Court
- Ⓑ Dune's Edge Campground
- Ⓔ Horton's Camping Resort
- Ⓔ North of Highland Camping Area
- Ⓔ North Truro Camping Area
- Ⓐ Peter's Pond Park
- Ⓕ Shawme Crowell State Forest

Note: Items with the same letter are located in the same town or area.

Hyannis (508-775-4110) brews its own beer, has a varied menu (everything from appetizers and burgers to shrimp cervesa—shrimp sautéed in draught beer), and reasonable prices ($4.50–$11.95).

In Provincetown, for a different sort of dining experience, try **Old Reliable Fish House** at 229 Commercial Street (508-487-9742). It has a mixed menu of Portuguese and Yankee specialties. The restaurant is on the water with outdoor seating in season, and dinner prices range from $8 to $12 for regular entrées, and start at $14 for lobsters. **Ciro & Sals** on Kiley Court is known statewide for sumptuous northern Italian creations. Prices are $9 to $20, and reservations are strongly recommended (508-487-0049).

Vorelli's at 226 Commercial Street also serves Italian as well as seafood, and has a nice atmosphere. Dinner entrées range from $14 to $18. The restaurant also has a raw bar (508-487-2778). Also on Commercial Street, **The Mew's**, which was once a stable (508-487-1500), and **Pepe's** (508-487-0670) are popular for seafood, while **Cafe Blase** (508-487-9465) serves good sandwiches at moderate prices, and has a pleasant sidewalk cafe in the summertime. There is no shortage of sub shops and pizza joints in town, and ice cream lovers are bound to be tempted by Provincetown's many ice cream parlors.

LODGING

Sandwich makes a wonderful place to base yourself when exploring the inner Cape. Sure accommodations are plentiful in nearby Hyannis, but Sandwich is more convenient to sights, almost as conveniently located to beaches, and has a lot more charm than Hyannis. On Sandwich's Main Street, the **Dan'l Webster Inn** (508-888-3622 or 800-444-3566) will bathe you in four-star comfort you won't have to sell your soul for. Double rooms run from $89 to $325 per night depending on the season, and children under 12 stay free in the same room with their parents. Reservations are strongly recommended.

Sandwich also has choice bed and breakfasts in the town center. Across from the Dan'l Webster, friendly hosts greet you at the **Captain Ezra Nye Guesthouse** (800-388-2278 or 508-888-6142) built in 1829. Rates are $85 to $105 per night including breakfast, are quite reasonable for the area. The **Isaiah Jones Homestead** (508-888-9115 or 800-526-1625), also on Main Street, is elegantly furnished with four-poster beds and other Victorian pieces. Modern conveniences are not overlooked, as one room has its own Jacuzzi tub. Doubles range from $75 to $125 in low season and $95 to $155 in high season.

You'll find a wide assortment of motor inns and cottages along scenic 6A in Sandwich. On the upper end is the mock Tudor-style **Earl of Sandwich Motor Manor** (508-888-1415 or 800-442-3275), with doubles ranging from $45 to $85. The attractive cedar-shingled **Spring Garden Motel** (508-888-0710) with flowering window boxes, a swimming pool, and cozy, comfortable rooms is in East Sandwich on the edge of a tidal marsh. Continental breakfast is included in the room rate, and rooms start at $68 in high season, and $50 in low season. If you would like to wake up to a rooster crowing and other sounds of a working farm, **Wingscorton Farm Inn** (508-888-0534), across the road from the Spring Garden Motel, offers fine accommodations ($115 to $150 per night including a full breakfast). For those traveling on a budget, the **HyLand Youth Hostel** at 465 Falmouth Road in nearby Hyannis is not too far from the ferryboat docks. The hostel is open all year and also offers facilities for families and couples. Beds start at $12 per person. Call (508) 775-2970 for information.

In Provincetown, the **Victorian Anchor Inn** at 175 Commercial Street has a wonderful porch for people-watching, an attractive garden in front, and oceanview rooms that rent for about $110 to $135 in the summer, and for $85 to $95 in the off-season. Town facing rooms go for $95 to $110 in the summer, and $75 during low season. Tower rooms are $125 during the summer, $85 off-peak, and the inn is open throughout the year (508-487-0432). Also open year-round is the **White Wind Inn** just across the street. Doubles go for $60 to $165. Call (508) 487-1526 for reservations. The **Somerset Guesthouse** on the corner of Commercial and Pearl streets has reasonable rates. Rooms with shared baths range from $65 to $85 in the summer, and $55 to $65 off season. Doubles with private baths go for $85 to $105 in the summer, and $70 to $80 in the winter (508-487-0383). All inns listed are convenient to downtown Provincetown.

Route 6A in nearby Truro has a string of cottages and motels on the beach. Accommodations there vary in quality, but are an option if you want to stay on the beach, or if you are traveling with a family and find in-town bed and breakfasts too expensive for your whole crew. If you have trouble finding lodging in the area, try calling Provincetown's Chamber of Commerce, (508) 487-3424, for assistance. Budget travelers should be aware that the **Little America Hostel** in Truro has accommodations for about $12 per person per night (508-349-3889), but that the hostel is only open during the summer months.

CAMPING

Shawme Crowell State Forest on Route 130 in Sandwich has 280 sites and is open April through November (508-888-0351), and campsites are much less expensive than at most other campgrounds on the Cape. **Peter's Pond Park** in Sandwich has both tent and trailer sites. Located on a freshwater pond, the campground is open seasonally mid-April through mid-October. Sites start at $17 per night (508-477-1775).

    Coastal Acres Camping Court on the West Vine Street Extension is the closest campground to downtown Provincetown. They do have a three-night minimum stay requirement for reservations, but you could call on the day of your arrival and see if they have space available (508-487-1700). Sites cost $20 for a tent and $27 for RV hookups. The campground is open April through October. **Dune's Edge Campground** off U.S. 6 is just a little farther from town but still convenient, and borders on sand dunes of the National Seashore (508-487-9815). Sites start at $19 per night, and the campground is open May through September. In North Truro there are three campgrounds you might try if Coastal Acres and Dunes Edge are full. They are **Horton's Camping Resort** (starting at $16 per site; 508-487-1220 or 800-252-7705), **North of Highland Camping Area** ($18 per site; 508-487-1191), and **North Truro Camping Area**, which is open all year ($7.50 per person $15 per site minimum; 508-487-1847).

NIGHTLIFE

The **Cape Cod Melody Tent** in Hyannis features well-known singers, comedians, and rock groups throughout the summer. Call (508) 775-9100 for schedule and ticket information.

SIDE TRIPS FROM CAPE COD

If you have time to spend in the area, the Cape Cod National Seashore has enough beautiful coastline to occupy nature enthusiasts and beach bums alike for many a day. There is always a new dune to investigate. Whale-watching is also an agreeable pastime in this part of the world. The *Portuguese Princess* shuttles eager marine mammal watchers daily from Provincetown, April through November, to view the whales in their natural habitat. Call (508) 487-2651 or (800) 442-3188 for reservations. Tickets start at about $17.50 per person.

18
PLYMOUTH AND THE SOUTH SHORE

The South Shore is the term used to refer to the towns that stretch along the shore from Boston south to Cape Cod—towns such as Quincy, where two United States presidents were born, and pretty coastal villages such as Duxbury, Cohasset, and Hingham. Yet it is Plymouth, some 35 miles south of Boston, that is the most celebrated of South Shore towns. And rightly so—it was in Plymouth that the Pilgrims settled in 1620, beginning the first real colonization of our country.

Today the Pilgrims' legacy can be explored at multiple sights in and around Plymouth such as Plimouth Plantation, the *Mayflower II*, Pilgrim Hall, and Plymouth Rock. For those preferring natural attractions to manmade ones, the South Shore boasts a number of wildlife sanctuaries, the World's End Reservation in Hingham, and Atlantic beaches—Duxbury Beach is a favorite among local beachcombers. ◥

PLYMOUTH

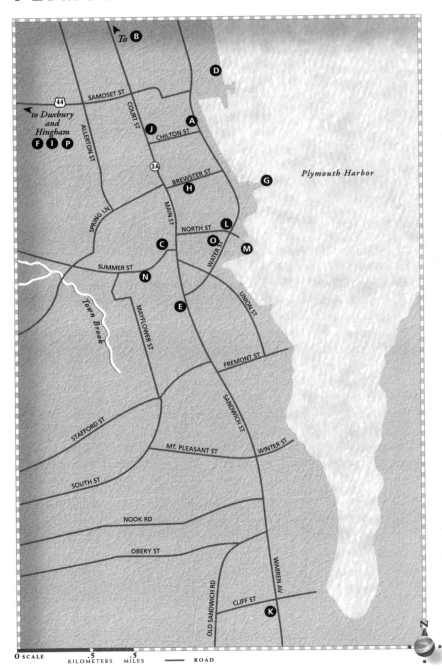

Plymouth Harbor

to Duxbury and Hingham

To **B**

D

A

J

G

H

L

C

O

M

N

E

K

SAMOSET ST
COURT ST
CHILTON ST
ALLERTON ST
BREWSTER ST
MAIN ST
NORTH ST
WATER ST
SPRING LN
SUMMER ST
MAYFLOWER ST
UNION ST
FREMONT ST
SANDWICH ST
STAFFORD ST
MT. PLEASANT ST
WINTER ST
SOUTH ST
NOOK RD
OBERY ST
OLD SANDWICH RD
WARREN AV
CLIFF ST

Town Brook

F **I** **P**

44

3A

0 SCALE
KILOMETERS .5 MILES .5 ROAD

N

Sights

A Antiquarian House

B Cordage Park Marketplace

C Court House and Museum

D Cranberry World

E Howland House

F John Alden House

G *Mayflower II*

H Mayflower Society Museum

I Old Burying Ground

J Pilgrim Hall Museum

K Plimouth Plantation

L Plymouth National Wax Museum

M Plymouth Rock

N Sparrow House

O Spooner House

P World's End Reservation

A PERFECT DAY ON THE SOUTH SHORE

My day would begin at Plimouth Plantation, where the Pilgrim life of 1627 has been recreated. For lunch, I'd feast on a fried clam platter from Wood's—getting take-out so I could picnic on the harbor. In the afternoon, I would take Route 3A north through Duxbury, Marshfield, Cohasset, and Hingham—possibly detouring from the main road to look at some of the South Shore's elegant homes. Next I would visit the Adams home in Quincy before heading to Boston for my evening meal and overnight accommodation.

SIGHTSEEING HIGHLIGHTS

★★★ **Plimouth Plantation and the** *Mayflower II* • Both the plantation and the ship are run by the same nonprofit organization. The plantation is a living museum exemplifying everyday seventeenth-century Pilgrim life and that of nineteenth-century Native Americans in the neighboring Wampanaog Settlement. In the Pilgrim village of thatched cottages, costumed guides play the parts of the original settlers tending to their farm animals, gardens, and everyday chores. They claim to know nothing of modern times but are happy to explain how and why things were done in 1627. The *Mayflower II* is docked in Plymouth Harbor adjacent to Plymouth Rock several miles away. Since historians aren't really sure what happened to the original *Mayflower*, this replica was built in England in the 1950s. On board, costumed guides relate the events of the fateful 1620 voyage, and you can see the cramped conditions under which the Pilgrims traveled. Hours: *Mayflower II* and Plimouth Plantation are open daily April through November from 9 a.m. to 5 p.m. The *Mayflower II* is open until 6:30 p.m. from late June through Labor Day. Admission to the plantation is $15 for adults, $9 for children. Admission to the ship is $5.75 for adults, $3.75 for children 5 to 12. Combination tickets are $18.50 for adults, $16.50 for seniors and students, $11 for children 5 to 12. (Half day)

★ **Plymouth Rock** • There is nothing extraordinary about this enshrined rock other than the fact that it symbolizes the Pilgrims' first settlement and thus is a cornerstone of American colonization. Visiting Plymouth Rock is probably comparable to kissing the Blarney Stone—all true patriots should make a pilgrimage once in a lifetime for their country's sake, whether it's engrossing or not. (½ hour)

✱ **Cranberry World** • Outside the museum building is a small cranberry bog where you can see how this one of only three native American fruits is grown. Inside there are exhibits on how the tangy fruit is harvested, and its uses through the years. Since the museum is operated by the Ocean Spray company, there is no charge for admission, and of course samples of cranberry refreshments are also free. Hours: Daily 9:30 a.m. to 5 p.m., May through November. Address: 225 Water Street in Plymouth. (½ hour)

✱ **Cordage Park Marketplace** • The marketplace, now filled with factory outlet stores and boutiques, is of interest because it stands on the site of a nineteenth-century rope manufacturing plant. The Plymouth mill was the world's largest and employed an army of workers. The prints and photographs on display throughout the marketplace will give you some sense of the factory's magnitude. Cordage Park is on Route 3A about 1 mile north of downtown Plymouth. (1 hour)

✱ **Pilgrim Hall Museum** • The museum, which is on the National Register of Historic Places, houses actual personal belongings of the Pilgrims, including Governor Bradford's Bible, and Myles Standish's sword. Hours: Year-round from 9:30 a.m. to 4:30 p.m. daily, except for Christmas and New Year's Day. Admission is $5 for adults, $4 for seniors, $2 for children 6 to 15. Address: 75 Court Street on Route 3A in the center of Plymouth. (1 hour)

✱ **Plymouth National Wax Museum** • Overlooking Plymouth Rock and harbor from atop Coles Hill, the museum re-creates events in Pilgrim history using wax figures. Hours: Daily 9 a.m. to 5 p.m., March through November. Admission is $5 for adults, $2 for children. (1 hour)

✱ **Pilgrim Path** • In addition to leading you to the *Mayflower II*, Plymouth Rock, and the Pilgrim Hall, this trail will lead you to other historic buildings throughout Plymouth. You'd need to spend a lot of time in Plymouth if you want to see them all, but here's a sampling of what's available:

Sparrow House was built in 1640 and is the oldest house in Plymouth. Now the museum houses rotating exhibits and a craft gallery, and admission is by donation. Hours: Daily except Wednesday 10 a.m. to 5 p.m., late May through late December. Address: 42 Summer Street.

The **Court House and Museum** on Town Square operated as a municipal building longer than any other court house in America. Hours: Daily during the summer, and admission is free. **Howland House** at 33 Sandwich Street is the only house still standing in Plymouth which an original Pilgrim actually lived in. Tours are given by costumed guides. Hours: Daily from 9 a.m. to 5 p.m. (tours are given from 10 a.m. to 4:30 p.m.), late May through mid-October. Admission is $2.50 for adults, $2 for students and seniors, 50 cents for children 6 to 12.

The **Spooner House**, built in 1749, was the home of Bourne Spooner, founder of the Plymouth Cordage Company. The house remained in the Spooner family until 1954, and many of the original furnishings are on display. Open from late May through mid-October. Admission is $2.50 for adults, 50 cents for children.

The lovely **Antiquarian House** at 126 Water Street was frequented by Daniel Webster and has a number of unusual octagonally shaped rooms. It is also open from late May through mid-October and admission is charged. The **Mayflower Society Museum**, with eighteenth-century furnishings, is also housed in a beautiful home and dates to 1745. It is the headquarters of the General Society of Mayflower Descendants. Hours: Non-members can visit the office and library Monday through Friday from 1:30 p.m. to 3:30 p.m. Admission is $2.50 for adults and 25 cents for children. Address: 4 Winslow Street.

For a map and complete listing of sites along the Pilgrim Path, contact the Plymouth Area Chamber of Commerce at 91 Samoset Street, Plymouth, MA 02360.

John Alden House • You can visit the home of the famous Mayflower couple, John and Priscilla Alden. Hours: Tuesday through Sunday late June through early September. Admission is charged. Address: 105 Alden Street in Duxbury.

Massachusetts Audubon Society • The society operates four wildlife sanctuaries on the South Shore. Phone: (617) 837-9400.

Old Burying Ground • On Chestnut Street in Duxbury, this is the cemetery where Myles Standish is buried along with other passengers from the *Mayflower*.

World's End Reservation • This 250 acres of shoreline park in

Hingham was designed by Frederick Law Olmstead, whose work you may have seen in the Boston Public Gardens as well as at other locations on your New England trip.

FITNESS AND RECREATION

Plymouth has a public beach with a bathhouse, parking lot (for up to 200 cars), and lifeguards are on duty. The 5-mile long Duxbury Beach is probably the most popular beach for swimming on the South Shore. It also has lifeguards and facilities, and its parking lot holds up to 1,400 cars. There is a fee to park at both beaches.

FOOD

In Plymouth, **McGrath's Restaurant** (508-746-9751) overlooking the harbor in downtown is a popular spot for seafood, and prices are moderate. Restaurants are plentiful all along Water Street at the waterfront. There are also informal eat-in or takeout seafood shacks out on the piers. Try **Wood's** (508-746-0261) on Town Pier where a fried clam plate will easily satisfy two hungry appetites. The John Carver Inn's informal **Hearth 'n Kettle Restaurant** (see below) is family friendly with a children's menu, and toys to keep kids occupied during meals. If you're further up the coast, **Kimball's by the Sea** (617-383-6650) at 124 Elm Street, overlooking the water in Cohasset, is known for its seafood.

LODGING

Plymouth is perhaps the town on the South Shore best equipped to handle overnight visitors. If you're visiting sights closer to Boston, it is probably just as easy to stay in the city. In Plymouth, **The Pilgrim Sands Motel**, on Route 3A, is a popular lodging choice because of its oceanfront location and proximity to Plimouth Plantation. Doubles start at $50 in low season, and run from $85 to $115 in summer (508-747-0900 or 800-729-7263). The **Sheraton Plymouth at Village Landing** at 180 Water Street is adjacent to the Village Landing Marketplace, not far from Plymouth Rock. Double rooms start around $100 per night, and it is best to make reservations several weeks ahead during the summer (800-325-3535). The **Governor Bradford Motor Inn** is right on Plymouth's waterfront. Motel style rooms have refrigerators and coffee makers, and range from $58 to $89 for double occupancy (800-332-1620

PLYMOUTH

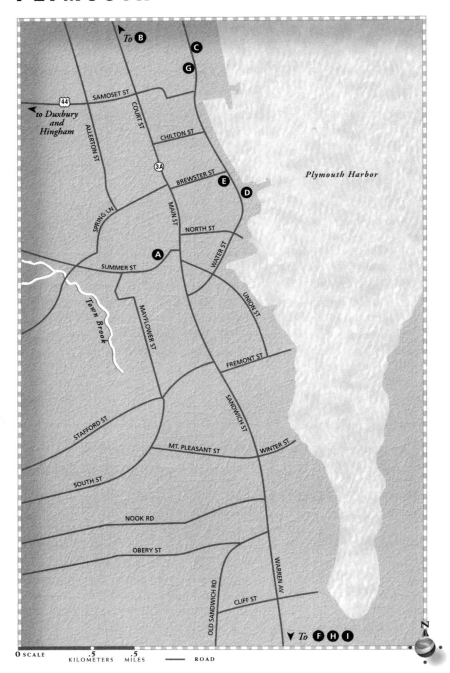

To **B**

C

G

44

to Duxbury
and
Hingham

SAMOSET ST

COURT ST

ALLERTON ST

CHILTON ST

3A

BREWSTER ST

E

D

Plymouth Harbor

SPRING LN

MAIN ST

NORTH ST

A

WATER ST

SUMMER ST

Town Brook

MAYFLOWER ST

UNION ST

FREMONT ST

SANDWICH ST

STAFFORD ST

MT. PLEASANT ST

WINTER ST

SOUTH ST

NOOK RD

OBERY ST

WARREN AV

OLD SANDWICH RD

CLIFF ST

▼ *To* **F** **H** **I**

N

0 SCALE .5 .5
KILOMETERS MILES ——— ROAD

Food

Ⓐ Hearth 'n Kettle Restaurant (at John Carver Inn)

Ⓑ Kimball's by the Sea

Ⓒ McGrath's Restaurant

Ⓓ Wood's

Lodging

Ⓔ Governor Bradford Motor Inn

Ⓐ John Carver Inn

Ⓕ The Pilgrim Sands Motel

Ⓖ Sheraton Plymouth at Village Landing

Camping

Ⓗ Indianhead Campground

Ⓘ Myles Standish State Forest

or 508-746-6200). The **John Carver Inn** in Plymouth's town center is run by the same people who operate the fine Dan'l Webster Inn in Sandwich. Doubles start at about $60 in low season, $85 in high season, and children under 18 can stay for free if they are in the same room with their parents. Call (508) 746-7100 or (800) 274-1620 for reservations.

CAMPING

Indianhead Campground, off Route 3A, south of Plymouth, is the closest camping area to Plymouth's attractions. The campground has complete hookups and recreational facilities including miniature golf, aquabikes, canoes, and rowboats. Sites start at $20 per night for two. Call (508) 888-3688 for reservations. **Myles Standish State Forest**, about 10 miles from Plymouth off Route 58 in South Carver, has 475 campsites plus swimming, hiking, boating, and fishing. Sites are about $12 per night. Call (508) 866-2526 for information.

19

NEW ENGLAND FESTIVALS

E ach New England state has its share of folk festivals ranging from arts and crafts fairs to lobsterfests. These regional events are a fun way to soak up local culture, and I've listed some of the area's best and most colorful below.

Connecticut

May
Lobsterfest, Mystic Seaport Museum, Mystic

June
Sea Music Festival, Mystic Seaport, Mystic

August
Connecticut River Raft Race, Haddam Meadows State Park, Haddam
Native American Festival, Haddam Meadows State Park, Haddam

September
Harbor Festival, New London

October
Chowderfest, Mystic Seaport Museum, Mystic

December
First Night, Hartford
Victorian Christmas, Gillette Castle State Park, Deep River
Christmas at Mystic Seaport, Mystic

Write Tourist Events, Department of Economic Development, 865 Brook Street, Rocky Hill, CT 06067, for a complete list of Connecticut events.

Maine

January
New Year's Eve Celebration, Portland
Happy New Year's Champagne Cup, Sunday River Ski Area, Bethel

June
Old Port Festival, Old Port, Portland

July
Seafood Festival, Bar Harbor
Great Schooner Race, Rockland Harbor, Rockland
Annual Dulcimer Festival, Bar Harbor
Rockport Folk Festival, Rockport
Arcady Music Festival, Mt. Desert

August
Lobster Festival, Rockland
Maine Arts Festival, Portland

December
Christmas Prelude, Kennebunkport

Contact the Maine Publicity Bureau at 97 Winthrop Street, Hallowell, ME 04347 (207-289-2423), for the most current events calendar.

Massachusetts

January
First Night New Year's Eve Celebration, Boston

March
St. Patrick's Day Parade, South Boston

April
The Boston Marathon, Boston
Daffodil Festival, Nantucket
Reenactment of Paul Revere's Ride, Boston
Reenactment of the Battle of Lexington and Concord, Lexington

May
Art Newbury Street, Boston
Salem Seaport Festival, Salem
Wool Days, Sturbridge Village
Boston Kite Festival, Franklin Park, Boston

June
Dairy Festival, Boston
Cape Cod Chowderfest, Hyannis

July
Boston Pops Concert and Fourth of July Fireworks Display, The Esplanade, Boston

Bastille Day, Marlborough Street, Boston
Chowderfest, Boston
Tisbury Street Fair, Martha's Vineyard
Edgartown Regatta, Martha's Vineyard
Marblehead Race Week, Marblehead
Stockbridge Antique Show, Stockbridge
Yankee Homecoming Days, Newburyport
USS Constitution Turnaround, Boston
Harborfest, Boston

August
Annual Festival of Shaker Crafts and Industries, Hancock Shaker Village
Mayflower Lobster Festival, Plymouth
Marshfield Fair, Marshfield
Annual Sandcastle and Sculpture Day, Nantucket

September
Cambridge River Festival, Cambridge
Eastern States Exposition, West Springfield
Bourne Scallop Festival, Buzzard's Bay
Essex Clamfest, Essex
Old Deerfield Craft Fair, Deerfield
Cranberry Festival, Harwich
Waterfront Festival, Newburyport
Cape Ann Road Race, Gloucester

October
Head of the Charles Regatta, Charles River, Cambridge
Mt. Greylock Ramble, Adams

November
Hammond Castle Museum Medieval Feast, Gloucester
Plimouth Plantation Thanksgiving Day, Plymouth

December
Christmas Stroll, Nantucket
Chowderfest, Vineyard Haven, Martha's Vineyard
Christmas at Hancock Shaker Village, Hancock

For more information on "Bay state" festivals, contact the Commonwealth of Massachusetts Office of Travel and Tourism, 100 Cambridge Street, 13th Floor, Boston, MA 02202.

New Hampshire

February
Dartmouth Winter Carnival, Hanover
Chocolate Festival, Mt. Cranmore, North Conway

April
Old Man of the Mountain Race, Attitash, Bartlett

June
Mt. Washington Road Race, Mt. Washington
Annual Fiddler's Contest, Lincoln
Jazz Festival, Portsmouth

July
Mid-summer Arts and Crafts Fair, Loon Mountain, Lincoln

September
World Mud Bowl Championships, Hog Coliseum, North Conway
Highland Games, Loon Mountain, Lincoln

October
Fall Foliage Festival, Loon Mountain, Lincoln

December
Candlelight Stroll, Strawberry Banke, Portsmouth

For more detailed information on New Hampshire festivals, contact the State of New Hampshire, Office of Vacation Travel, P.O. Box 856-RC, Concord, NH 03301 (603-271-2666).

Rhode Island

January
Polar Bears Dip, New Year's Day, Newport Beach, Newport

June
Block Island Race Week, Block Island
Outdoor Art Festival, Newport
Taste of Block Island Seafood Festival, Block Island
Great Chowder Cook-off, Newport Yachting Center, Newport

July
Black Ships Festival, Newport
Newport Music Festival, Newport Mansions, Newport
Virginia Slims Tennis Tournament, Newport Casino, Newport

August
JVC Jazz Festival at Newport, Fort Adams
Great Gatsby Ball, Rosecliff, Newport

September
Newport International Boat Show, Newport

November
Block Island's Annual Shopping Stroll, Block Island

December
Christmas in Newport, Newport

Call or write the Newport Tourism and Convention Authority, P.O. Box 782, Newport, RI 02840 (401-849-8048), for a free descriptive brochure of Newport County's numerous cultural events.

Vermont

March
Maple Festival, Woodstock

April
Festival of Quilts, Rutland

May
Lilac Sunday, Shelburne Museum, Shelburne
Spring Farm Festival, Billings Farm Museum, Woodstock
Mayfest, Bennington

June
Hot Air Balloon Festival, Quechee
Cow Appreciation Day, Billing Farm Museum, Woodstock

July
Vermont Lumberjack Roundup, Rutland

August
Fools-A-Float, Burlington
Scottish Festival, Quechee
Bennington Battle Day Weekend, Bennington
Summer Festival and Craft Fair, Woodstock

September
Vermont State Fair, Rutland
Shelburne Harvest Festival, Shelburne
Stratton Arts Festival, Stratton Mountain

December
Wassail Festival, Woodstock
Festival of Christmas Trees, Stowe

The Vermont Chamber of Commerce, Box 37, Montpelier, VT 05601
(802-223-3443), can provide you with additional information about
ongoing activities and events in the state.

APPENDIX

METRIC CONVERSION CHART

1 U.S. gallon = approximately 4 liters
1 liter = about 1 quart
1 Canadian gallon = approximately 4.5 liters

1 pound = approximately $1/2$ kilogram
1 kilogram = about 2 pounds

1 foot = approximately $1/3$ meter
1 meter = about 1 yard
1 yard = a little less than a meter
1 mile = approximately 1.6 kilometers
1 kilometer = about $2/3$ mile

90°F = about 30°C
20°C = approximately 70°F

Planning Map: New England

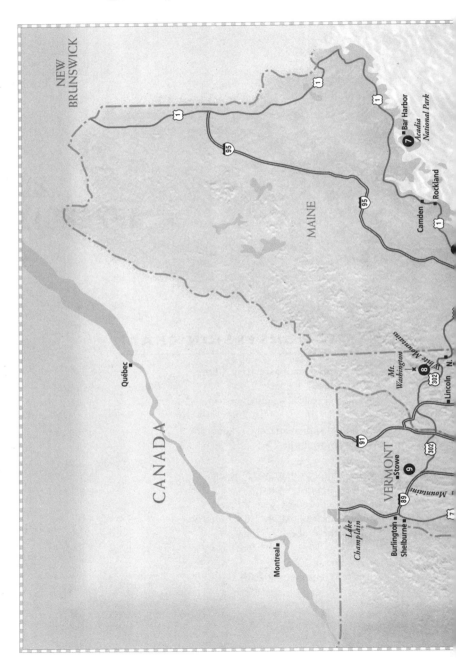

You have permission to photocopy this map.

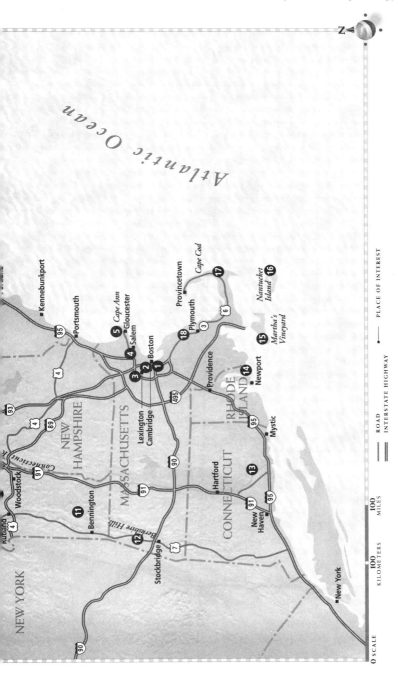

N

SCALE
0   100   100
  KILOMETERS MILES

ROAD
INTERSTATE HIGHWAY
PLACE OF INTEREST

Atlantic Ocean

NEW YORK

NEW HAMPSHIRE

MASSACHUSETTS

CONNECTICUT

RHODE ISLAND

Kennebunkport
Portsmouth
Cape Ann
Gloucester
Salem
Boston
Lexington
Cambridge
Provincetown
Cape Cod
Plymouth
Providence
Newport
Nantucket Island
Martha's Vineyard
Mystic
Hartford
New Haven
New York
Bennington
Woodstock
Rutland
Stockbridge
Berkshire Hills
Connecticut

95 93 89 4 91 90 495 6 3 7 95 91

INDEX

Maps Index

Other Books from John Muir Publications

Rick Steves' Books

Asia Through the Back Door, 400 pp., $17.95
Europe 101: History and Art for the Traveler, 352 pp., $17.95
Mona Winks: Self-Guided Tours of Europe's Top Museums, 432 pp., $18.95
Rick Steves' Baltics & Russia, 144 pp., $9.95
Rick Steves' Europe, 528 pp., $17.95
Rick Steves' France, Belgium & the Netherlands, 256 pp., $13.95
Rick Steves' Germany, Austria & Switzerland, 256 pp., $13.95
Rick Steves' Great Britain, 240 pp., $13.95
Rick Steves' Italy, 224 pp., $13.95
Rick Steves' Scandinavia, 192 pp., $13.95
Rick Steves' Spain & Portugal, 208 pp., $13.95
Rick Steves' Europe Through the Back Door, 480 pp., $18.95
Rick Steves' French Phrase Book, 176 pp., $5.95
Rick Steves' German Phrase Book, 176 pp., $5.95
Rick Steves' Italian Phrase Book, 176 pp., $5.95
Rick Steves' Spanish Phrase Book, 176 pp., $5.95
Rick Steves' French/German/Italian Phrase Book, 320 pp., $7.95

A Natural Destination Series

Belize: A Natural Destination, 344 pp., $16.95
Costa Rica: A Natural Destination, 380 pp., $18.95
Guatemala: A Natural Destination, 360 pp., $16.95

For Birding Enthusiasts

The Birder's Guide to Bed and Breakfasts: U.S. and Canada, 416 pp., $17.95
The Visitor's Guide to the Birds of the Central National Parks: U.S. and Canada, 400 pp., $15.95
The Visitor's Guide to the Birds of the Eastern National Parks: U.S. and Canada, 400 pp., $15.95
The Visitor's Guide to the Birds of the Rocky Mountain National Parks: U.S. and Canada, 432 pp., $15.95

Unique Travel Series

All are 112 pages and $10.95 paperback, except Georgia and Oregon.
Unique Arizona
Unique California
Unique Colorado
Unique Florida
Unique Georgia ($11.95)
Unique New England
Unique New Mexico
Unique Oregon ($9.95)
Unique Texas
Unique Washington

Travel+Smart™ Trip Planners

All are 256 pages and $14.95 paperback.
American Southwest Travel+Smart™ Trip Planner
Colorado Travel+Smart™ Trip Planner (avail. 9/96)
Eastern Canada Travel+Smart™ Trip Planner
Hawaii Travel+Smart™ Trip Planner
Kentucky/Tennessee Travel+Smart™ Trip Planner (avail. 9/96)
Minnesota/Wisconsin Travel+Smart™ Trip Planner (avail. 10/96)
New England Travel+Smart™ Trip Planner
Pacific Northwest Travel+Smart™ Trip Planner (avail. 8/96)

Other Terrific Travel Titles

The 100 Best Small Art Towns in America, 256 pp., $15.95
The Big Book of Adventure Travel, 384 pp., $17.95
Indian America: A Traveler's Companion, 480 pp., $18.95
The People's Guide to Mexico, 608 pp., $19.95
Ranch Vacations: The Complete Guide to Guest and Resort, Fly-Fishing, and Cross-Country Skiing Ranches, 528 pp., $19.95
Understanding Europeans, 272 pp., $14.95
Undiscovered Islands of the Caribbean, 336 pp., $16.95
Watch It Made in the U.S.A.: A Visitor's Guide to the Companies that Make Your Favorite Products, 328 pp., $16.95
The World Awaits, 280 pp., $16.95

Automotive Titles

The Greaseless Guide to Car Care, 272 pp., $19.95
How to Keep Your Subaru Alive, 480 pp., $21.95
How to Keep Your Toyota Pickup Alive, 392 pp., $21.95
How to Keep Your VW Alive, 464 pp., $25

Ordering Information

Please check your local bookstore for our books, or call 1-800-888-7504 to order direct and to receive a complete catalog. A shipping charge will be added to your order total.

Send all inquiries to:
John Muir Publications
P.O. Box 613
Santa Fe, NM 87504